THE
OUTDOOR
SWIMMING
GUIDE

THE OUTDOOR SWIMMING GUIDE

OVER 400 OF THE BEST LIDOS, WILD SWIMMING AND OPEN AIR SWIMMING SPOTS IN ENGLAND, WALES & SCOTLAND

EDITED BY
KATHY ROGERS

Vertebrate Publishing, Sheffield
www.v-publishing.co.uk

THE OUTDOOR SWIMMING GUIDE

EDITED BY **KATHY ROGERS**

First published in 2021 by Vertebrate Publishing. Reprinted in 2022.

 Vertebrate Publishing, Omega Court, 352 Cemetery Road, Sheffield S11 8FT, United Kingdom.
www.v-publishing.co.uk

A CIP catalogue record for this book is available from the British Library.

ISBN 978-1-83981-106-7

Front cover: Wild swimming in the Lake District. © *James Kirby*

Back cover: (L–R) Bude sea pool. © *www.paulmeyler.co.uk* / Tinside lido. © *Jay Chard* / Janet's Foss. © *Louise Kibler, @viewswithlou* / West Lake at Colwick Country Park. © *Cameron Bonser*

All other photography copyright as credited.

Design and production by Jane Beagley & Cameron Bonser, Vertebrate Publishing.

Vertebrate Publishing is committed to printing on paper from sustainable sources.

Printed and bound in Europe by Latitude Press.

Contents

Introduction

Growing up in Devon, in the summer we would abandon the busy beaches for Dartmoor's peaty pools. We would splash in tree-fringed rivers and lie lizard-like on mossy boulders. We would cycle the canal to the Lock Cottage, take the ferry across the Exe to lounge poolside at Topsham Outdoor Swimming Pool.

Indoor swimming was about lessons, lengths and endless verrucas; outdoor swimming was like walking or running or scrambling – just another way of moving through the world, of being in the open air. The very best summer afternoons are about blue skies, bare feet and damp hair. Whether in dappled sunshine or spiky rain, outdoor swimming still offers childlike joy. You'll discover outdoor swimming destinations on the flanks of mountains, on boggy moors, among farmland and woods, by the seashore and even in the very middle of Britain's biggest cities.

This guide offers you the opportunity to discover the wondrous places to swim outside in England, Scotland and Wales. Whether you've never before swum under blue skies or you begin each day with a dawn dip, it reveals the gentle rivers, friendly lidos, mermaid tarns and open swim clubs in every corner of this water-drenched island.

Please don't take good care of this book. Cram it in your backpack or jam it in your glovebox. Sit on it when the grass is wet, use it as a tiny umbrella or an impromptu plate at your post-dip picnic, circle your favourite spots and pore over it in the pub. We want this book to become your dog-eared companion, sticky with ice cream, squidged midges and squelchy mud. We hope that you will take this book on your adventures, and when you've visited the places in this guide, find a few more secret swim spots of your own.

ACKNOWLEDGEMENTS

We would like to thank Poonam Ahirwar, Jessica McElhattan, Alice Noel, Eleanor Quinn, and Rebecca Wales who researched the swim spots, and wrote the descriptions for this guide. Thanks also to Suzanna Cruickshank and Ella Foote who provided invaluable editorial feedback on the book. We also appreciate the help that we have received from lidos and swimming pools, open swim organisations and keen swimmers and photographers, who have provided information and advice, and inspirational photography. We are particularly grateful for the help from busy volunteers who work tirelessly to operate community-run pools and for those pioneering exciting new open swim venues.

About this book

The Outdoor Swimming Guide provides details of more than 400 outdoor swimming spots (including lidos and outdoor pools, wild swims and open water areas) in England, Scotland and Wales.

All of the listed locations are turn-up-and-swim spots (although pre-booking is always advisable at popular lidos during the summer and has been a requirement during the Covid-19 pandemic); very few require membership (and those that do often offer it at a nominal fee on the day). The guide provides information on how to get there, when to go, what to expect, food and drink, public transport, parking and other local amenities. It also offers practical information on outdoor swimming:

- How to get started
- Health and safety and the law
- Kit.

This book divides outdoor swimming spots into three types; lidos or outdoor pools (highlighted in **blue**), wild swim spots (highlighted in **green**) and open water swims (highlighted in **purple**).

All the locations listed offer the opportunity for an outdoor swim. In addition, we have listed spots that offer:

- Paddling – areas shallow enough (below 0.5 metres) to paddle, particularly for children.
- Plunge pool – a deeper area, often near a waterfall, where it is possible to submerge yourself and tread water, but there may be little space for swimming.

LIDOS AND OUTDOOR POOLS

Lidos and outdoor pools are built environments that have been constructed for the primary purpose of swimming. These include urban outdoor pools, small community lidos and tidal pools. There is a huge variation among outdoor pools: some are lifeguarded, some are not; some encourage picnics and even barbecues, some run strictly time-limited swim sessions; most discourage or prohibit smoking, alcohol (and drugs) and glass bottles or containers – many also frown on photography; most lidos and outdoor pools charge for entry, and some also charge for other facilities, such as showers or lockers. Whatever the rules and regulations, most outdoor pools offer friendly and scenic venues for a relaxing swim, and are beloved by locals and lido tourists alike.

Opening hours – lidos and outdoor pools often only open during summer months (generally between May and September). Some only open at weekends or during the early evening, particularly where the pool is shared with a local school. Opening hours are often subject to change, and may be dependent on pool maintenance, the weather or availability of volunteers – it is always advisable to check that a lido will be open before you visit.

Heated or unheated – not all lidos are heated, and even those that are increasingly are experimenting with cold or colder winter swimming sessions.

Volunteers – many lidos are community-run operations that rely heavily on volunteer effort (some lidos are privately run, or run by or on behalf of the council).

Disabled facilities – most pools now offer level or ramped access to the poolside, but many offer limited accessibility. Pools may lack accessible changing areas (or you may be asked to use the disabled toilet) and there may not be accessible ways to enter the water. Many lidos recognise this as a high priority, so it is worth contacting them to check the current situation.

Tidal pools – tidal pools, designed to be filled by an incoming tide, can be a great and safer alternative to sea swimming. It is inadvisable to swim in tidal pools at high tide, when walls may be overtopped; check tide tables before visiting. Always keep an eye on the tide (and your belongings!).

The 1930s was the golden age of lido building, and many surviving lidos are historical assets, with listed status. Founded in 2015, Historical Pools of Britain celebrates and champions Britain's historical pools – *historicpools.org.uk*

BUSCOT WEIR. © *ANYWHEREWEROAM.COM*

unlifeguarded; they often lack life-saving equipment and may be remote and difficult for rescue services to reach.

Particularly in the mountain regions of Wales and Scotland, you may face a long hike over challenging terrain to reach wild swim spots; you will need strong hillwalking and navigation skills to reach some remote locations safely.

OPEN WATER SWIMMING

Open water swimming is swimming in open waters (such as rivers and lakes) in supervised conditions. Generally there are specific sessions (as well as a charge to attend) and lifeguards. There may be ramps or jetties, as well as natural-water entry points; many venues offer toilets and changing rooms, a cafe and on-site parking. Open water swim venues usually offer one or more courses, marked out by buoys, and sometimes run induction or introductory courses. Open water swimming is sometimes permitted in reservoirs, disused quarries or pits, where wild swimming is advised against or not permitted. Open water swimming is a good opportunity to experience swimming in wild waters with safety precautions. Some open water swim venues operate all year round, although many require you to wear a wetsuit when the water temperature falls. Many also require you to wear a brightly coloured swim cap.

WILD SWIM SPOTS

Wild swim spots are places to swim in rivers, lakes and waterfalls. We have only included locations where it legally possible to reach the water's edge (there are public or permissive rights of way, or the area is accessible to the general public). All of these spots are suitable for swimming although some are small plunge pools and some are long river stretches; many offer waterside spots suitable for paddling. We have not generally included disused quarries, gravel pits, canals or reservoirs. *The Outdoor Swimming Guide* does not list sea swimming spots (although it does include tidal pools). Wild swim spots are almost always

Open water swimming venues may partner with the National Open Water Coaching Association (NOWCA). To swim at NOWCA venues, you must sign up in advance for a membership; annual adult membership is £15 in 2022. Because you cannot walk up and swim at NOWCA venues, they are not included in this guide but they are a good option for open water swimmers looking for a regular and affordable local swim spot; details of NOWCA swim spots can be found at *nowca.org*

Symbols

Public transport – there are bus, railway or other public transport services within a kilometre of the swim spot, with frequent daily services (usually hourly, but at least four daily in more rural locations). The access section provides more information on public transport connections.

Parking – there is parking available within a kilometre of the swim spot. This may be on-street parking or a car park (charges may apply).

Food and drink – for lidos and open swim spots, this indicates that there is food and drinks (hot and cold) available at the swim spot or adjacent to it. For wild swims, this indicates that there is somewhere (pub, restaurant or kiosk) selling food and drink within a kilometre.

Toilets – for lidos and open swim spots, there are toilets on-site. For wild swims, there are public toilets (not in a pub or cafe) within a kilometre; details of the location are usually provided in the description, but these facilities may not always be open.

Changing rooms – there are changing rooms on-site. These may be communal or open to the air; there may not be showers or lockers. Only for lidos and open swim spots.

Heated – the pool is heated. Lidos may not always be heated; they often offer cold water swims in the winter. Sometimes, not all pools on-site are heated, and pools may be gently warmed rather than heated to standard swimming pool temperature. Only used for lidos/outdoor swimming pools.

Accessibility – the swim spot has level or ramped access to both the water and other facilities. It has accessible changing areas and toilets and accessible ways to enter the water (a wet chair or hoist, or for open swim spots a hard-surfaced slipway). The access section of each swim spot description provides further information, but you are advised to contact the lido or open swim spot to get current information on accessibility. This symbol is not used for wild swim spots.

YOUR FIRST OUTDOOR SWIM

No one is too young, too old or too inexperienced to enjoy an outdoor swim. Outdoor swimming is for everyone – you don't even need a swimming costume. If you are a non-swimmer or a novice, or would just benefit from brushing up on rusty skills, many outdoor pools offer swimming lessons, both for children and adults. Every summer, Swim England and the Royal National Lifeboat Institution (RNLI) offer Swim Safe sessions (*swimsafe.org.uk*), teaching children vital open water swimming skills. Open water swimming venues often provide inductions and introduction to open water sessions. You could hire a wild swimming guide, who will not only offer invaluable expertise on safely swimming in open water but also insider info on the best local spots. Consider joining a club (there are many informal local swim groups as well as organised athletic clubs) or taking a swim holiday.

Safety

Outdoor swimming is not an inherently dangerous activity. Despite tragic, well-publicised incidents of drowning in open water every year, outdoor swimming is a low-risk hobby. The National Water Safety Forum collates annual statistics; in the UK in 2020, there were 254 fatal incidents in outdoor water, 85 of which occurred in coastal or shore waters. Of the 254 deaths, 77 involved swimming-related activities (including 9 from jumping or diving in, and 15 related to water play); 89 people died while walking or running near open water. A 2011 Royal Society for the Prevention of Accidents (RoSPA) report identified open water swimming as a relatively low-risk activity; diving, boating and even fishing were all significantly higher risk. Young males are particularly at risk of accidental drowning in open water; alcohol or drugs are often a factor in accidents. The key to staying safe in open water is to know the risks, respect your abilities and learn what to do in an emergency.

Prepare – find out about your swim spot in advance. Investigate the water quality, currents and any site-specific hazards. Check the weather forecast. Prepare your kit – not just for your swim, but also for afterwards. Know what to do in an emergency.

Know your limits – you are responsible for your own safety. Don't swim too far or for too long. Don't succumb to peer pressure or the influence of the group. Acclimatise gradually.

Dip, don't jump – scope out your swim spot. Locate the entry and exit points, and where the water is shallow or deepens. Identify any life-saving equipment near the water. Look for underwater (or water's edge) hazards. Assess the current using twigs or leaves. Don't jump into the water (unless you have ascertained it is currently safe to do so – water conditions change), and enter with caution.

Don't swim alone – swim with a friend, a guide, a club or where there are lifeguards. If you do swim alone, consider taking a spectator. Experienced swimmers may decide to swim alone, in more remote or isolated spots – if you do so, always let someone know where you are.

Watch out – for anglers, canoeists, kayakers, paddleboarders and boats. In popular areas, always wear a brightly coloured swim cap. If swimming in or visiting open water spots with children, ALWAYS know where they are and what they are doing.

Don't swim – in floodwaters or stagnant water, or during thunderstorms. Box weirs are very dangerous because of circulating currents. Be cautious about swimming in canals, urban wild waters and reservoirs, or in adverse weather conditions. Be cautious about swimming at night or in poor visibility, unless you are an experienced wild swimmer and familiar with the location.

Warm up – get out of the water before you get too cold, and be prepared to warm up as soon as you leave the water. Have towels or drying robes within easy reach. Take plenty of warm clothes – layers are best. Don't forget your hands, feet and head. Eat something and have a hot drink. Consider taking a camping stove or hot flask.

You can find more information on safety in the water at:

- *www.outdoorswimmingsociety.com*
- *www.nationalfirechiefs.org.uk/Be-Water-Aware*
- *www.rlss.org.uk*
- *rnli.org*

EMERGENCIES

FLOAT TO LIVE

If you find yourself in difficulty in the water, try to lie on your back, extend your arms and legs, and float. This gives you the opportunity to bring your breathing under your control, lessens the likelihood that you will inhale or ingest water and allows you to assess the situation and call for help.

Know what to do in an emergency. Brush up on your first aid skills; consider learning some lifeguarding and water rescue skills. Don't place yourself in danger to rescue someone else.

Dial 999 or 112 to contact the emergency services; ask for the coastguard if you are in a coastal area. If you are in a remote countryside area, ask for the 'Police – Mountain Rescue'; do not attempt to contact Mountain Rescue directly. Be prepared to provide your name, location and details of what has occurred. Know how to use your phone to determine your exact location (for example, with SARLOC or Phone Find). Emergency services can also be contacted by SMS text – useful if you have low battery or intermittent signal. You can register by sending an SMS message, 'register', to 999. Emergency SMS should only be used when voice call contact with emergency services is not possible.

HEALTH & SAFETY

Outdoor swimming offers many health benefits – it may improve the immune system, mental health and circulation as well as increasing general fitness. Regular swimmers have reported alleviation of symptoms relating to conditions as diverse as the menopause, depression and joint inflammation. There are some risks, particularly associated with open or wild waters; many are avoidable by taking sensible precautions and most are readily treatable. Avoid swimming near **sewage outlets**, and do not swim if the water does not look clean. **Blue-green algal bloom** can be toxic, and is particularly dangerous for dogs – check for local warnings and do not swim if in doubt. **Cover cuts and scrapes** with a waterproof plaster or dressing. Consider wearing water shoes if the underwater surface is pebbly, sharp or uneven. **Wet surfaces are slippery**, particularly when covered with mud or weeds – be cautious about falling in or near water.

You should seek advice from your GP, pharmacist or other medical practitioner if you suspect you are suffering from an infection or other condition as a result of swimming.

Swimmer's ear (*otitis externa*) – an infection in your outer ear canal, usually bacterial; symptoms include itching, fluid discharge and redness. Dry your ears thoroughly after swimming, and don't swim in unclean water. If left untreated the condition may become chronic or cause hearing loss.

Surfer's ear (*exostosis*) – abnormal bone growth resulting from prolonged exposure to cold wind and water. If you swim for prolonged times in chilly conditions, consider protection to keep your ears warm and dry, such as earplugs, a wetsuit hood or swim cap.

Swimmer's itch (*cercarial dermatitis*) – a rash reaction to microscopic parasites, often nicknamed 'duck fleas', in the water. They may be more common on sunny days and in slow-moving water. Although uncomfortable, the condition usually clears in a few days.

Cryptosporidiosis/E. coli – swimming in water polluted by sewage, or livestock excrement, can cause vomiting and diarrhoea. Don't swim near sewage outlets or intensively farmed areas, avoid swallowing water while swimming and clean your hands thoroughly before eating or drinking.

Leptospirosis/Weil's disease – a serious, but rare, infection that you can get from the urine (in water or soil) of infected animals, such as rodents, pigs and livestock. Symptoms of Weil's disease include high temperature, headaches, nausea, aching muscles, red eyes and loss of appetite – seek medical advice promptly if you encounter any of these symptoms after open water swimming. Do not swim in flood water, stagnant water or in urban areas; cover cuts before entering the water and shower after swimming. Leptospirosis is generally readily treated with antibiotics, but Weil's disease can cause liver or kidney complications and may be fatal.

Cold shock – a series of cardiorespiratory reactions caused by sudden immersion in cold water, including gasping, hyperventilation and panic. It may cause a heart attack, due to vasoconstriction. Be prepared for your body's physiological response to cold water, acclimatise yourself gradually, do not jump into cold water.

Hypothermia – a dangerous drop in your body temperature; symptoms include shivering, sluggishness, slurred speech and confusion. Hypothermia can progress rapidly and may be fatal. Do not stay too long in water, and if you experience symptoms of hypothermia, leave the water and warm up immediately. Be mindful of symptoms of hypothermia in other swimmers. Your core temperature will continue to fall after you leave the water, as the effects of vasoconstriction ease, which can lead to afterdrop; this may manifest as shivering or feeling faint several minutes or more after leaving the water.

Muscle cramps – sudden, painful muscle contractions; they may impair your ability to swim. They can be caused by fatigue or overuse – if you experience cramps while swimming, float until they pass, and then consider leaving the water.

SWIMMING & THE ENVIRONMENT

Wild swimming is the perfect opportunity to enjoy the nature around you, but be mindful of the impact that your enjoyment can have on the environment, both in and out of the water and particularly on the water margins.

Leave no trace – take all your rubbish (and any other litter you encounter) home with you.

Fire – be extremely careful with cigarettes and barbecues. You need the permission of the landowner to have a barbecue, and in some areas, such as the Peak District National Park, landowners have banned the use of barbecues.

Don't disturb wildlife – don't approach wild animals or uproot or damage plants. Keep your dog under control at all times.

Seasons – in spring and summer, avoid swim spots where you may disturb nesting birds. In autumn and winter, avoid salmon rivers where fish eggs may be buried.

Sites of Special Scientific Interest (SSSIs) and nature reserves – be cautious about swimming in protected environments. Do not swim in SSSI areas where swimming is discouraged to protect the environment.

Potions and lotions – whatever is on your skin will end up in the river. Don't use soap or shampoo at wild swim spots; consider covering up or using eco-friendly sunscreens and insect repellents.

Biosecurity – Check, Clean, Dry – check your swimwear and yourself for live organisms. Clean all your kit and dry it thoroughly. It is important to prevent the spread of organisms, particularly non-native invasive species, between locations.

Travel – consider the impact of your travel to swim spots. All the swim spot listings have details of how to reach them by public transport, if this is feasible; if you do drive, park with consideration. Do not obstruct roads, gates or rights of way; do not park on private property, verges or in pub or shop car parks (without permission).

The Environment Agency publishes details of water quality at specified bathing spots at *environment.data.gov.uk/bwq/profiles*

WILD SWIMMING: THE LAW

There is no clear legal right to swim in open waters in the UK. There is an undisputed right to wild swim:

- In the sea and tidal waters
- In Scotland, where it is enshrined in the Outdoor Access Code.

There may be a legal right to wild swim:

- In navigable waters (for example, on all rivers that can be navigated by boats)
- Where the water is crossed by, or can be entered from, a public right of way.

Swimming is often permitted, or at least tolerated, sometimes by long-established local tradition. Entering the water to swim where there is no legal right is usually trespassing, currently a civil offence; you may be liable for any damages caused as a result of your actions. Byelaws or other local regulations may regulate swimming in certain areas, such as the River Thames in the city of London or reservoirs; swimming in such locations may be a criminal offence. If asked to leave the water by a landowner, representative of the landowner or police, it is often best to leave promptly even if you believe that you have a legal right to swim there.

'No Swimming' signs may represent an attempt by the landowner to limit liability for any accidents that happen in the water; they do not necessarily have legal standing.

KIT LIST

Swimming is an affordable pastime, requiring little in the way of kit. What you need will depend on where you swim, when you swim, your sensitivity to cold and what type of swimming you do. Experiment with the kit that suits you best, and ask other swimmers for advice on what they find useful. Outdoor swim centres and lidos often have kit available to borrow or hire.

- Swimsuit/trunks
- Wetsuit
- Goggles
- Swimming cap
- Thermal accessories (gloves and socks)
- Tow float/dry bag
- Changing robe/sports towel
- Whistle
- Earplugs
- Phone case
- Waterproof roll-top bag
- Swimming shoes
- Throw line

UPDATES

If you have any updates for *The Outdoor Swimming Guide*, please do drop us a line at **lidos@v-publishing.co.uk**

GLOUCESTER

67
68
69 61 64 66
    62 65
    63

60

58 59
57 BRISTOL   54 BATH
56   55   53
    52
    51
    50

7
8
6   48 49

5   39   47 46
                           44 45
        38   40   43
EXETER 37   42
36 35   BOURNEMOUTH
                           41
9 10 11
12 13
        31 32
14 28 29 33 34
16 15   27 30
   17 26 24
        25 23
        22
LOOE   18 21
        19
        20

2
1 FALMOUTH

XIV

South-West England

BUDE SEA POOL. © WWW.PAULMEYLER.CO.UK

JUBILEE POOL. © *LYRA & MOTH PHOTOGRAPHY*

JUBILEE POOL

50.1150, -5.5317 / Battery Road, Penzance, Cornwall, TR18 4FF / 01736 369224 / Swimming and paddling / www.jubileepool.co.uk

The striking Jubilee Pool is the UK's largest art deco, seawater lido and juts from the Cornish coast into the Atlantic Ocean. Opened in 1935, the pool was cleverly designed to cope with the full ferocity of the Cornish seas; the lido is triangular in shape and comprises a main pool, a geothermal pool and a learner pool. The pool has a strong commitment to sustainability, implementing a plastic-free policy and pioneering geothermal heating and low chemical use. The lido was seriously damaged in storms in 2014, and its restoration was only made possible by determined community support. You can top off your visit with food from the cafe, which specialises in local produce, and enjoy views from the terraces of golden sands stretching towards St Michael's Mount.

Access

Access via ladders, steps and ramp. Ramped access to poolside; accessible toilets and changing room; hoist (main pool), ramp (geothermal pool). Penzance railway station a kilometre away; Market Jew Street stop, 600 metres away, served by frequent buses to Heamoor, Mousehole, St Ives and other local towns. Parking on the promenade as well as St Anthony's car park.

HAYLE OUTDOOR SWIMMING POOL

50.1890, -5.4225 / King George V Memorial Walk, Hayle, Cornwall, TR27 4BL / 01736 752568 Swimming / www.hayletowncouncil.net/your-council/outdoor-swimming-pool

Kids can really make a splash at Hayle Outdoor Swimming Pool – there is a four-lane slide into the pool's shallow end. The once-unheated pool now enjoys gentle warming from a solar cover, which can boost the water temperature above 20 °C on warm summer days. The friendly, twenty-five-metre-long pool in the heart of Hayle offers grassy lawns and poolside picnic benches, or the chance to indulge in a cream tea at the pool's charming Cafe Riviere. The seaside town of Hayle is famed for its five kilometres of golden sand dunes, the Towans, but you could choose instead to explore the Family Activity Trail around the Copperhouse Pool, which starts by the swimming pool.

Access

Access via ladders, handrailed steps and slide. Ramped access to poolside. Hayle railway station 600 metres away; St Elwyn's Church bus stop, opposite pool, served by buses to Penzance, Cambourne and Truro approximately every two hours. Free on-site parking.

DOZMARY POOL. © JAMES LATUS

RESPRYN BRIDGE

50.4391, -4.6794 / Bodmin, Cornwall / Swimming

On the National Trust's Lanhydrock Estate in Bodmin, as the River Fowey rushes under Respryn Bridge it creates a magical swim spot. Wooden decking for fishing as well as grassy banks surround the water, which is one and a half to two metres deep, and a shingle beach rests by the footbridge. Swimmers should swim against the current, which can be quite rapid. Especially in the spring, when the forest floor is covered in a blanket of bluebells, this spot with riverside walks and easy access has an ethereal beauty which is hard to beat. The dramatically Gothic Lanhydrock House is a great place to stop for a bit of sightseeing, and also has a tearoom. Further choice for refreshments can be found in Bodmin.

Access

Access via shingle beach, muddy banks or wooden fishing decks. Paths by riverside – one leads to Bodmin Parkway railway station (two kilometres away), which also has bus services to Plymouth and Padstow. Parking at Respryn Bridge, less than 100 metres away; National Trust car park a kilometre and a half away.

DOZMARY POOL

50.5428, -4.5522 / Bolventor, Cornwall / Swimming and paddling

High on wild, bare Lorna Doone moors, reaching Dozmary Pool is an adventure in itself. Many legends are associated with this pool, including claims that it is the resting place of King Arthur's Excalibur. Even if Excalibur doesn't reveal itself, this is still a lovely spot for a dip: secluded and peaceful, the wild, perhaps haunted, moorlands which surround it have an ethereal feel. Grassy banks and small, pebbly beaches slope to the shallow water. Although the pool is generally cold, on a sunny day it feels as if the wide expanse of the blue skies go on forever. Learn more about the local legends at the nearby smugglers' haunt, the Jamaica Inn, which offers a museum and place to stay as well as food.

Access

Access via pebbly shores and grassy banks. Follow lane south from Jamaica Inn. Hourly buses to Bodmin and Launceston stop at Jamaica Inn, approximately a kilometre and a half away. Limited on-street parking in Bolventor, approximately a kilometre and a half away; do not park in passing places on narrow lanes.

BUDE SEA POOL. © WWW.PAULMEYLER.CO.UK

BUDE SEA POOL

50.8325, -4.5539 / Summerleaze Beach, Bude, Cornwall, EX23 8HJ / 01288 488118 / Swimming and paddling / *www.budeseapool.org*

Hidden beneath Bude's striated cliffs, the ninety-one-metre-long Bude Sea Pool was constructed in the 1930s to provide locals with a safe spot to swim in the sea. It's a steep journey down steps to the pool from the South West Coast Path, close to Summerleaze Beach. The pool is Bude's most popular tourist destination and is open all year around, and although Summerleaze Beach is lifeguarded in summer there are no lifeguards designated for the lido. You are advised not to swim in it at high tide. The pool's location, tucked beneath the cliffs and sheltered from the worst of the Atlantic Coast's weather, means that on summer days it is the perfect sunspot.

Access
Access via steps and a sloped beach. Pool is reached via steep cliff path, with steps. Bus stops on The Strand, 800 metres away, served by buses to Exeter (every two hours), Barnstaple, Plymouth and other local destinations. Paid parking at Summerleaze car park, 300 metres away.

ROCK SEA POOL

51.0407, -4.2430 / Westward Ho!, Devon / Swimming and paddling

At low tide, a submarine joy is revealed on the rocky beach at Westward Ho! – a square tidal pool reappears, freshly filled with seawater. The pool, a popular bathing spot since Victorian times, is just over a metre deep and has no facilities. Although the pool is the responsibility of Torridge District Council, volunteers also work tirelessly to ensure the pool is kept clean and free from debris. There are public toilets at the Slipway and Seafield car parks. This diamond pool lies just beneath the South West Coast Path, and while you may have to scramble over rocks to reach it, you should pause to explore the rock pools for sea anemones and hermit crabs. The town centre is a short stroll along the seafront, offering plenty of cafes for a post-dip fish and chips.

Access
Entry into water via steps at pool's shallow end. Frequent buses to Ilfracombe, Barnstaple from Nelson Road and Atlantic Way stops, 500 metres away. Paid parking at Seafield long stay car park.

WATERSMEET

51.2228, -3.7988 / Watersmeet, Devon /
Swimming and paddling

In the shadow of Watersmeet House sits
a stretch of river perfect for a tranquil dip.
Rocks litter the entrance to the small plunge
pools, with a canopy stretching overhead.
The surrounding ancient woodland is rich in
wildlife, and you may spot otters, buzzards
or herons. In Barton Wood on the eastern
branch of the river there are waterfalls, and
a further kilometre and a half upstream lies
Long Pool, a deep, fifty-metre stretch of river
overgrown with ferns and infused with a
mystical atmosphere. For further exploration,
the Two Moors Way and Coleridge Way follow
the River Lyn into Lynmouth via the gorge and
the South West Coast Path is a kilometre away.
The tearoom at Watersmeet House offers
afternoon teas and warm pasties.

Access
Access via stony foreshore and steep, mossy
banks with rocks. Approximately three kilometres away, buses to Barnstaple (and
Minehead in summer) stop in Lynmouth a
few times a day. Pay-and-display parking at
Watersmeet House.

COW CASTLE, RIVER BARLE

51.1235, -3.7258 / Simonsbath, Somerset /
Swimming and paddling

A beautiful wild swimming spot set in a scenic
and remote area within Exmoor National
Park, this stretch of the River Barle lends itself
to both paddling and swimming. Along the
centre of the river there is a pleasant, hidden
pool with crystal-clear water that reaches a
depth of approximately a metre and a half.
The closest facilities, including a pub, and
car park, are approximately three kilometres
away in Simonsbath. This swim spot, in the
shadow of the Iron Age hill fort of Cow Castle,
makes a perfect stop on the Two Moors Way,

which follows the river between Withypool
and Simonsbath; it is worth a climb to the top
of Cow Castle for the views, even if only the
faintest traces of the hill fort remain.

Access
Entry into water via sloping, grassy banks
and convenient stepping stones. Not easily
accessible via public transport: closest buses
seven kilometres away in Exford, for services to
Minehead. Free parking in Simonsbath, three
kilometres away.

CULLEVER STEPS POOL

50.7131, -3.9764 / Belstone, Devon /
Swimming and plunge pool

Cullever Steps Pool is a small, shallow plunge
pool in a natural amphitheatre under the
flanks of Scarey Tor. Just downstream from
Cullever Steps, this swim spot is surrounded
by grassy banks and rocks which lead into
the cold water. The pool is not easy to reach,
requiring a bumpy drive along narrow roads
(or a cross-country hike) and a walk along
the tufty and often boggy riverbanks, but the
reward is a tranquil spot and undisturbed
swim in Dartmoor's enchanting moors. The
charming village of Belstone is nearby, where
the Tors Inn is a great stop for a bite to eat.

Access
Access via rough stony and grassy banks. Walk
from Cullever Steps on grassy trails by river.
Buses from Okehampton, Exeter and Bude
stop several times a day at Belstone, two and
a half kilometres away. Roadside parking at
Rowtor car park, a kilometre and a half from
swim spot.

SHILLEY POOL. © STEPHEN FOSTER

SHILLEY POOL

50.7049, -3.9101 / Throwleigh, Devon / Swimming and plunge pool

Many streams and rivers bubble to life through the marshy ground of South Tawton Common, and one is Blackaton Brook. The water cascades down from dangerously boggy Raybarrow Pool, one of Dartmoor's most infamous mires, into the dammed Shilley Pool. With grassy banks and flat rocks the water is easy to access, and you can enjoy a plunge pool approximately a metre deep. The wide, flat rocks will provide a warm platform for a post-dip picnic on sunny days. This sheltered spot is one of Dartmoor's best-kept secrets, and a trip here can be combined with a walk up Cosdon Beacon, a granite-domed hill that offers panoramic views from the English to Bristol channels on fine days. The closest pubs and cafes are in South Zeal.

Access
Grassy banks and wide, flat rocks to access water. Buses from Cheriton Bishop to Oke-hampton stop at Moor View once each way daily. Grassy parking area near Moor Farm, north of Throwleigh, approximately a kilometre from pool; follow footpath along south side of river (not public right of way); bridleway access north of river from lane at Moorside.

SALMON LEAPS

50.6923, -3.8101 / Drewsteignton, Devon / Swimming

The River Teign flows through woodland to Salmon Leaps, a pool beneath the twentieth-century Castle Drogo. The river flows into three Victorian stone plunge pools which provide an exhilarating tumble, but the strong current means these are not suited to children. You should avoid swimming here between October and January, when salmon leap the weir as they travel to their easily disturbed spawning grounds, In spring and summer, the stunning scenery makes Salmon Leaps the perfect place to reconnect with nature. Refreshments can be found at Castle Drogo's tearooms, less than one kilometre away but a steep climb or, approximately one and half kilometres each way, the Mill End Hotel upstream and the Fingle Bridge Inn downstream. You can also enjoy a dip at the nearby Fingle Bridge, a deep gorge surround-ed by thick and enchanting woodland.

Access
Access via grassy banks. Buses from Moreton-hampstead to Exeter stops at Castle Drogo a few times a day, just over a kilometre away. Paid parking at Castle Drogo (free for National Trust members) and Fingle Bridge (with toilets); roadside parking by Fingle Bridge; although Castle Drogo is closer there is a steep climb from the river.

MORETONHAMPSTEAD COMMUNITY SWIMMING POOL. © *SAM FABIAN-MILLER*

CHAGFORD POOL

50.6811, -3.8326 / Rushford, Chagford, Newton Abbot, Devon, TQ13 8DA / 01647 432929 / Swimming and paddling / *www.chagfordpool.co.uk*

Stretching along the banks of the tree-fringed River Teign, Chagford Pool draws its water from the river. Dug out by local residents in 1933, the thirty-four-metre-long pool remains very much a community effort. Recent improvements include heating and showers; there is a small paddling pool in addition to the main pool. There is a grassy sunbathing area and poolside seating. You are welcome to bring your own food, but there is also a poolside Tea Shed. This serene pool in the midst of green fields offers a lido experience in a wild environment.

Access

Entry to pool via handrailed steps and ladders. Level access to poolside. A kilometre away, buses leave from Lower Street to Exeter every three hours, as well as Okehampton and Newton Abbot. On-site parking; overflow parking in field.

MORETONHAMPSTEAD COMMUNITY SWIMMING POOL

50.6611, -3.7687 / Court Street, Moretonhampstead, Devon, TQ13 8LG / 01647 440276 / Swimming and paddling / *www.moretonpool.co.uk*

Moretonhampstead's pool is a community-run, twenty-five-metre lido situated on the eastern edge of Dartmoor. Open from May to September, the pool is heated by air source heat pumps and solar power. With a sectioned-off shallow end plus a separate small toddler pool, this is a great place for all the family to enjoy. The pool's timetable offers lane swimming sessions, technique tuning, aqua fit and water polo sessions, as well as general swim sessions which offer a variety of toys and floats for children to play with. The lido itself is surrounded by grassy areas, picnic tables and a sun terrace, making it an ideal place to spend a relaxing afternoon. There is also a small on-site shop selling hot and cold refreshments. To extend your day out, Moretonhampstead Motor Museum rests a short walk away.

Access

Access via steps and ladders. Level access to poolside; accessible toilets and changing facilities. Paid on-site parking at Court Street car park, which also has a bus stop (frequent services to Exeter, also Newton Abbot and Plymouth).

COWSIC WATERFALL POOL

50.5606, -3.9715 / Two Bridges, Devon / Swimming

The River Cowsic tumbles through waterfalls and small plunge pools to meet the River Dart near Two Bridges. If you follow the riverside path towards Beardown Farm, you will find secluded spots to swim among the verdant woodland. This isolated moorland is not easy to reach; you are close to the sinister Lych Way, or Way of the Dead, as it winds its way past the deserted gunpowder factory at Powder Mills and the oaks of Wistman's Wood. It may be a scramble down to the riverbanks and may be a stretch too far for younger children, but the effort required to reach the spot means that you are likely to enjoy it in peace. The Two Bridges Hotel offers fine dining but also cream teas on the lawn.

Access

Access via steep, grassy and muddy banks – follow the footpath towards Beardown Farm from Two Bridges. Buses from Tavistock, Plymouth, Exeter stop at the Two Bridges Hotel stop a few times a day, 500 metres away. Parking at Wistman's Wood car park, across road from Two Bridges Hotel, 500 metres away.

CRAZY WELL POOL

50.5165, -4.0011 / Princetown, Devon / Swimming

High on the moors of Dartmoor, Crazy Well Pool is a pool fed by a natural spring. Grassy and sometimes steep banks lead to the water, and the depths are often cold. Once the shelves on the water's edge drop away the pool feels bottomless – indeed, local tales long claimed that it was. More recent evidence suggests the water is around four and a half metres deep; it was probably excavated as part of the area's tin mines. This exposed and supposedly haunted pool has uninterrupted views across the atmospheric moors, and a trip here can be combined with a visit to the Crazywell Cross, allegedly the marker of an ancient track. Refreshments can be found at the Plume of Feathers Inn, five kilometres away in Princetown.

Access

Access via steep, tussocky slopes and small beach area. Buses to Tavistock run every two hours from Princetown, five kilometres away. Nearest parking at Whiteworks or Norsworthy Bridge car parks, just under three kilometres away. Clear paths detour north from bridleway between Whiteworks and Raddick Hill, or south from Devonport Leat path.

MAGPIE BRIDGE

50.5138, -4.1116 / Horrabridge, Devon / Swimming

Magpie Bridge, also known as Bedford Bridge, is a small pool on the fast-flowing River Walkham, which winds its way through some of Dartmoor's most stunning scenery. Rocks litter the entrance to the water and willow, oak and hazel trees create an emerald archway over the swim spot, making it the perfect place to escape the bustle of nearby Horrabridge. The pool is just deep enough for a refreshing swim, although care should be taken with the weeds which populate the river. After admiring the surrounding grassland, in which chamomile can be spotted, refreshments can be found at the Leaping Salmon in Horrabridge. The Drake's Trail cycling and walking route offers a pleasant and convenient route into the village, or to Plymouth or Tavistock for those wanting to combine a day's cycling with a cool dip.

Access

Access via gently sloping, grassy banks; reached on foot from footpath to south of river from Bedford Bridge, which connects with Drake's Trail. Frequent buses to Plymouth and Tavistock from Bedford Bridge stop, less than 100 metres away. Parking at Bedford Bridge car park (toilets now closed), less than 100 metres away.

MOUNT WISE SWIMMING POOLS. © *JAY CHARD*

CADOVER BRIDGE

50.4637, -4.0357 / Shaugh Prior, Devon / Swimming and paddling

In the heart of Dartmoor, Cadover Bridge forms one of the more popular pools on the River Plym. Flat, grassy banks provide access to the clear and shallow water, meaning this is a great place to bring children for a paddle. However, watch out for slippery rocks and sharp stones on the riverbed. Surrounded by scenic moorland views, this is an idyllic place for a day spent sunbathing. If you follow the footpath a couple of kilometres downstream into North Wood, you'll discover a waterfall and deep pool perfect for shaded swimming. Cadover Bridge is also a good starting point for walks across the moors and ancient woodlands, and when your feet are tired you can find

refreshments at the White Thorn Inn, or there is often an ice cream van in the Cadover Bridge car park.

Access

Access via mossy, grassy banks and shingly beaches. White Thorn Inn bus stop in Shaugh Prior is served by buses to Plymouth approximately four times a day, two kilometres away. Parking 300 metres away at Cadover Bridge car park.

MOUNT WISE SWIMMING POOLS

50.3656, -4.1733 / James Street, Plymouth, Devon, PL1 4HG / 01752 306265 / Swimming and paddling
www.everyoneactive.com/centre/ Mount-Wise-Swimming-Pools

While their glamorous neighbour, Tinside Lido, may garner the attention,

the white-walled Mount Wise Swimming Pools offer an alternative seaside pleasure. Free to enjoy, in addition to the main swimming pool there is a shallower pool with beach-style entry and a fun pool, complete with fountains, stepping stones and a bubble pool. Enjoy stunning seafront views and the opportunity to glimpse the stern grey ships as they sail in and out of the Royal Navy dockyard. The unheated, saltwater pools are next to a seaside cafe should you need a post-dip hot drink.

Access

Entry to water via ladders, beach-style entry. Level access to poolside. Frequent buses from Prospect Row to Plymouth centre and Derriford, 500 metres away; Devonport railway station two kilometres away. Free parking on James Street.

TINSIDE LIDO. © JAY CHARD

TINSIDE LIDO

50.3633, -4.1421 / Hoe Road, Plymouth, Devon, PL1 3DE / 01752 261915 / Swimming / *www.everyoneactive.com/centre/tinside-lido*

The blue stripes and generous curves of Tinside Lido, beneath the candy-striped Smeaton's Tower on Plymouth Hoe, epitomise the glamour of the 1930s art deco lido. Behind the whitewashed walls on the expansive sun terraces, you could mistakenly believe you are on the decks of a cruise ship as you gaze across the waves of Plymouth Sound. The pool retains many of its period features, with helpful modern additions such as a lift. The unheated, seawater pool offers inflatable fun sessions and starlit open air cinema evenings, as well as a well-regarded lido cafe. It is hard to believe that this pool was closed and derelict between 1992 and 2005, but it now offers the perfect opportunity to fall in love with the British seaside all over again.

Access
Access via steps and ladders. Lift provides access to level poolside; accessible changing rooms and toilet; hoist available. Frequent buses to local destinations from Royal Parade, just under a kilometre away; coach station a kilometre away; Plymouth railway station two kilometres away. Paid parking on promenade.

SALCOMBE SWIMMING POOL

50.2379, -3.7776 / Onslow Road, Salcombe, Devon, TQ8 8AG / 07746 248187 / Swimming / *www.facebook.com/Salcombe.Swimming.Pool*

On the outskirts of the golden-sanded tourist honeypot of Salcombe, Salcombe Swimming Pool is a functional pool for the local community. There is little space here for poolside lounging, but volunteers work hard to ensure that this summer-opening, heated pool is a great resource for the community. The twenty-five-metre pool is run by the Salcombe & District Swimming Pool Association, a registered charity founded in 1930. Facilities include changing rooms, showers and a foyer area offering a selection of hot and cold drinks, plus snacks. A trip here can be combined with a visit to Fort Charles, a sixteenth-century artillery castle built under the orders of King Henry VIII.

Access
Access via steps and ladders; wheelchair access to poolside may be restricted due to space. Hourly buses to Kingsbridge, Salcombe centre from Main Road, adjacent to lido. On-site parking.

SHOALSTONE SEAWATER POOL. © *CHRIS SLACK*

DARTMOUTH OUTDOOR POOL

50.3468, -3.5953 / Milton Lane, Dartmouth, Devon, TQ6 9HW / 07706 730947 / Swimming / *www.dartmouthpool.weebly.com*

Dartmouth Outdoor Pool is a treasured, community-run, heated lido tucked away at the top of the town just alongside Dartmouth Academy. The twenty-five-metre-long lido is open to the public every day from the end of May to the first weekend of September, with public swimming sessions taking place from 9 a.m. to 5 p.m. The pool also runs early morning swims and adult-only sessions in the evening, as well as hosting swimming galas, fundraising barbecues and children's birthdays. The lido is staffed by lifeguards during the summer season and offers changing facilities with warm showers. Also on-site is a grassy outdoor area ideal for picnicking on, plus a small shop selling a range of hot and cold drinks, snacks and swimming accessories. Venturing a short distance into Dartmouth provides plenty of refreshment options.

Access
Entry into pool via steps and ladders. Level access to poolside. Buses to Plymouth and centre of Dartmouth stops outside lido hourly. Academy car park available outside school hours; also on-street parking.

SHOALSTONE SEAWATER POOL

50.4012, -3.4987 / Berry Head Road, Brixham, Devon, TQ5 9FT07799 414702 / Swimming / *www.shoalstonepool.com*

A popular bathing spot since Victorian times, the Shoalstone Seawater Pool is a fifty-three-metre lido sunk into a rock promontory in the fishing port of Brixham. The pool is free to use but relies on donations to survive. Never actually closed, there are lifeguards during the summer but swimming in winter is not generally encouraged. Overlooking the pool is a picnic green and extensive decks, with sunloungers and deckchairs available to hire; there are also a number of beach huts on-site which can be rented on a season-by-season basis. Refreshments are available to purchase from the Water's Edge kiosk and Shoals restaurant. With its sparkling turquoise seawater, social shallow end and striking white buildings, this is a stunning pool in a special location.

Access
Entry to pool via ladders and steep ramp; steps to poolside. Frequent buses from Torquay, Paignton and Newton Abbot stop in Brixham centre, two kilometres away; 17 bus connects town to Berry Head Road. Paid on-site parking – profits go towards pool costs.

BUCKFASTLEIGH OPEN AIR POOL. © BUCKFASTLEIGH OPEN AIR POOL

DARTINGTON SWIMMING POOL

50.4475, -3.7118 / Shinner's Bridge, Dartington, Totnes, Devon, TQ9 6JD / 07940 938015 / Swimming / *www.dartington-swimmingpool.co.uk*

Tucked next to the wooded Bidwell Brook, the unheated Dartington Swimming Pool is a popular post-school swim spot for local families. It was originally dug out by volunteers in the 1970s, and the twenty-metre-long pool remains dependent on the hard work of volunteer villagers. The pool opens from May to September, generally only in the afternoons. On-site facilities include a tuck shop, changing rooms and toilet. The lido is next to a grassy play area with climbing frames and table tennis, and there are plenty of places to grab a bite to eat nearby. Those looking for a different post-dip experience could learn how to make their own gin at the Devon Gin School, just across the road from the lido.

Access

Entry into pool via ladders. Level access to poolside; accessible toilet. Frequent buses to Plymouth, Newton Abbot, Totnes stop at Shinners Bridge stop, 300 metres away; closest railway station is Totnes, three kilometres away. Paid parking at Bidwell Brook car park, adjacent to lido.

STAVERTON WEIR, RIVER DART

50.4611, -3.7075 / Staverton, Devon / Swimming and paddling

The River Dart between Staverton and Dartington offers plenty of opportunity for swimming, and Staverton Weir, close to the heritage railway station, is a popular summer spot. Those who venture a few hundred metres downstream will discover the wide, tranquil, willow-fringed Still Pool. A small, sandy beach gives access to the water, but there is a rope swing for the adventurous. The deep, dark

waters provide a mystical feel, and lucky swimmers may see a dipper. For a trip back in time, take the steam railway from Totnes and jump off at Staverton (or the Nappers Halt request stop) for an idyllic dip. Ginger beers (or craft cocktails) all round at the fifteenth-century Sea Trout Inn afterwards!

Access

Access via grassy banks and sandy beach, with rocks to jump from. Public footpath from Staverton railway station to weir, north bank of river; also paths on south bank. Staverton and Nappers Halt heritage railway stations less than a kilometre away, also buses to Totnes from here. Parking at Staverton Play Park, a kilometre away.

BUCKFASTLEIGH OPEN AIR POOL

50.4797, -3.7797 / Victoria Park, Plymouth Road, Buckfastleigh, Devon, TQ11 0DB / 01364 642222 / Swimming *www.buckfastleighpool.co.uk*

Buckfastleigh Open Air Pool is a colourful little pool (just twenty-one metres long) tucked into a corner of Victoria Park, which also boasts a skate park and adventure play area. While Victoria Park offers plenty of picnic space the pool itself is compact, with little spare space around the edges, although there is a small sun

ASHBURTON SWIMMING POOL. © *CARA GRIFFITHS, SANDINMYPOCKETS.COM*

deck. The lido's timetable comprises of a variety of sessions, including early morning lane swimming, family swims and fun sessions for kids. The reception area doubles as a tuck shop for those wanting a sweet treat. A trip here could be combined with a day out at Buckfast Abbey or lunch at the Riverford Field Kitchen, and it's an easy detour from the A38 main road en route to Plymouth or Cornwall.

Access

Entry to water via ladder; access to pool involves steps and tight spaces. Bus stop at lido with frequent buses to Newton Abbot and Exeter, also nearby X38 service to Plymouth. Paid on-site parking.

ASHBURTON SWIMMING POOL

50.5158, -3.7519 / Whistley Hill, Love Lane, Ashburton, Devon, TQ13 7DW / 01364 641094 / Swimming
www.ashburtonpool.com

Open from May to September each year, Ashburton Swimming Pool is a heated, twenty-one-metre lido situated in a small town on the south-eastern edge of Dartmoor. The pool was built in 1924 as part of the Golden Lion Hotel before it was eventually taken over by Teignbridge District Council as a public lido. The pool is managed by volunteers from the local community and runs a variety of swimming activities including general swimming, lane swimming, women-only sessions and aqua fit classes. Alongside the lido is a grassy park area featuring picnic tables and benches. There is also a small on-site cafe selling drinks, snacks and swimming essentials such as goggles, floats and armbands. The proceeds from the cafe go towards the Friends of Ashburton Swimming Pool fund to help with future developments. Further refreshments can be found at the Silent Whistle pub.

Access

Access via steps and ladders. Level access to poolside. Frequent buses to Exeter, Newton Abbot, Totnes from Eastern Road, 300 metres away. Pay-and-display car park in town centre, 500 metres away.

WELLSFOOT ISLAND

50.5162, -3.8268 / Holne, Devon / Swimming and paddling

Nestled deep in Holne Woods, Wellsfoot Island is a secret island which gives respite from the River Dart. The rusty, peaty water is just deep enough to swim in, although the algae-laden boulders beneath the water's surface are sometimes slippery. Once you reach the velvety, copper sand of the island, a canopy of trees and abundance of flowers await you. The River Dart slows into a gentle meander here, and as you gaze up at the high cliff which flanks the water it feels as if you could be the only person in the world. The Church House Inn provides refreshments in the picturesque village of Holne; there is also a community-run tearoom.

Access
Access via grassy banks and red, sandy beach. Follow cycle lane north from Holne to reach riverbank. Bus to Newton Abbot stops once daily on Wednesdays from Church House Inn in Holne, less than a kilometre away. Limited street parking in Holne; do not block passing places. Newbridge car park approximately three kilometres away.

HORSESHOE FALLS

50.5200, -3.8200 / Holne, Devon / Swimming and plunge pool

For those who want a wooded swim slightly closer to the car park than Sharrah Pool, Horseshoe Falls is a small, horseshoe-shaped waterfall set by a series of deep plunge pools. Grassy banks and rocks lead into the water, which has a sudden drop in depth, but if you make your way up to the waterfall it will give you a refreshing natural massage. Or for those seeking a thrill, just upstream there is a rope swing. Encased in an enchanting woodland, this spot is as peaceful as it is stunning. Refreshments can be found in Holne at the Holne Community Shop & Tearoom or the Church House Inn.

Access
Access via rock slab, pebbly beaches and muddy banks. Not easily reached by public transport: one bus on Wednesday from Newbridge to Tavistock Inn in Poundsgate, 500 metres away. Parking at Newbridge car park, 500 metres away.

SPITCHWICK COMMON

50.5253, -3.8140 / Poundsgate, Devon / Swimming and paddling

Spitchwick Common is a charming, accessible stretch of river surrounded by woodland. Grassy flats lead to the rocky riverbank, which gives way to clean, peaty water. The water gets deeper on the far side, and behind this a cliff looms. A search will reveal rough-cut granite steps which lead down to clear pools. This is one of Dartmoor's most cherished swim spots, but it has become busy in recent years – despite this, it is a refreshing diversion from the Two Moors Way long-distance trail, which crosses Newbridge. This is in an ideal place to combine with a trip to Buckfast Abbey, and refreshments can be found at the Tavistock Inn in Poundsgate.

Access
Access via shallow, grassy slopes. Tavistock to Dawlish bus, nicknamed 'England's rarest bus service', stops at Newbridge on the fifth Saturday in summer months; 672 service to Newton Abbot stops once daily on Wednesdays. Newbridge car park 350 metres away; follow footpath along north bank of river to reach Spitchwick Common.

SHARRAH POOL

50.5300, -3.8396 / Poundsgate, Devon / Swimming and paddling

Surrounded by enchanting woodland, Sharrah Pool is a secluded pool where the River Dart and Dart Gorge meet. Around 100 metres across, there are sandy patches which allow easy access into the deep, crystal-clear water.

You may find the chill of the water a shock as you tiptoe in, owing to the calm current flowing through. Confident swimmers can surf the 'Sharrah Chute', by jumping from the Elephant Rock into the cascade. The Holne Woods which surround the pool give it a magical feel, and there are plenty of large rocks to enjoy a picnic on after your swim. Alternatively, you can walk two kilometres to one of England's oldest pubs, the Tavistock Inn.

Access

Access via sandy beaches and granite slabs. Only accessible on foot, through National Trust's Holne Woods. Poorly served by public transport: one bus on Wednesday to Poundsgate/Tavistock Inn from Newton Abbot, two kilometres away. Newbridge car park two and a half kilometres away.

BOVEY TRACEY SWIMMING POOL

50.5869, -3.6779 / Recreation Ground, Newton Road, Bovey Tracey, Devon, TQ13 9BD / 01626 832828 / Swimming and paddling / www.boveyswimmingpool.org.uk

Bovey Tracey is a charming market town on the edge of Dartmoor. Its charity-run, twenty-five-metre-long lido is beloved by locals; schoolchildren created colourful poolside mosaics

for the pool, which celebrated its fiftieth anniversary in 2019. In addition to the main pool, which is heated to 28 °C, there is a three-metre-square toddler's pool. Other facilities include a sun terrace, a spectator area and a well-stocked kiosk selling plenty of drinks, snacks and ice creams. The pool offers swimming lessons, inflatable fun sessions and, although it is usually only open in the summer, festive swims complete with polar bears.

Access

Entry into water via ladders. Level access to poolside; accessible changing facilities and toilet; hoist available. Hourly buses to Exeter and Newton Abbot from Dolphin Square, 300 metres away. Parking at recreation ground adjacent to lido.

CHUDLEIGH COMMUNITY POOL

50.6025, -3.6010 / Lawn Drive, Chudleigh, Newton Abbot, Devon, TQ13 0LS / 07886 128349 / Swimming / www.chudleighpool.org.uk

In the heart of the pretty little wool town of Chudleigh, the community-run swimming pool is nestled next to the primary school. The small pool is heated to a balmy 28 °C, and an arched wooden shelter provides a poolside refuge whatever the weather. Not all lidos are historic – Chudleigh's

BOVEY TRACEY SWIMMING POOL. © *JOHN STEER*

was built in 1997, and utilises solar panels as well as being low chlorine. There is always something going on at this pool in the summer, with twenty-four-hour swims and music and drama fundraising events. Venturing a short distance into Chudleigh provides a variety of refreshment options.

Access

Entry into water by ladders. Level/ramped access to poolside; accessible changing rooms and toilet. Hourly buses to Newton Abbot from Memorial stop, 300 metres away. School car park available outside school hours; otherwise street parking.

TOPSHAM OUTDOOR SWIMMING POOL. © *SARAH THELWALL*

KINGSTEIGNTON SWIMMING POOL

50.5583, -3.6016 / Meadow-croft Drive, Kingsteignton, Newton Abbot, Devon, TQ12 3PB / 01626 366480 / Swimming and paddling / *www.kingsteigntonswimming-pool.org.uk*

In 1972, Kingsteignton held carnivals, sponsored knits and tea dances to kick off a fundraising campaign for a local lido; the pool was finally built in 1979. Fundraising has continued ever since, including for the toddler's pool, a new boiler and pool liner, and currently replacement sand filters. There is a seating area around the pool for spectators and an on-site kiosk selling hot and cold drinks, confectionery and ice creams, and the pool has good accessibility with sloping steps and a hoist. On the edge of a small town, this lido is testament to what can be achieved through coffee mornings, teddy tombolas,

plant sales and dogged determination; even the local canine population has been helping out on sponsored walks.

Access

Entry to pool via ladders and handrailed steps. Level access to pool; accessible changing rooms and toilets; hoist available. Frequent buses to Exeter and Newton Abbot from Exeter Road, on opposite side of playing field. On-site parking.

TEIGNMOUTH LIDO

50.5484, -3.4914 / Eastcliff Walk, Teignmouth, Devon, TQ14 8TA / 01626 779063 / Swimming / *www.teignbridgelei-sure.co.uk/swim/teignmouth-lido*

On Teignmouth's seafront, next to the Royal Corinthian Yacht Club, the twenty-five-metre Teignmouth Lido is one of three operated by Teignbridge District Council (the others are Buckfastleigh and Ashburton

– see pages 14 and 15). Built in 1976, the heated lido operates in the summer months. The lido offers a variety of swimming activities including lane swimming sessions, adult-only sessions, fun sessions and family aqua fit sessions. As well as the pool, there is also a small play area and an on-site refreshment kiosk. The Eastcliff Cafe is next to the pool, and the quaint seaside town of Teignmouth has plenty to entertain the whole family, including the Grand Pier. The pool is closed for the 2021 season in order to undergo energy-efficient modernisation.

Access

Entry into water via steps and ladders. Level access to poolside; accessible toilet. Teignmouth railway station 300 metres away; buses from Exeter, Dawlish and Newton Abbot can be caught from town centre, 300 metres away. Paid parking at East Cliff car park, across the railway line from the lido.

TOPSHAM OUTDOOR SWIMMING POOL

50.6846, -3.4651 / Fore Street, Topsham, Exeter, Devon, EX3 0HF / 01392 874477 / Swimming / www.topshampool.moonfruit.com

When Devon's beaches are tiled with towels, you can seek out a special spot to sunbathe on the patio of Topsham's twenty-five-metre-long lido, tucked among semi-detached houses and just behind the railway station. Built in 1979, the community-run, heated pool remains a beloved local swim spot and is open from April to September, although it also offers New Year's Day swim sessions. With its friendly cafe (well stocked with cake), family fun inflatable sessions and dawn swims for the dedicated, Topsham Outdoor Swimming Pool offers something for everyone. Topsham is an attractive town on the Exe Estuary, with plenty of pubs; the historic Bridge Inn was the first pub officially visited by the Queen. The port town offers Dutch-style housing, antiques shopping and the Topsham Museum with its Vivien Leigh exhibition to explore. It is the perfect stop on a day out cycling the Exe Estuary Trail.

Access
Access via ladders and handrailed steps. Level access to poolside. Topsham railway station 200 metres away. Nelson stop, 100 metres away, served by frequent buses to Exeter and Exmouth. Limited parking at Matthews Hall Car Park; further parking at quayside.

CORNWALL HOUSE OUTDOOR POOL

50.7345, -3.5294 / 21 St German's Road, Exeter, Devon EX4 6TG / 01392 722515 / Swimming / www.sport.exeter.ac.uk/facilities/swimmingpools

A functional pool primarily for Exeter's student population, the Cornwall House Outdoor Pool nonetheless welcomes the general public and offers a quiet oasis on the green fringes of this historic city. The twenty-five-metre-long lido, on the University of Exeter's Streatham Campus, is open seven days a week during the summer months and runs a variety of sessions including lane swimming and recreational swimming, plus family swims with small inflatables and floats. Although the pool itself does not offer refreshments, there are plenty of places on and about campus to grab a bite to eat, all of them catering for a student budget.

Access
Entry into pool via ladders. Level access to poolside; limited changing facilities. University campus well-served by high-frequency buses to city centre. Less than one kilometre to St James Park railway station; a kilometre and a half to Exeter St David's.

Limited visitor parking on university campus.

FLUXTON WEIR, RIVER OTTER

50.7376, -3.2837 / Ottery St Mary, Devon / Swimming and paddling

Near the pretty village of Ottery St Mary is a calm stretch of the River Otter near Fluxton Weir, which has its own natural flume section and a rope swing. The paths on the east banks of the river rise above the floodplains, so it is easier to reach on the western side. Once through the dropping willows which frame the water, the surrounding luscious fields provide a place to dry off. There is a deep pool nearly two kilometres north of the weir at a sharp bend in the river. Knights Farm Shop offers takeaway hot drinks and cakes, as well as local produce, and Ottery St Mary has plenty of refreshment options, including the Rusty Pig and Lamb & Flag pubs.

Access
Access via sandy beach area and gentle, grassy slopes; easy footpath between Ottery St Mary and Tipton St John along the western banks. Frequent buses to Exeter (less frequent services to Honiton, Axminster and Sidmouth) from Ottery St Mary, two kilometres from the deep pool. Paid parking at Canaan Way car park, three kilometres away.

CLYST HYDON SWIMMING POOL

50.8042, -3.3815 / Clyst Hydon, Cullompton, Devon, EX15 2NT / Swimming / *www.sites.google. com/site/clysthydonswimmingclub*

A green-edged pool up a wooded track dug into Devon's rolling farmland, Clyst Hydon Swimming Pool is a friendly little pool on the edge of a small village. The pool was founded when the local squire dammed the river; a more permanent structure was built in the 1950s. The community-run pool is unheated but offers a warm welcome; check out their occasional swimming brunches, offering a fried breakfast after your swim. There is a slide and small paddling pool, as well as plenty of grass to play on. The pool relies entirely on volunteers, and may close during bad weather or due to staffing shortages. The Five Bells Inn, next to the lido, offers sandwiches and hearty pub lunches.

Access

Access via ladders and a slide. Poolside not level, and access to pool itself requires crossing rough terrain. Difficult to reach by public transport: Whimple railway station eight kilometres away. Free parking at village hall, at bottom of track.

WIVEY POOL

51.0405, -3.3183 / The Recreation Ground, Wiveliscombe, Somerset, TA4 2TA / 01984 624720 / Swimming / *www.wiveypool.net*

The volunteer-run Wivey Pool is deep in the green West Country farmlands, on the edge of the historic town of Wiveliscombe. One of Somerset's oldest pools, the twenty-seven-and-a-half-metre-long lido opened in 1927, and remains a popular summertime destination. Traditionally the heated pool only opens in the summer season, but they have been experimenting with autumn and winter swims (with warm mince pies afterwards). There are picnic spots and a sunbathing deck poolside, and hot drinks available from the kiosk.

Access

Access via ladders (diving permitted). Level/ramped access to poolside. The Square stop, 700 metres away, is served by buses to Taunton approximately every three hours. Small car park on-site; free car park near recreation ground.

TINTINHULL SWIMMING POOL

50.9749, -2.7147 / Tintinhull, Yeovil, Somerset, BA22 8PW / Swimming and paddling / *www. tintinhullparishcouncil.gov.uk/ Swimming_Pool_22592.aspx*

Built in the 1930s, Tintinhull Swimming Pool is a small, narrow lido operated and maintained by the village's parish council. In its early days, the pool's water – drawn from a local borehole – had a tendency to turn green, a problem solved by modern filtration systems. Beside the main pool is a separate toddler pool, plus space for picnics and sunbathing. There are no lifeguards at the pool, although at least one volunteer 'pool opener' at any session will have received first aid and resuscitation training. The lido is generally open from May to September each year, although opening hours depend on volunteer availability. The pretty honey-coloured village is also home to the formal Tintinhull Gardens, run by the National Trust, where there are tearooms; the village also has a pub, the Crown and Victoria, serving food.

Access

Entry into water via steps and ladders. Level access to poolside; accessible changing areas but no accessible toilet. Regular buses to Yeovil depart from Head Street, 500 metres south of lido. Parking at village hall, a few hundred metres away.

WIVEY POOL. © *WIVEY POOL*

WAREHAM BRIDGE

50.6836, -2.1094 / Wareham, Dorset / Swimming and paddling

As the River Frome winds its way through Wareham, one of the only remaining Saxon walled towns in England, it widens to a popular swimming spot under Wareham's South Bridge. Stony steps and muddy banks slope leisurely to the river, which is deep enough for swimming but not for jumping in. Swimmers should watch out for other river users, such as small boats and kayaks. The grassy areas and benches dotted around make this a slice of serenity in the bustling Dorset town. The Old Granary and Quay Inn pubs overlook the swim spot, but there is ample choice for refreshment in Wareham; there are public toilets by the Howards Lane car park.

Access

Access via stony steps and muddy banks. Frequent buses to Poole, Swanage and Weymouth from town centre, less than a kilometre away; Wareham railway station just over one kilometre north. Pay-and-display car park by bridge, several other car parks within 500 metres of swim spot.

FIDDLEFORD MANOR

50.9216, -2.2860 / Fiddleford, Dorset / Swimming

Fiddleford Manor is a quiet millpond in the shadow of a historic manor house believed to have been built in the fourteenth century by the Sheriff of Somerset and Dorset. Grassy banks and shallow weir steps give easy access to the water, which is channelled by three old sluice gates. The water is often invitingly warm in summer months. A swim here is a dive into the heart of Thomas Hardy Country, and with ancient woodlands surrounding you it is not difficult to lose yourself in the romance of the countryside. A dip here can be combined with a trip to the eponymous manor house, and afterwards the Fiddleford Inn offers hearty meals. The Stour Valley Way offers a pleasant walking route from Fiddleford into Sturminster Newton.

Access

Access via shallow steps and grassy banks. Buses from Sturminster Newton to Gillingham, which has a railway station, stop a few times a day three kilometres away. Free parking at Fiddleford Manor.

COLBER BRIDGE

50.9277, -2.3105 / Sturminster Newton, Dorset / Swimming and paddling

As the River Stour winds its way through the limestone Blackmore Vale, it opens up to a calm, reedy stretch of water by Colber Bridge. The grassy fields which flank the river extend to banks to the water, although these can sometimes be muddy and may have a drop to the river. The serene, deep water flows under the ornate wrought-iron bridge, and as you enjoy a long swim either up or downstream you may spot a kingfisher or demoiselle dragonfly. This stretch of river is also used by a local angling club, so be sure to check for anglers before climbing in. After a relaxing float, Sturminster Newton, once home to Thomas Hardy and his wife Emma, has plenty of tearooms and pubs on Market Cross; there are also public toilets in the Station Road car park.

Access

Access via muddy, grassy and sometimes steep banks. Footpath from The Row leads to Colber Bridge and river; Stour Valley Way path offers access to eastern banks. Buses from town centre to Gillingham, which has a railway station, stop a few times a day. Pay-and-display car parks in town centre, less than a kilometre away.

CUTT MILL

50.9480, -2.3199 / Hinton St Mary, Dorset / Swimming and paddling

Cutt Mill was once home to generations of millers, but now its ruins preside over a pool on the River Stour popular with local swimmers. Grassy banks with a small drop provide access, and the water has shallow patches but deepens by the weir. The farmland which flanks the swim spot is rich in wildlife, with common sandpipers and sedge warblers often making an appearance in summer. As the clear, slow-moving water engulfs you, this spot has the feel of a scene that has stopped in time. The shallow waters are perfect for a splash, but it is dangerous to jump from the ruins into the river. Hinton St Mary offers refreshments at the White Horse Inn, and further choice can be found down the road in Sturminster Newton.

Access

Access via grassy banks. Follow Hardy Way or Stour Valley Way from Sturminster Newton, or Leigh Lane near Hinton St Mary. Buses to Sturminster Newton and Gillingham (which has a railway station) stop regularly at Hinton Bus Shelter, just over a kilometre away. Limited on-street parking in Hinton St Mary; car parks in Sturminster Newton.

SHAFTESBURY OASIS SWIMMING POOL

51.0081, -2.1939 / Barton Hill, Shaftesbury, Dorset, SP7 8DQ / 01747 853181 / Swimming / *www.shaftesbury-oasis.com*

Tucked away on a residential street, Shaftesbury Oasis is a heated community outdoor pool run by the council. The small, enclosed pool (twenty-three metres long by nine metres wide) is brightly decorated. This family orientated lido offers inflatable session for children on Friday afternoons but also lane swimming and early morning and evening adult-only sessions for those seeking calmer waters. Poolside space is limited, but you can purchase hot and cold drinks from the snack kiosk.

Access

Entry to pool via steps. Level access to the poolside; facilities may be challenging due to space. Frequent buses to Salisbury from Town Hall stop on High Street, 500 metres away. Limited street parking; do not block ambulance access. Angel Lane pay-and-display car park less than a kilometre away.

WEST LYDFORD, RIVER BRUE. © *GOWILDGOWEST*

TISBURY SWIMMING POOL

51.0669, -2.0847 / Weaveland Road, Tisbury, Wiltshire, SP3 6HJ / 01747 870896 / Swimming / *www.tisburyswimmingpool.co.uk*

The friendly Tisbury Swimming Pool is Wiltshire's only heated lido. The small pool (twenty-three metres long) is popular, particularly during the family friendly afternoons. This is not a linger-all-day lido – the day is timetabled into sessions that include public swimming, lane swimming, adults only and parent and baby. When the lifeguards go home for the day, the pool has been known to host the occasional pool party, often with a fancy-dress theme. Refreshments, including hot drinks and ice lollies, are available to purchase on-site. There are also toys available for children to play with in the pool, and there is plenty of room for sunbathing. To extend your day out, the fourteenth-century ruins of Old Wardour Castle lie five kilometres away.

Access
Entry into water via ladders. Level access to poolside. Tisbury railway station approximately a kilometre away; buses from High Street, 300 metres away, to Salisbury stop a few times a day.

WEST LYDFORD, RIVER BRUE

51.0843, -2.6233 / West Lydford, Somerset / Swimming

In the shadow of West Lydford's Church of St Peter, a 100-metre stretch of the River Brue is a tranquil spot for a dip. Steep grassy slopes offer a muddy scramble to the water, and as you float in the calm current you can gaze at the seventeenth-century bridge. You can admire the flower-lined waters, watch out for demoiselle dragonflies in the spring or simply sunbathe on the riverbanks in a spot which will make you feel as if you have stepped into a postcard. After your dip, refreshments can be found at the Cross Keys Inn.

Access
Access via steeply sloping grassy and muddy banks. Buses between Wincanton and Street at A37 and B3153 crossroads every two hours, approximately a kilometre away. Limited street parking on road near church in West Lydford.

GREENBANK POOL

51.1272, -2.7377 / Wilfrid Road, Street, Somerset, BA16 0EU / 01458 442468 / Swimming and paddling / *www.greenbank-pool.co.uk*

The philanthropy of shoe-making family the Clarks has left its mark in diverse ways on the pretty Somerset village of Street; in 1934, feminist Alice Clark bequeathed Greenbank Pool to the local women as a safe space to swim, far from the rowdy men splashing, often unclothed, in the River Brue. The leafy lawns behind white art deco pool buildings are now a popular family picnic spot. The thirty-metre-long pool is heated to a cosy 30 °C, and there is a splash park as well as a shallow paddling area to keep the kids cool. There's a friendly kiosk if you fancy an ice cream in the Somerset sunshine. If a visit to Street's Clarks Village factory outlet doesn't appeal, the mystical Glastonbury Tor is approx-imately four kilometres away. The summer-opening Greenbank Pool is closed until 2022.

Access
Entry to water via ladders. Level/ramped access to poolside (may have to cross grass); accessible changing facilities and toilet; hoist available. Regular buses to Yeovil, Taunton, Bridgwater and Shepton Mallet stop 300 metres away. On-site parking.

SHEPTON MALLET LIDO

51.1912, -2.5527 / Shaftsgate Avenue, Shepton Mallet, Somerset, BA4 5YA / 01749 347851 / Swimming and paddling / *www.fusion-lifestyle.com/centres/shepton-mallet-lido*

Shepton Mallet's lido is framed not by trees, but the towering tanks of the Brothers Cider factory next door – recycled heat from the plant was once used to heat the pool water. The twenty-five-metre-long pool is accompanied by a splash area, full of fountains and water jets, and a shallow children's pool. Tucked in among houses and a trading estate, this lido is a blue oasis with grassy lawns and an undercover balcony area for those looking to relax. It offers moonlight swims for those seeking to swim beneath the stars. Ice creams are available from the well-stocked on-site shop, which also offers a good range of swim kit.

Access
Entry into water via ladders. Ramped access to poolside. Regular buses to Street, Yeovil, Frome and Bath can be caught from town centre, 500 metres away. On-site parking.

GREENBANK POOL. © *SARAH THELWALL*

FARLEIGH HUNGER-FORD, RIVER FROME

51.3178, -2.2826 / Farleigh Hungerford, Somerset / Swimming and paddling / *farleighswimming.co.uk*

Farleigh Hungerford, home to the Farleigh and District Swim-ming Club, is an eighty-metre stretch of gravel-bottomed river, up to just under two and a half metres in depth. Steps and ladders provide access to the water, and there is shallower, if slippery, access from the weir. You must be a member of the Swimming Club to swim (annual family membership, for up to six, is £25 in 2021 – membership can be purchased at Stowford Manor Farm). The grassy meadows offer plenty of space for sunbathing, although dogs are not allowed on-site. The site is open from May to Sep-tember and occasionally out of season. During the season, there is a Portaloo and open changing stall available. After

DUNDAS AQUEDUCT. © SHUTTERSTOCK/ANDY BALLARD

DUNDAS AQUEDUCT, RIVER AVON

51.3619, -2.3101 / Monkton Combe, Somerset / Swimming and paddling

On the outskirts of Bath, the nineteenth-century Dundas Aqueduct carries the Kennet and Avon Canal over the River Avon and is a popular spot for canal boats and day trippers. Fewer people visit the tree-fringed river beneath the aqueduct, but the lush riverbanks offer the perfect peaceful wild swim spot in the shadows of the aqueduct's towering arches. If you're lucky, you might even spot a heron or kingfisher on the banks of this calm river. There are plenty of picnic spots and benches by the canal, and spots to paddle as well as swim. The Angelfish Restaurant is a short walk away. This is also a perfect destination for cyclists: the NCN 4 cycle route follows the canal right into Bath.

Access

Access via grassy banks, small beach areas and pontoon. River can be accessed from aqueduct via a path down to boathouse, opposite side from basin. Frequent buses to Brassknocker Basin from Salisbury, Trowbridge and Bath stop next to aqueduct. Pay-and-display car park at Brassknocker Basin.

your dip you can visit the ruins of the fourteenth-century Farleigh Hungerford Castle, and enjoy a cream tea at Stowford Manor Farm.

Access

Access via steps, ladders, and weir; jumping permitted, but not diving. Difficult to reach by public transport; Avoncliff railway station approximately three kilometres away. Free parking in field by swim spot.

AVONCLIFF

51.3396, -2.2797 / Avoncliff, Wiltshire / Swimming and paddling

Near John Rennie's towering Avoncliff Aqueduct, a fun family swim spot can be discovered above the five-foot-high weir on the River Avon. In the shadow of an old mill-house, the deep and calm river pool is the perfect spot to splash around on a summer's day.

The perfect day trip from Bristol, this spot offers a rope swing, grassy picnic spots and flat, shallow paddling areas. The river is swimmable up to historic Bradford-on-Avon. This popular stretch is also frequented by kayakers and canoeists, so keep an eye out and consider wearing a bright swim cap. Refreshments can be found at the waterside Cross Guns pub. There are also plenty of pubs and cafes in Bradford-on-Avon – a walk along the canal towpath from the town will allow you to visit the fourteenth-century stone Tithe Barn on the way.

Access

Access via gently sloping, grassy banks and stone-slabbed weir. Avoncliff railway station just across the aqueduct, offering services to Bristol, Exeter and London. Limited free parking near aqueduct – consider walking the two kilometres along towpath from Bradford-on-Avon.

CLEVELAND POOLS. © *BEN HOLMES*

CLEVELAND POOLS

51.3909, -2.3474 / Hampton Row, Bath, Somerset, BA2 6QS / 07836 252569 / Swimming and paddling / *www.clevelandpools.org.uk*

Cleveland Pools is Britain's oldest outdoor pool; the semi-circular lido, with its Georgian crescent-style buildings, was built in 1815. It closed in 1978, briefly becoming a trout farm in the 1980s. After a seventeen-year campaign, the Cleveland Pools Trust have rescued the lido, with the help of the National Lottery; it is scheduled to reopen in 2022. The restored pools will offer a children's pool and splash area, a kiosk, space to sunbathe, Georgian-style changing cubicles and improved accessibility. This tree-fringed pool, on the outskirts of historic Bath, promises the very best of past and present in a Georgian lido, rejuvenated for the twenty-first century; in the meantime, you will have to satisfy yourself with a wild swim at nearby Kensington Meadows.

Access
Access via steps. Accessibility unclear, but the restoration has a commitment to improved accessibility and access. Frequent buses to city centre on Beckford Road, 300 metres away; Bath Spa railway station two kilometres away. No on-site parking – swimmers encouraged to arrive on foot, bike or bus (or boat!), but Podium car park a kilometre and a half away.

KENSINGTON MEADOWS, RIVER AVON

51.3911, -2.3483 / Bath, Somerset / Swimming

Hidden in the heart of the historic city of Bath is a stretch of the River Avon adjacent to the nature reserve of Kensington Meadows. It is a delight to discover this secret spot to escape the tourists that crowd the city streets and to cool down after a busy day of sightseeing. This spot is just across the river from the Cleveland Pools, the Georgian lido that is currently undergoing restoration. This stretch of the river is often busy with kayakers, boats and other river users so consider a brightly coloured cap and tow float. The wide, flat meadows are perfect for a picnic and offer panoramic city views. For a full day out, the Royal Crescent and Roman Baths are both within walking distance, and there is a variety of pubs and cafes throughout the city.

Access
Access via grassy banks. Bath city centre approximately a kilometre and a half away; Bath Spa railway station two kilometres. Frequent buses to Bath centre on London Road, 500 metres away (also buses to Devizes and Chippenham). Pay-and-display car parks on Avon Street and Charlotte Street; limited on-street parking.

RISING SUN, RIVER CHEW. © *GRACE HAINES*

RISING SUN, RIVER CHEW

51.3718, -2.5522 / Pensford, Somerset / Swimming and paddling

In the shadow of the Grade-II-listed Pensford Viaduct, the River Chew opens to create a shallow pool perfect for paddling. Grassy banks slope gently into the water and provide sun-soaked areas to enjoy a picnic. With plenty of shallow areas, this is an ideal spot to bring children after exploring the tranquil Chew Valley. Although there are no facilities at the spot itself, food and drink can be found at the Rising Sun, whose beer garden overlooks the River Chew.

Access

Access via grassy banks (follow the lane by Rising Sun or footpath on opposite side of river). Frequent buses to Street, Bristol, Wells and Bath stop in Pensford village centre, less than a kilometre away. Limited on-street parking; alternate parking at village hall, 500 metres away.

YATTON, RIVER YEO

51.3826, -2.8587 / Yatton, Somerset / Swimming

Between the M5 motorway and the West Coast Main Line railway, you'll find a bracing swim spot in the horseshoe curves of the River Yeo. The perfect day trip from Bristol, this steep-banked section of the water offers privacy and seclusion. Nestled among Somerset's green farmland, this spot is characterised by its crystal clear and reedy water, although the river may run low after a dry spell. A dip here and sunbathe on the lush surrounding fields will be sure to leave you refreshed, and afterwards nearby Yatton offers plenty of opportunity to get a bite to eat.

Access

Entry to water via steep-sided banks; a scramble may be required. Yatton railway station two kilometres away via Wemberham Lane; swim spot is easy to reach by bike. Frequent buses to Bristol from railway station. Nearest parking at railway station.

CLEVEDON MARINE LAKE. © *LAURA NESBITT*

CLEVEDON MARINE LAKE

51.4351, -2.8699 / Salthouse Fields, Old Church Road, Clevedon, Somerset, BS21 7TU / 01275 877180 / Swimming and paddling / *www.clevedonmarinelake.co.uk*

The expansive Clevedon Marine Lake is the largest tidal infinity pool in the world, containing 30 million litres of seawater. The lake is shared with canoeists, model boat enthusiasts and even zorbers, so consider taking a brightly coloured swim cap. The lake's calendar provides details of events and overtopping (you should not swim when the water overtops the perimeters, in stormy weather or if a red flag is flying). The lake has no lifeguards and is only one metre deep at its fringes, so diving is not permitted, and there are public toilets near the neighbouring coastguard station. Since its opening in 1929, the pool has welcomed long-distance swimmers and challenge events, but more importantly it offers swimmers a blissful opportunity to float and watch the sun set over the Bristol Channel in bracingly chilly saltwater. The nearby Salthouse Bar & Restaurant can provide refreshments.

Access
Access via handrailed steps; do not use slippery slipway. Level/ramped access to poolside. Frequent buses to Bristol on Elton Road, in front of lake. Paid on-site parking at Salthouse Fields car park.

PORTISHEAD OPEN AIR POOL

51.4939, -2.7716 / Esplanade Road, Portishead, Somerset, BS20 7HD / 01275 843454 / Swimming and paddling / *www.portisheadope-nairpool.org.uk*

A 1960s lido, Portishead Open Air Pool offers striking concrete architectural details to rival its 1930s siblings. Familiar to many as the star of *Ty's Great British Adventure*, which documented its refurbishment in 2009, this volunteer-run, biomass-heated, thirty-three-metre lido, standing on high cliffs, will still take your breath away. You can swim, splash in the children's pool, sunbathe on the terraces or enjoy views over container ships on the Bristol Channel. The community-run cafe offers fresh fruit as well as hot drinks, snacks, sweets and light meals. Post-swim, you could enjoy a stroll along the beach or Portishead Lake Grounds next to the lido or head to the marina for a waterfront lunch.

Access
Access via ladders and handrailed steps. Level access to poolside; accessible (wet room) changing areas and toilets. Frequent buses to Bristol, Weston-Super-Mare and Nailsea from town centre, less than a kilometre away. On-street parking and car park adjacent to lido.

BRISTOL LIDO. © SARAH THELWALL

PORTISHEAD OPEN AIR POOL. © SARAH THELWALL

BRISTOL LIDO

51.4597, -2.6114 / Oakfield Place, Clifton, Bristol, BS8 2BJ / 01179 339530 / Swimming / *www. lidobristol.com*

Once, lidos were synonymous with glamour, and Bristol Lido is an elegant, heated pool that unabashedly showcases an exclusive allure. Nestled among Clifton's Georgian terraces, the Victorian pool no longer languishes in disrepair but is now a spa facility offering saunas, massages and spa treatments, and a fine dining Mediterranean restaurant. Primarily a members facility, the lido offers some public sessions as well as spa-and-swim and swim-and-eat packages. The lido occasionally offers family fun sessions, but generally is open to over-eighteens only. If you want to make a weekend of it there are plenty of nearby attractions to explore, including Bristol Zoo, the museum and art gallery, and Isambard Kingdom Brunel's masterpieces, the iron *SS Great Britain* and Clifton Suspension Bridge.

Access

Entry to pool via ladders. Level/ramped access to poolside; accessible wet room changing areas and toilet. Less than a kilometre to Clifton Down railway station; frequent buses to city centre from Victoria Rooms stop, 300 metres away. Parking limited; pay-and-display car parks near Bristol Museum, 700 metres away.

WOTTON OUTDOOR SWIMMING POOL

51.6360, -2.3548 / Symn Lane, Wotton-under-Edge, Gloucestershire, GL12 7BD / 01453 842086 / Swimming / *www.wottonpool.co.uk*

Wotton Outdoor Swimming Pool is a little pool, dedicated to swimming and not much more. With its ingenious concertina roof, you can swim in a greenhouse on colder days and enjoy wide, blue skies when the weather is warmer and the roof is pushed back. There is little space for lounging by the eighteen-metre-long pool, and nothing more than changing rooms and toilets in the way of facilities (although despite the challenges of charitable funding, recent renovations have seen the addition of a disabled toilet and accessible changing area). It's a short stroll to the village's cafes and pubs should you need a post-dip refresher. The pool began its life in the 1950s as a hands-on construction project for school pupils, supervised by teachers and local engineers, and it remains an invaluable community resource rather than a destination day out.

Access

Entry via ladders. Level access to poolside; accessible changing area and toilet. Buses to Yate (which has a railway station), Dursley, and occasionally to Gloucester from village centre, a few hundred metres away. On-street parking; pay-and-display car park across road.

STRATFORD PARK LIDO

51.7499, -2.2252 / Stratford Road, Stroud, Gloucestershire, GL5 4AF / 01453 766771 / Swimming and paddling / *www.everyoneactive.com/centre/stratford-park-leisure-centre*

The blue, wedding-cake fountain identifies Stratford Park Lido as one of the 1930s art deco generation of pools, although its glamour has faded. The fifty-metre, spring-fed outdoor pool retains its concrete, Grade-II-listed parabolic diving board, although it is now rarely in use. The waters were only heated for three brief years before the boiler was melted down to contribute to the war effort. The expansive patios and lawn next to the pool are rarely busy. The lido continues to exist due to the unfailing commitment of local volunteers, who are proactive about planning for the future of the pool whoever manages it. The cold-water pool currently opens on summer afternoons; there is a cafe in the neighbouring leisure centre. The lido is in the midst of Stratford Park, which has an arboretum, lawn bowling green and miniature railway in addition to extensive play areas.

Access
Access via ladders (and occasionally diving board). Level access to poolside; accessible changing rooms and toilets. Frequent buses to Stroud centre, Gloucester and other local destinations outside South Gloucestershire and Stroud College, next to lido; Stroud railway station approximately a kilometre away. On-site parking.

LAKE 32 OUTDOOR CENTRE

51.6574, -1.9619 / Spratsgate Lane, Cirencester, Gloucestershire, GL7 6DF / 01285 861202 Swimming and paddling / *www.ukwatersports.co.uk*

A neighbour to the open water swimming venue at the Cotswold Country Park, Lake 32 offers open water swimming on a naturally fed, freshwater lake nestled in the stunning Cotswold Water Park. Grassy banks and small beaches not only give easy access to the clear water, but also provide space to sunbathe and admire the surrounding woodland. The 1,000-metre lake contains shallows for older children to splash in but reaches a depth of up to four metres. Swimming is available seven days a week (although you will have to pay a nominal membership fee), but your dip falls in designated areas of the lake to ensure space for kayakers, paddleboarders and other water sports enthusiasts. A popular venue for triathlon training, it also hosts moonlight swims. This family-friendly spot has a seasonal cafe, and is the perfect place for a day out.

Access
Access via grassy banks and small beaches. Buses to Cirencester and Malmesbury stop a few times a day at Somerford Keynes, a kilometre and a half away; closest train station, Kemble, approximately six kilometres away, via Thames Path. On-site parking.

COTSWOLD COUNTRY PARK AND BEACH

51.6614, -1.9635 / Spratsgate Lane, Shorncote, Cirencester, Gloucestershire, GL7 6DF / 01285 868096 / Swimming and paddling / *www.cotswoldcountryparkandbeach.com*

Cotswold Country Park and Beach comprises two lakes formed through gravel extraction, dotted within the bigger Cotswold Water Park. Sandy beaches lead to a crystal-clear lagoon, with shallows for paddling as well as deeper sections to stretch your legs in. Swim sessions are available all year around, although only members can swim in the winter. First-time swimmers must undergo a short induction; you are advised to pre-book. Brightly coloured caps are mandatory as well as tow floats if you do not wear a wetsuit. With an inflatable water park, various water sports and go-karts there is plenty at the park to keep the family entertained. Alternatively, there are barbecue pits available to hire

WATERLAND OUTDOOR PURSUITS. © *DANIEL_JAMES_PIX*

if you fancy a post-swim feast. The Beach Shack provides seasonal refreshments on-site, but more choice can be found in nearby Somerford Keynes.

Access

Access via sandy beaches. Ramped access to water; accessible toilets and changing rooms. Buses to Cirencester and Malmesbury stop a few times a day at Somerford Keynes, a kilometre and a half away; closest train station, Kemble, approximately six kilometres away, via Thames Path. On-site parking (paid, but free during swim session).

BUSCOT WEIR

51.6802, -1.6680 / Lechlade-on-Thames, Gloucestershire / Swimming and paddling

Built in 1790, Buscot Weir is a deep pool on National Trust land. Grassy, and sometimes muddy, banks lead into the water. The weir is lined with weeping willows,

which not only give it the feel of a scene straight out of a picture book, but also create an enclosed spot. The trees also provide natural platforms to jump from, and swimmers young and old can enjoy the plunge into the calm water. This is a popular spot with families, and although there are shallow edges the water deepens in the middle, so this would be suited to older children. The Buscot Tearoom is a lovely spot for lunch. Although not easy to reach by public transport, the weir is the perfect swim spot for those hiking the Thames Path National Trail.

Access

Access via grassy, muddy banks. Closest public transport is Lechlade-on-Thames, three kilometres away, for buses to Cirencester and Swindon a few times a day. National Trust pay-and-display car park at Buscot Village, less than a kilometre away.

CHEESE WHARF

51.6841, -1.6766 / Lechlade-on-Thames, Gloucestershire / Swimming and paddling

Cheese Wharf is a deep pool on the River Thames, within National Trust land; once a loading dock for twenty tonnes of Cotswolds cheese a day, it is now a roadside glade ideal for a serene swim. Grassy banks provide access to the water, but there are rope swings frequented by swimmers of all ages. Among buttercup-filled fields and weeping willows, it is difficult not to be thrilled by the picture-perfect views which envelope you. The Buscot Tearoom provides refreshments in the nearby village, or the Trout Inn is less than a kilometre up the road.

Access

Water accessed from grassy banks and rope swing. 77 bus to Cirencester stops near Trout Inn, approximately four times daily. Limited parking on-site; more parking found at Lechlade Riverside car park (via Thames Path) and Buscot Lock and Weir.

CIRENCESTER OPEN AIR SWIMMING POOL. © *MICHAEL ATHIENITES*

LECHLADE, RIVER THAMES

51.6880, -1.7049 / Lechlade-on-Thames, Gloucestershire / Swimming and paddling

On the outskirts of the Cotswolds town of Lechlade-on-Thames, you can discover great swim spots in the Riverside Park, close to the Grade-II-listed Round House. The proximity to the town and the easy-to-access location makes this a popular spot for visitors with families, and the surrounding meadows make for great picnic spots. The water can reach around two metres in depth, but silty shallows can be found near the river's edge. Adventurous swimmers can jump off the Halfpenny Bridge, approximately one kilometre downstream, into the river; the bridge marks the start of the navigable Thames. Plenty of cafes and pubs can be found in Lechlade-on-Thames, and there are toilets on Oak Street in the town centre.

Access

Water accessed from silty shallows and grassy banks. 76 and 77 buses to Cirencester and Swindon stop in town centre, just under two kilometres away, a few times a day. Parking at Riverside car park, less than a kilometre away.

CIRENCESTER OPEN AIR SWIMMING POOL

51.7187, -1.9746 / Riverside Walk, Cirencester, Gloucestershire, GL7 2EF / 01285 653947 / Swimming and paddling / *www.cirenopenair.org.uk*

With the castellated turrets of Cecily Hill Barracks as its backdrop, Cirencester Open Air Swimming Pool is one of the oldest lidos in England, having opened in 1869. Next to Cirencester Park, the pool is a firm favourite with locals and has been operated and managed by a dedicated group of volunteers since 1973. There is a separate paddling pool and a small water slide for children, in addition to the twenty-eight-metre-long, heated pool which is filled with natural spring water. Generally, half the pool is dedicated to lane swimming and half to general swimming, but there is timetabled lane swimming as well as family friendly and inclusive swim sessions. Very much a community-centred pool, the large patio area encourages companionable lounging and the lido's tuck shop offers hot or cold drinks and snacks.

Access

Access via ladders (and a children's slide). Level/ramped access to poolside; accessible changing facilities and toilet. Frequent buses to Gloucester, Stroud and Swindon from town centre, a kilometre away. Pay-and-display Abbey Grounds car park 500 metres away, further car parks in town centre.

SANDFORD PARKS LIDO. © *GINA DRUMMOND*

SANDFORD PARKS LIDO

51.8934, -2.0700 / Keynsham Road, Cheltenham, Gloucestershire, GL53 7PU / 01242 524430 / Swimming and paddling / *www.sandfordparkslido.org.uk*

Sandford Parks Lido is a Grade-II-listed, heated outdoor swimming pool in the heart of regency Cheltenham; among the distinctive period features that it retains are its crescent buildings and wedding-cake fountain. Set in four acres of landscaped grounds, the fifty-metre-long lido originally opened in 1935 and remains a popular family destination, offering a children's pool, paddling pool and play area as well as the main pool. A variety of refreshments are available from the pool's in-house cafe. The lido (run by a charitable trust) takes full advantage of its stunning setting by hosting concerts, film screenings and outdoor theatre, as well as an end-of-season dog swim. The lido is set among the ornamental delights of Sandford Park, perfect for a picnic.

Access
Access via ladders, slides and handrailed steps. Ramped/level access to poolside; accessible changing room; hoist available. Frequent local buses to Cheltenham centre, Leckhampton, Gloucester and Cirencester stop on College Road and Sandford Road, less than a kilometre away; Cheltenham Spa railway station two kilometres away. Paid on-site parking.

BATHURST POOL

51.7196, -2.5410 / High Street, Lydney, Gloucestershire, GL15 5DY / 01594 842625 Swimming / *www.bathurstpool.co.uk*

Hidden away in green fields almost in Wales, the vibrant Bathurst Pool may be one of Gloucestershire's best-kept secrets. Originally given as a present to the inhabitants of Lydney and Aylburton by the Bathurst family in 1920, this thirty-eight-and-a-half-metre, largely unheated, outdoor pool, run by volunteers, opens during the summer months (solar panels offer gentle warmth to the water). Near the banks of the River Severn, pretty sails flutter over the patio areas to offer protection from the sun; you are encouraged to bring a picnic but there is a fully stocked on-site shop offering snacks, drinks and ice creams. As of 2021, the pool does not accept card payments (cash and cheque only).

Access
Access via ladders. Level access to poolside. Two kilometres away, Tesco bus stop served by regular buses to Chepstow and Gloucester; Lydney railway station is a kilometre and a half away, via Mead Lane off A48. On-site parking (in a field).

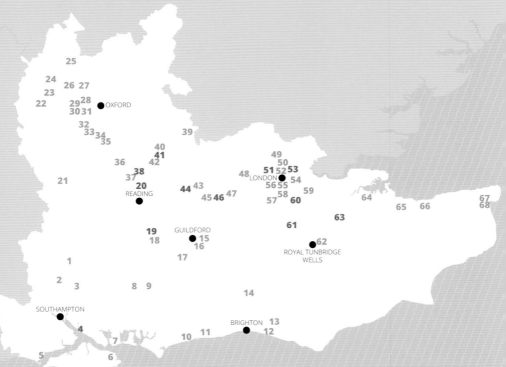

25

24
23
26 27
22
29 28
30 31 ● OXFORD

32
33 34
35
39

40
41
36 42

38
37
21
20
READING

43
44
45 46 47

49
50
51 52 53
48 LONDON ●
56 55 54
58 59
57 60

19
18
GUILDFORD
15
16

61

63

17

62
ROYAL TUNBRIDGE
WELLS

64

65 66

67
68

1

2
3
8 9

14

SOUTHAMPTON ●

4

BRIGHTON 13
12

5
6
7
10 11

South-East England

SHILLINGFORD BRIDGE. © ANYWHEREWEROAM.COM

CHILBOLTON COW COMMON. © SHUTTERSTOCK/INVISIBLE EDIT

CHILBOLTON COW COMMON

51.1624, -1.4493 / Wherwell, Hampshire / Swimming and paddling

The River Test cuts a wide swathe through the historic Chilbolton Cow Common. Long a summer bathing destination for local families (and also popular with anglers), there are gentle, sloping beaches perfect for paddling near the footbridge where the Test Way crosses; the current becomes stronger in deeper sections of the river. The common is now a nature reserve and SSSI, so take special care and consider swimming somewhere else if it is busy; you should not have barbecues here. There are places to eat a short walk downstream at Wherwell.

Access
Access via sandy, sometimes gravelly or pebbly beaches; river can be reached via Test Way footpath. Occasional buses (twice daily) from Wherwell to Andover, 700 metres away. Limited street parking in Wherwell.

HOUGHTON, RIVER TEST

51.0843, -1.5122 / Houghton, Hampshire / Swimming and paddling

Located just south of the small, idyllic village of Houghton, this swimming spot is ideal for families looking for a shallower swimming location suitable for younger swimmers. The wide ford eventually deepens downstream and the cold water reaches the perfect depth for swimming. The rural surrounding areas of this swim spot make it very popular on a sunny summer day, but it is beautiful when the spring wild flowers are blooming. Be cautious of upsetting the anglers who often fish here. Few amenities are located in this area, however the Boot Inn can be found 800 metres to the north where swimmers can stop for some classic pub food. Alternatively, you can follow the Clarendon Way trail through John of Gaunt's Deer Park to the nearby village of King's Somborne.

Access
Water accessed from pebbled shallows and low, grassy banks. Buses leave twice a day to Winchester from Houghton Village Hall stop, 300 metres away. Roadside parking 150 metres to the west.

HOUGHTON, RIVER TEST. © *SHUTTERSTOCK/INVISIBLE EDIT*

COMPTON LOCK, RIVER ITCHEN

51.0272, -1.3222 / Shawford, Hampshire / Swimming and paddling

Just outside of Twyford, this popular spot is loved by visitors due to its picturesque location and easy accessibility. The water is clean and deep with a gentle current, and the now-disused lock is shaded by lush trees. The neighbouring meadows are ideal as spots for picnics and sunbathing for swimmers looking to relax after a dip in the sometimes-weedy water. With the Hockley Meadows Nature Reserve to the south and the Hockley Viaduct to the north, this area is full of interesting opportunities for visitors to experience after their swim. For those looking for a bite to eat, the Bridge Inn is a short walk away and is loved for its traditional pub food.

Access
Water accessed from raised concrete banks, wooden steps and grassy riverbank. Itchen Way runs along river between Shawford and Winchester; footpaths from Compton and Northfields. Shawford railway station 500 metres south. Limited roadside parking available.

ANDARK LAKE

50.8802, -1.2911 / Oslands Lane, Lower Swanwick, Southampton, SO31 7EG / 01489 885811 / Swimming / *andarklake.co.uk*

Andark Lake is a purpose-built lake for diving that is also available for other water sports, including open water swimming. This friendly venue, next to the River Hamble on the outskirts of Southampton, has great facilities including a shop, cafe and new purpose-built changing facilities, as well as a strong commitment to accessibility and environmental sustainability. The lake is filled from a borehole, and water quality is tested regularly. For those visiting the seaside, this is a great and safe alternative if you don't fancy tackling the waves.

Access
Beach and pontoon entry; handrailed slipway. Accessible changing rooms and toilets. Frequent buses to Portsmouth, Southampton on Bridge Road/A27, by entrance to lake. Bursledon railway station a kilometre away. On-site parking.

LYMINGTON SEAWATER BATHS

50.7532, -1.5284 / Bath Road, Lymington, Hampshire, SO41 3SE / 01590 678882 / Swimming / *www.lymingtonseawaterbaths.org.uk*

Opened in 1833, the gigantic (110-by-50-metre) Lymington Seawater Baths are the oldest open air seawater baths in the UK – although the town was a popular bathing destination before the baths were dug out. In this filtered, seawater pool, next to the sailing club's bobbing masts, you may find yourself in the company of crabs and shrimps. It is not the sedate retreat it once was – you can try paddleboarding or zorbing, tackle the inflatable obstacle course or relax in a hot tub as well as swimming in the pebble-bottomed pool. There are also swimathons and swim-with-your-dog sessions. If you don't fancy an ice cream, you can treat yourself to fish and chips from the pool's kiosk.

Access
Access via ladders and handrailed steps. Level access to poolside; accessible toilets and changing facilities; no hoist. Lymington Town railway station a kilometre away; Bath Road paid car park adjacent to baths.

WATERSIDE POOL

50.7306, -1.1500 / The Esplanade, Ryde, Isle of Wight, PO33 1JA / 01983 563656 / Swimming and paddling / *www.watersidepool.co.uk*

Next to the golden sands of Ryde Beach, you can enjoy the glass-walled Waterside Pool. The pool is open to the skies when the sun is shining, but has a retractable roof that covers the water when the storm clouds gather. In addition to swimming, you can take part in water workouts, swimming lessons and Octopush (or underwater hockey); there is also a poolside sauna to enjoy. Perhaps the best time to swim is in the evening when the roof is open, offering a fine view of the stars. Snacks and hot drinks are available from the pool's kiosk, but alternatively you could enjoy an ice cream on the seafront; you are also close to Ryde's cafes and pubs. Ryde Pier is less than a kilometre from the pool, so this would make a great day trip from Portsmouth.

Access
Access via ladders and handrailed steps. Level access to poolside; accessible changing rooms and toilets; hoist available. Ryde Esplanade railway station and Ryde Pier (ferry from Portsmouth) 800 metres away. On-site parking.

HILSEA LIDO

50.8363, -1.0761 / London Road, Hilsea, Portsmouth, Hampshire, PO2 9RP / 07903 823347 / Swimming and paddling / *hilsea-lido.org.uk*

If the entrance of Hilsea Lido seems strangely familiar, it may be because local filmmaker Ken Russell used it as a 'holiday camp' in the 1975 musical *Tommy*. Though less bustling than in its heyday, this elongated pool near Portsmouth Harbour is still beloved by the local community. Originally filled with seawater, its now-fresh water remains unheated. With two shallow ends, there is a four-and-a-half-metre-deep diving pit near the centre, with a two-metre-high diving platform. You are welcome to bring a picnic, or you can take advantage of the neighbouring Blue Lagoon for home-made cake or buttered crumpets. This historic lido may have lost a little of its glamorous sheen, but volunteers have worked tirelessly to restore the diving platform, unblock the drains, give the art deco buildings a lick of paint, plant a pretty flower garden and offer a warm welcome.

Access
Access via ladders and diving platform. Level access to poolside; accessible facilities are limited – large changing area, but no specifically accessible toilets; no hoist.

PETERSFIELD OPEN AIR POOL. © *BILL SPENCE*

Frequent local buses stop outside lido to Fareham, Southsea and Portsmouth city centre; Cosham railway station a kilometre away. On-site parking.

PETERSFIELD OPEN AIR POOL

51.0043, -0.9320 / Heath Road, Petersfield, Hampshire, GU31 4DZ / 01730 265143 / Swimming / *petersfieldpool.org*

Petersfield Open Air Pool opened in 1962, and heating was added in 1969. The colourful, volunteer-run pool is open from April to September, although they offer unheated weekend swims through winter and spring and even provide a poolside firepit to warm by. The twenty-five-metre pool has a diving board and a pleasant, sheltered poolside area to relax. They run swim lessons and coaching, junior-only sessions and at the popular midnight swims you can celebrate post-dip with a glass of fizz. In addition

to a snack kiosk, if you fancy food the poolside barbecue is often fired up for evening and weekend swim sessions. At the heart of the South Downs, Petersfield is the perfect base from which to explore the hilly national park.

Access

Access via ladders and handrailed steps. Level access to poolside; accessible changing rooms and toilets; no hoist. Petersfield railway station 800 metres away. Paid parking available adjacent to lido.

SANDY BAY

50.9890, -0.7329 / Midhurst, West Sussex / Swimming and paddling

On the edge of the chalky South Downs, the meandering River Rother makes for a great swim spot on a sunny afternoon. If you follow the golden Castle Causeway from Midhurst town centre across the water meadows you will discover a grassy path to the

Sandy Bay. This small beach, near the Cowdray Heritage Ruins, offers easy, sloping access to the water, which has a gentle current. The water is shallow here, generally never deeper than a metre and a half, and the sandy beach is perfect for a picnic. There are public toilets next to the bus station, and plenty of cafes in Midhurst's medieval town centre. You can also swim fifteen kilometres downstream to near Lower Fittleworth with its picturesque bridge, but beware of tricky currents near the arches.

Access

Access via the gently sloping, sandy beach. Grassy path leads down to the river from track junction near the tower – from town centre, follow path to bridge, then follow track upstream to a grassy path which leads to swim spot. Frequent buses to Chichester, Worthing, Guildford and Petersfield from bus station, 500 metres away. Pay-and-display car park next to bus station.

SALTDEAN LIDO. © *FUSION LIFESTYLE*

ARUNDEL LIDO

50.8531, -0.5513 / Queen Street, Arundel, West Sussex, BN18 9JG / 01903 884772 / Swimming and paddling / *www.arundel-lido.com*

Under the turrets of Arundel Castle, Arundel Lido certainly offers a swim with a view. This heated pool also offers a lot more than just swimming; with its mermaid swim classes, bootcamp on the lawn and dementia-friendly coffee mornings there is something for everyone. There is also a children's pool and plenty of places to picnic when you've tired of the water. Although the lido is open from May to September it also offers festive swims in December. If you don't fancy a hot chocolate at the pool cafe, a stroll across the River Arun will take you to the town's historic centre.

Access

Access via ladders and easy steps with handrails. Level access to poolside; accessible changing rooms and toilets; hoist available (you are advised to call ahead). Frequent buses to Worthing and Shoreham-by-Sea stop outside lido; Arundel railway station 700 metres away. Pay-and-display car park adjacent to lido.

FINDON SWIMMING POOL

50.8681, -0.4084 / St John the Baptist Primary School, School Hill, Findon, West Sussex, BN14 0TR / Swimming / *findonswimmingpool.co.uk*

The fifteen-metre, colourful Findon Swimming Pool opens for one brief hour a day between May and September. A school swimming pool that is open to the public, it still primarily attracts children who love to splash down the slide into the warm water. The pool can accommodate a maximum of forty swimmers and no food or drink is allowed in the pool area, but this is a great local resource for Sussex children to enjoy through the summer. Run entirely by volunteers, this lido is a friendly spot at the heart of the village community. There is a cafe and a pub a few minutes' walk away in the village centre.

Access

Access via ladders and slide. Wheelchair access to pool is difficult with level, but limited, poolside space and few facilities. Findon served by frequent buses from Worthing; approximately five kilometres to West Worthing railway station. School car park available at weekends/during school holidays; street parking in village.

PELLS POOL. © ROB READ

SALTDEAN LIDO

50.8012, -0.0421 / The Oval Park, Saltdean Park Road, Saltdean, Brighton, East Sussex, BN2 8SP/ 01273 069984 / Swimming and paddling / *saltdeanlido.org*

Saltdean, which has recently gone extensive restoration, is the epitome of Britain's 1930s seaside lidos, and retains its art deco glamour. Saltdean was a holiday resort built with dreams of just what the British seaside could be, and the lido was at the heart of that vision. While there is still work ongoing, you can sunbathe by the white prow of the 1930s lido building or take a dip in the impossibly blue waters of the curved pool. At Saltdean, the whole family is catered for: there is a paddling pool for toddlers complete with a fountain, and, not content with an end-of-season doggy swim, September is Dogtember at Saltdean – dogs can jump, splash and slide into the water alongside their owners. Hot drinks and snacks are available at the lido kiosk; Whitecliffs Cafe is just across the road.

Access

Access via handrailed, shallow steps and ladders. Frequent bus services to and from Brighton on Marine Drive, adjacent to lido. On-site parking.

PELLS POOL

50.8773, 0.0097 / Brook Street, Lewes, East Sussex, BN7 2BA / 01273 472334 / Swimming and paddling / *www.pellspool.org.uk*

The spring-filled Pells Pool opened in 1860, and is the oldest freshwater lido in the country. Unheated, the mornings tend to be reserved for lane swimming, with family fun sessions as the water warms throughout the day. With film nights, midnight swims and the Midsummer Madness weekend, this is a volunteer-run lido at the heart of its community. In recent years, the summer season has been extended into October, allowing a rare opportunity to enjoy a cold-water lido swim in autumn. Wetsuits are encouraged on colder days and under-sixteens are not permitted to swim if the temperature falls below 15 °C. The on-site kiosk sells hot drinks and snacks, and the tree-fringed lawn is perfect for a picnic. It is a short walk to the historic town centre, with plenty of cafes and pubs.

Access

Access via ladders. Level access to poolside; accessible toilets and changing rooms; handrailed, ramped access to water – wheelchair available to borrow. Lewes railway station 800 metres away; Lewes well served by buses from Eastbourne and Brighton. Paid car parks and metered street parking nearby, but often busy.

GUILDFORD LIDO. © *FREEDOM LEISURE*

BURGESS HILL LIDO

50.9648, -0.1533 / Triangle Way, Burgess Hill, West Sussex RH15 8WA / 01444 876000 / Swimming and paddling / *www.placesleisure.org/centres/the-triangle*

Burgess Hill's historic lido closed in 1998, and the Triangle Leisure Centre opened in 1999 to offer a modern replacement for the lost facility. A changing village stands between the indoor pool, the fun pool, and the lido; you can use all three pools, so can splash down the chutes into the fun pool and then float, via the lazy river, into the sun in the lido. You may struggle to swim lengths in this small, often busy and irregularly shaped pool, but it is a great choice for families, who may want to spend some time doing some focused swimming before having a relaxed session outside. There is a small cafe on-site. The leisure centre is located on the green fringes of Burgess Hill, and the Woolpack pub can provide refreshments.

Access
Access via handrailed steps. Level access to poolside; accessible changing rooms and toilets; hoist available for all three pools. Frequent bus service to Burgess Hill centre from lido; approximately three kilometres to Burgess Hill railway station. On-site parking.

GUILDFORD LIDO

51.2474, -0.5696 / Lido Road, Guildford, Surrey, GU1 1HB / 01483 449108 / Swimming and paddling / *www.freedom-leisure.co.uk/centres/guildford-lido*

Tucked between the expansive Stoke Park and the curving River Wey, you can find the 1930s Guildford Lido. In summer, the heated, fifty-metre pool offers lane swimming and family friendly swim sessions. The pool remains open for 'cold' weekend swims over winter; unlike other lidos offering cold water winter swims, Guildford employs some heating to ensure the water temperature does not drop below 10 °C. There are slides to enjoy (although these incur an additional charge) and a children's pool. Relax on the landscaped lawns post-dip, with an ice cream from the lido's snack kiosk. Guildford Lido is due to close for major refurbishment over the winter of 2021.

Access
Access via ladders, slides and shallow, handrailed steps. Level access to poolside; accessible changing rooms and toilets; hoist available. Approximately a kilometre to London Road (Guildford) railway station; shortcut through Stoke Park. On-site parking.

FRENSHAM GREAT POND. © *SHUTTERSTOCK/GRAHAM PRENTICE*

WEY NAVIGATION

51.2220, -0.5770 / Shalford, Surrey

The Wey Navigation cuts through green pastures and has long been a popular swim spot, although there have been attempts to discourage swimming in the area. With sandy beaches, this quiet stretch of gentle water in wooded countryside is the perfect day trip from London. You may face a bit of a scramble to get in and out of the water over steep, slippery, muddy banks, but there is always a better spot on a sandy beach if you follow the footpath a little further along the river. You can visit Ye Olde Ship Inn, a rest stop for pilgrims and seafarers since the sixteenth century, near the ruins of the historic St Catherine's Chapel.

Access
Access via steep, grassy banks and sandy beaches. Frequent buses to Guildford on A3100 main road near St Catherine's Lock, 800 metres away; Shalford railway station two kilometres away. Limited on-street parking.

FRENSHAM GREAT POND

51.1575, -0.7916 / Frensham, Surrey / Swimming and paddling

Set in heathered Surrey countryside owned by the National Trust, the stunning Frensham Great Pond is loved for its vast, sandy beaches and clean, shallow water. Well suited for beginners or for families wanting a day out, the lake, created in the thirteenth century, is a great introduction to swimming under the open sky. Swimming is permitted in two designated areas and water quality is monitored from April to September by the Environment Agency; be sure to check the water quality before your trip. Conservation areas are fenced and should not be disturbed. Picnics are popular but barbecues are not permitted, so for those wanting a hot meal Frensham Pond's snack bar can be found on-site. There are also public toilets by the Central car park in Farnham.

Access
Water accessed from sandy beach. Frequent buses to Aldershot and Haslemere on A287, at entrance to park. On-site parking.

ALDERSHOT LIDO. © *SARAH THELWALL*

ALDERSHOT LIDO

51.2356, -0.7468 / Guildford Road, Aldershot, Hampshire, GU12 4BP / 01252 323482 / Swimming and paddling / *www.placesleisure.org/centres/aldershot-lido*

At Aldershot Lido, the focus is firmly on fun, with colourful water slides spiralling into the water as well as a sandpit, toddlers' pool and a traditional lido fountain. Opened in 1930, the the newly refurbished lido is one of the UK's largest outdoor pools, with enough space for lane swimming, splash-about fun and a diving platform. The historic lido was host to pentathlon events during London's 1948 Olympic Games. Set in attractive grassy parkland, you are encouraged to bring your own picnic and enjoy the scenery (no alcohol allowed). The pool is unheated, so expect a shock if you slide down the chutes into the water on a grey day. You can get a hot chocolate or toasted sandwich at the on-site cafe if you need to warm up.

Access

Shallow, sloping entry, with steps to sit on, as well as ladders, slides and diving boards. Level access to poolside; accessible toilets and changing facilities; hoist available. Two kilometres to Aldershot railway station; frequent 15 (Tices Meadow) bus connects lido to town centre. On-site parking.

THE QUAYS

51.2948, -0.7370 / Coleford Bridge Road, Mytchett, Camberley, Surrey, GU16 6DS / Swimming / *www.quayswim.co.uk*

If you like an early morning dip in the orange glow of sunrise, The Quays is the spot for you: it offers early morning and evening swims on Mondays, Tuesdays, Thursdays and at the weekend between April and September. In Farnborough, this spring-fed lake is surrounded by lush woodland. The Quays offers a countryside feel, it is close to Farnborough's town centre, with a railway station, shops and restaurants close at hand. Lifeguards patrol the water on kayaks and, with varied swim circuits, beginners are well catered for. Hot water is available for you to make your own hot drinks, but for a bite to eat the nearby Kingfisher on the Quay is a popular spot for visitors to stop after enjoying the refreshing water.

Access

Water accessed via gentle slopes and ramp. Approximately one kilometre to Farnborough North railway station; frequent buses to Farnborough centre from Coleford Bridge Road and Rectory road, less than one kilometre. On-site parking.

HORSESHOE LAKE ACTIVITY CENTRE

51.3522, -0.8238 / Mill Lane, Sandhurst, Berkshire, GU47 8JW / 01252 871808 / Swimming / *horseshoelakeactivitycentre.co.uk*

Horseshoe Lake Activity Centre is a water sports centre where you can enjoy a range of activities, including yoga on the water. With modern facilities and clean water all wrapped up in a wild setting, the lake – one of several flooded gravel pits in the area – is a great spot for open water swimming. Beginners are welcome here and there are lifeguards on standby during swim sessions; children (from the age of eight) can swim with adult supervision. The Activity Centre hosts various classes and competitions for swimmers and is loved for its friendly and inclusive environment. Picnics are recommended with plenty of green spaces available to relax on after a swim. With an on-site Italian cafe, plenty of countryside walks around the lakes and with great wildlife-spotting opportunities, this is an ideal place for a full day out.

Access

Water accessed via small, sandy beach. Accessible toilet; ramped access to changing rooms; ramped access to water. Frequent buses to Farnborough at White Lion stop in Yateley, just over a kilometre away. Crowthorne and Sandhurst railway stations approximately a kilometre and a half away (both via Three Castles Path). On-site parking.

NORTHCROFT LIDO

51.4031, -1.3333 / Northcroft Lane, Newbury, Berkshire, RG14 1RS / 01635 31199 / Swimming and paddling / *www.leisurecentre.com/ northcroft-leisure-centre*

At a hefty seventy-two metres long, Northcroft Lido is certainly a great pool for lovers of lane swimming. The lido is part of a large leisure complex which offers a gym, squash courts, minigolf, indoor pool and a children's play area. Although much changed, the outdoor pool here dates back to 1870, when swimming was segregated by sex. The lido offers a toddlers' paddling pool and expansive tree-fringed lawn to lounge on, and a leisure centre cafe. It's a short stroll into the historic centre of the market town of Newbury.

GRAFTON LOCK, RIVER THAMES. © *BILL NICHOLLS*

Access

Access via ladders. Level access to poolside; accessible changing rooms and toilets; hoist available. Newbury railway station a kilometre away. On-site parking.

GRAFTON LOCK, RIVER THAMES

51.6913, -1.6084 / Radcot, Oxfordshire / Swimming

In the middle of the beautiful Oxfordshire countryside, Grafton Lock offers stunning views on this remote and difficult-to-reach stretch of the River Thames. In a secluded area bordered by endless fields, the lock is home to cool water which is great for cooling off in hot weather. The current remains gentle unless there have been heavy rains, making this area perfect for beginners and those who prefer a more relaxing swimming experience. The nearest village is Radcot four kilometres downstream, where you'll discover Ye Olde

Swan. Here you can stop and enjoy a meal in the historic building or on grassy lawns looking over the water. You have to be dedicated to reach this wild swim spot, but it may be a great excuse for hikers on the Thames Path National Trail to rest their blistered feet.

Access

Entry into water from grassy bank. Difficult to access by public transport: occasional buses to Radcot from Oxford, four kilometres away. Limited on-road parking, may require walk of at least a kilometre. Accessible by boat.

MINSTER LOVELL

51.7993, -1.5309 / Minster Lovell, Oxfordshire / Swimming and paddling

In the shadow of the striking ruins of the fifteenth-century Minster Lovell Hall, a picturesque stretch of the River Windrush winds its way through the grounds. With easy access down sloping banks and shady spots for a picnic, this is a great place to take in the stunning scenery of the Cotswolds. The water is shallow enough for small children to paddle, and the water gets deeper (but only to approximately a metre) on the side farthest from the ruins for those wanting a swim. There are several pubs among the thatched cottages of Minster Lovell village, including the White Hart, and for a full day out the North Leigh Roman Villa is approximately ten kilometres away.

Access
Access via steep, grassy slopes. Go behind the church and through the ruins to reach the river. White Hart bus stop in Minster Lovell, a kilometre and a half away, has frequent buses to Burford, Witney and Cheltenham. Small car park (around eight cars) at top of narrow lane leading to St Kenelm's Church, but this fills up quickly.

THE LIDO AT CHIPPING NORTON

51.9392, -1.5404 / Fox Close, Chipping Norton, Oxfordshire, OX7 5BZ / 01608 643188 / Swimming and paddling / *chippylido.co.uk*

Built by the community in 1970, the volunteer-run 'Chippy Lido' offers aqua fit, poolside yoga, synchronised swimming, swim lessons and lifeguard training, as well as family and adult swim sessions. Along with the twenty-five-metre-long main pool, there is a shallow toddlers' pool and a slide if you'd prefer to make a swift entrance into the pool. The (short) season traditionally ends with a dog swim. If you don't fancy chips at the lido's friendly cafe

or a picnic on the lawn, it's a few minutes stroll into the centre of the charming Cotswolds town of Chipping Norton, where there are plenty of pubs and cafes to choose from.

Access
Access via ladders, handrailed steps and slide. Level access to poolside; accessible changing rooms and toilets; hoist available. Frequent bus services from Chipping Norton to Oxford, and hourly to Banbury. Limited on-site parking; free parking in town centre, less than a kilometre away.

WOODGREEN LEISURE CENTRE

52.0615, -1.3503 / Woodgreen Avenue, Banbury, Oxfordshire, OX16 0HS / 01295 262742 / Swimming and paddling / *www.leisurecentre.com/woodgreen-leisure-centre*

The outdoor pool at Banbury's Woodgreen Leisure Centre mixes business with leisure. The fifty-metre-long pool is perfect for swimming lengths, but the slide and aquasplash area are perfect for those just looking to have fun. The pool was built in 1939; an eightieth birthday celebration in 2019 saw staff dressed in period costume and admittance at eight pence, the 1939 price. Resisting closure in the 1990s, the council spent £1.4 million restoring it in 2008. The heated pool is only open in the summer, although the leisure centre has recently been trialling a 'chilly season' spring opening. The pool's timetable is split into sessions of two to four hours for lane swimming, aqua fit and general swimming, so this is not a venue to spend all day at, although there are grassy lawns where you can enjoy a coffee from the kiosk after your swim.

Access
Access via ladders. Level access/lifts to poolside; accessible changing rooms and toilets; hoist available. Frequent buses to Banbury centre and Neithrop on Park Road, adjacent to lido; approximately two kilometres to Banbury railway station. Free on-site parking.

THE LIDO AT CHIPPING NORTON. © *THE LIDO AT CHIPPING NORTON*

STONESFIELD, RIVER EVENLODE

51.8452, -1.4303 / Stonesfield, Oxfordshire / Swimming and paddling

Located in the stunning Cotswolds, this stretch of the River Evenlode is loved by visitors for its picturesque scenery and serene, gentle river. Shallower water can be found near the bridge where the cold water is the perfect depth for paddling. For those wanting to swim, a short walk downstream leads to deeper waters. You can explore the ruins of the riverside Roman villa and hunt for fossils in the Stonesfield slate; the very first fossil bones identified as a dinosaur were discovered in a nearby field in the nineteenth century. The last pub in Stonesfield, the White Horse, has closed although there is currently a high-profile campaign to reopen it as a community asset, so it's worth double-checking.

Access

Water accessed from stony shallows and grassy banks. Follow Oxfordshire Way, or footpath through Stockey Bottom, from Stonesfield. Frequent buses to Oxford and other local destinations from Prospect Close stop, 800 metres away. Parking in Stonesfield, less than a kilometre away.

WOODSTOCK OPEN AIR POOL

51.8486, -1.3394 / Shipton Road, Woodstock, Oxfordshire, OX20 1LW / 01993 811785 Swimming and paddling / *www.better.org.uk/ leisure-centre/west-oxfordshire/woodstock-open-air-pool*

The Woodstock Open Air Pool is a good example of a community-centred lido. The heated, twenty-five-metre-long pool, with grassy lawns and benches, also has a small paddling pool and a diving board, which can be used in quieter sessions. The snack kiosk is open only at busier times, offering hot and cold drinks as well as crowd-pleasing chips. Those wishing to make a day out of it could visit the nearby Blenheim Palace, Sir Winston Churchill's birthplace, with its formal gardens, rolling grounds and yew-tree-lined Marlborough Maze.

Access

Access via ladders and handrailed steps. Level access to poolside; accessible changing rooms and toilets; no hoist. Frequent buses to Oxford and Chipping Norton on Oxford Road (next to Blenheim Palace), approximately a kilometre away. On-site parking.

SUNNYMEAD BATHING PLACE. © *WWW.DRIVINGWITHDOGS.CO.UK*

SUNNYMEAD BATHING PLACE

51.7851, -1.2576 / Sunnymead, Oxfordshire / Swimming and paddling

Just north of Oxford, this little stretch of the River Cherwell is perfect for swimming thanks to its picturesque location, wide, open spaces and deep, cool water. Popular with kayakers and canoeists, this spot is never short on activity in the summer months. Fields lead to the banks of the river and the expansive parkland makes a great spot to relax or have a picnic after a swim. Sunnymead and Cutteslowe are two conjoined parks which together provide plenty of leisure facilities, including an orienteering route, miniature railway, paddling pool and miniature golf. If you cross beneath the A40 main road near the paddling pool you will find public toilets and a kiosk cafe (approximately a kilometre away).

Access

Access to grounds via slope with grassy banks at the water's edge. Good cycle links from city centre. High-frequency buses to Oxford city centre from Banbury Road, 800 metres away; also frequent services to Bicester and Banbury. Cuttislowe Park pay-and-display car park, just off A40, less than a kilometre away.

WOLVERCOTE BATHING PLACE

51.7809, -1.2959 / Wolvercote, Oxfordshire / Swimming and paddling

Tucked away amid overgrown trees and shrubbery, this is a popular swim spot for those wanting to cool off in the summer months. Wolvercote Bathing Place is south of the village of Wolvercote and has a history that dates back to the Victorian era. Now little more than a quiet offshoot from the River Thames, in its prime this was the location that visitors would flock to from all over Oxford. With the decline in river swimming, the council shut its bathing places in the 1990s; abandoned pools can also be found at Tumbling Bay and Long Bridges. The water is still ideal for swimming, although the surrounding area is not maintained by the council. There are public toilets in the car park, and the Trout Inn, beloved by fictional detective Inspector Morse, is just across the river.

Access

Access via concrete ramps and steps. Frequent buses to Abingdon-on-Thames, via Oxford centre, from Wolvercote village centre, less than a kilometre away. Parking adjacent in Port Meadow Godstow car park.

HINKSEY HEATED OUTDOOR POOL. © *FUSION LIFESTYLE*

PORT MEADOW

51.7739, -1.2901 / Oxford, Oxfordshire / Swimming, paddling and falling into rabbit holes

In 1862, an Oxford academic spent a lazy afternoon in Port Meadow telling tales about Alice to his friend's daughters, and this three-kilometre stretch of historic common land is a Wonderland for anyone looking for riverside picnics, boating adventures and a relaxing dip. It is easy to reach the cool waters of the River Isis via the shallow, sandy beaches. Oxford council has launched a bid to designate the area's bathing water so that water quality is safeguarded. To the north, you can explore the stunning ruins of the twelfth-century Godstow Abbey. For those wanting to fill up on some delicious food the extremely popular waterfront gastropub, the Trout Inn, can be found 200 metres away from the swim spot. There are public toilets in the Port Meadow Godstow car park.

Access

Easy access to water via sandy beaches. Easy access on foot or bike from city centre. Frequent buses to Abingdon-on-Thames, via Oxford centre, from Wolvercote village centre, less than a kilometre away; Oxford railway station, less than a kilometre south of swim spot. Pay-and-display car parks south of swim spot; free parking Godstow car park.

HINKSEY HEATED OUTDOOR POOL

51.7398, -1.2566 / Hinksey Park, Abingdon Road, Oxford, Oxfordshire, OX1 4RP / 03448 933222 / Swimming and paddling / *www.fusion-lifestyle.com/centres/hinksey-outdoor-pool*

Nestled in the green Hinksey Park on the college sports fields on Oxford's southern fringes, you'll discover Hinksey Heated Outdoor Pool. This hourglass-shaped pool devotes one half to lane swimming, and in the other half there is sloping, beach-style entry into the pool with a long handrail, as well as refreshing water fountains for family friendly swimming and lounging in the warm water. When the lawns are not being called into service as an outdoor gym or circuit class area, they are ideal for a post-dip picnic. When the moon is full, the pool stays open until midnight, although you'll need to be prompt to book an evening session. There is a poolside cafe offering hot drinks and paninis, and Oxford city centre is just under two kilometres away.

Access

Beach-style access to water, with handrail and ladders. Level access to poolside; accessible changing rooms and toilets; beach-style access to water, pool chair available. Frequent buses to Oxford centre, Abingdon-on-Thames and other Oxfordshire towns on Abingdon Road by Hinksey Park. Oxford railway station approximately two kilometres away. Hinksey Park car park approximately 250 metres away.

ABBEY MEADOWS OUTDOOR POOL. © *NICK BELL*

ABBEY MEADOWS OUTDOOR POOL

51.6698, -1.2767 / Abbey Close, Abingdon, Oxfordshire, OX14 3JE / 01235 529321 / Swimming and paddling / *www.better.org.uk/ leisure-centre/vale-of-white-horse/abbey-mead- ows-outdoor-pool*

On the banks of the Thames, in a green, grassy field, you can discover the delights of the L-shaped Abbey Meadows Outdoor Pool. With little more than the pool and changing rooms, this is the quintessential lido experience. The heated pool underwent a £1.3 million refurbish- ment in 2018, but retains its lazy riverside lido style, with plenty of tree-fringed lawns to lounge on. While there is no on-site cafe, you are only a few minutes' stroll from the centre of the charming market town of Abingdon-on-Thames. After your swim, you can enjoy Abbey Meadows with its splash zone, children's play area and wild flower meadow, or just take a leisurely stroll down the Thames to Abingdon Lock.

Access

Access via ladders, steps and beach-style entry. Level access to poolside, accessible changing rooms and toilets; no hoist. Approximately three kilometres from Radley and Culham railway stations; Abingdon well served by frequent buses from Oxford and Wantage. Pay-and-display car park for Abbey Meadows.

CLIFTON HAMPDEN, RIVER THAMES

51.6565, -1.2056 / Clifton Hampden, Oxford- shire / Swimming and paddling

Found just downstream from the village of Clifton Hampden, this stretch of the River Thames is great for families and first-time swimmers but also popular with boaters, so consider wearing a bright cap. Wide, green meadows give way to the tree-fringed river, making this the perfect spot to spend a summer's day. There are plenty of small, sandy beaches on the grassy banks. The water remains cool, but not too cold, and long-dis- tance swimmers can enjoy a lengthy swim in this stretch of the Thames downstream towards Dorchester and Shillingford. There is a pub, the Barley Mow, next to Sir George Gilbert Scott's red-bricked bridge in Clifton Hampden.

Access

Water accessible from grassy banks and sloping, sandy beaches. Follow Thames Path from Clifton Hampden Bridge. Buses to Abingdon-on-Thames via Culham and Didcot from village centre, 300 metres away, every two hours; Culham railway station two and a half kilometres away. On-street parking in Clifton Hampden, less than a kilometre from swim spot.

CLIFTON HAMPDEN, RIVER THAMES. © *SHUTTERSTOCK/CHRISLOFOTOS*

SHILLINGFORD BRIDGE

51.6247, -1.1431 / Shillingford, Oxfordshire /
Swimming

On the often-weedy banks of the River
Thames, you can enjoy a shady swim near the
picturesque, nineteenth-century Shillingford
Bridge. It is easy to follow the Thames Path
along the river and pick a pleasant spot to
stop off for a picnic and dip in the gentle, clean
water. This stretch of the river is popular with
boaters, who often choose to moor up at the
Shillingford Bridge Hotel; there may be broken
glass from summer revellers on the riverbanks
occasionally. The Shillingford Bridge Hotel
offers Sunday carveries and afternoon teas on
grassy lawns by the river; there is also the Shill
River Shack takeaway at the hotel, where you
can grab a burger or jacket potato.

Access
Access via grassy banks, occasionally overgrown by weeds; be wary of rubbish, particularly glass. Frequent buses to Oxford, Reading
and Henley-on-Thames in Shillingford, near
Kingfisher Inn, a kilometre away. Limited
on-street parking in Shillingford, a kilometre
away.

RIVERSIDE PARK AND POOLS

51.6014, -1.1189 / Crowmarsh Gifford, Wallingford, Oxfordshire, OX10 8EB / 02038 598208
Swimming and paddling / *www.better.org.uk/
leisure-centre/south-oxfordshire/riverside-park-
and-pools*

The heated, twenty-three-metre-long
Riverside Park and Pools is right next to the
River Thames, on the green fringes of the
Riverside campsite. There's a free splashpad
area adjacent to the lido, and you can reward
yourself with an ice cream from the kiosk after
your exertions. There is plenty of space by
the pool, including grassy lawns to lounge on.
A short stroll over the medieval Wallingford
Bridge will take you to the historic town centre,
with a good choice of places to eat and drink;
the grounds of the ruined eleventh-century
Wallingford Castle make a fantastic spot for a
picnic. Wallingford is also a great destination
if you want to combine a pool dip with a wild
swim in the River Thames.

Access
Access via ladders. Level access to poolside;
accessible changing rooms and toilets; hoist
available. Town centre (less than a kilometre
away) served by frequent buses to Reading,
Oxford and other towns on the Thames.
Pay-and-display parking on-site.

GORING AND PANGBOURNE. © SHUTTERSTOCK/STERLING IMAGES

WYCOMBE RYE LIDO. © FUSION LIFESTYLE

GORING AND PANG-BOURNE, RIVER THAMES

51.5072, -1.1107 / Goring, Oxfordshire / Swimming and paddling

Between Pangbourne and Goring with the Chilterns as your backdrop, you can enjoy this untouched part of the River Thames, beloved for its clean, refreshing water and the neighbouring expansive Hartslock Nature Reserve. North of Reading and a less-frequented area than other wild swimming spots along the Thames, this is great for a family day out and an easy excursion from London. There are plenty of grassy open spaces surrounding the river for relaxing and enjoying a picnic after a swim. The village of Goring lies two kilometres to the north, where there are a range of pubs and cafes available; nearby Pangbourne and Whitchurch-on-Thames also offer charming country-side pubs.

Access
Access from high, grassy banks and peaty inlets. Goring and Streatley railway station two and a half kilometres away; Goring and Streatley bus station located next door. Pay-and-display parking available in Goring, two kilometres away.

THAMES LIDO

51.4603, -0.9653 / Napier Road, Reading, Berkshire, RG1 8FR / 01182 070640 / Swimming / *www.thameslido.com*

Thames Lido is the luxury end of Britain's outdoor pool world. The lido began life in 1902 as King's Meadow, an Edwardian ladies' swimming bath, but fell into disrepair. It reopened in 2017 after three years of restoration. With a sauna, spa, Mediter-ranean restaurant and gloriously renovated lido buildings with tasteful modern extensions, this is very much a red-letter day out for adult

non-members. Children are allowed to swim during some afternoon sessions, but with no lifeguards each child must be accompanied by an adult. The lido is primarily for members, but opens for pre-booked swims in the afternoons, and spa–swim and dine–swim packages are on offer. If the city streets get too much for you, this luxurious lido nestled on the banks of the River Thames is a great day out from London.

Access
Access via ladders. All areas (except massage rooms) wheelchair accessible; accessible changing rooms and toilets. Reading railway station less than a kilometre away. Private car park for members/pre-booked packages. King's Meadow pay-and-display car park less than a kilometre away.

CAVERSHAM LAKES

51.4711, -0.9389 / Henley Road, Caversham, Reading, Berkshire, RG4 9RA / 07935 604463 / Swimming / *www.cavershamlakes.co.uk*

In disused gravel pits on the outskirts of Reading, Caversham Lakes is an easily accessible location, perfect for families to experience the vast water. There are three courses marked out at 400 metres, 750 metres and 1,500 metres, and the site is suitable for first-time as well as experienced open water swimmers. Swim sessions are available daily from May to September. You must wear a brightly coloured hat and use a swim float, and wetsuits are recommended. This man-made lake is also used for various other water-based activities including kayaking and an inflatable aqua park. A small cafe and lakeside bar are available on-site for visitors to refuel at (you are not allowed to bring your own food), and the surrounding grassy fields and wooded trails are great for exploring.

Access

Beach-style entry into water. Good accessible routes around the site; accessible changing rooms and toilets. Frequent buses to High Wycombe and Reading centre stop on Henley Road at entrance to lakes, 700 metres away; Reading railway station five kilometres. Free on-site parking.

CHESHAM MOOR GYM AND SWIM

51.6971, -0.6071 / Moor Road, Chesham, Buckinghamshire, HP5 1SE / 01494 776975 / Swimming / *cheshammoorfitness.org.uk/swim*

Rain or shine, even when the poolside paving stones need gritting, Chesham Moor's heated pool is open all year around. You can even enjoy a midnight swim, a poolside barbecue or the occasional bacon butty morning. The pool uses ionisation to sanitise the water, meaning that it is a great low-chlorine dip destination. There's not much room poolside for a picnic, but the lido is right next to the Chess Valley recreation area, Hodds Wood and Chesham Moor, so there is plenty of green space to explore after your swim. Built in 1912, this lido offers historic charm and modern facilities. The Pheasant pub is a short walk away and can provide refreshments.

Access

Access via ladders and handrailed steps. Level access to poolside, accessible changing rooms and toilets; hoist available. Chesham Underground station a kilometre away; hourly bus services to Little Chalfont, Amersham and Chesham centre stop outside lido. On-site parking.

WYCOMBE RYE LIDO

51.6234, -0.7391 / The Rye, Bassetsbury Lane, High Wycombe, Buckinghamshire, HP11 1QX / 01494 769472 / Swimming and paddling / *www.fusion-lifestyle.com/centres/wycombe-rye-lido*

On the outskirts of High Wycombe, this large, 1950s lido sits on the edge of the expansive green space of the Rye. The heated, thirty-three-metre main pool opens all year around, although the toddlers' pool is generally only open in the warmer summer months. There's a lido cafe, waterside sauna and grassy areas to picnic on. The pool offers early morning swims and evening dips in the illuminated water. You would be sensible to book at this popular pool, particularly in the summer if you want to enjoy a sunny dip with Wycombe's green hills as backdrop. A variety of further refreshment options can be found in High Wycombe.

Access

Access via ladders and steps, with handrail. Level/ramped access to poolside; accessible changing rooms and toilets. Frequent local bus services to Uxbridge, Slough and Watford stop near the Rye, less than a kilometre away. High Wycombe railway station less than a kilometre away. Paid on-site parking.

HURLEY ISLAND, RIVER THAMES. © *ANYWHEREWEROAM.COM*

MARLOW OPEN WATER SWIM

51.5758, -0.7459 / Westhorpe Farm, Westhorpe Farm Lane, Little Marlow, Buckinghamshire, SL7 3RQ / 07730 552161 / Swimming / *www.marlowopenwaterswim.co.uk*

You can enjoy open water swimming at Westhorpe Lake on Monday and Wednesday evenings as well as weekend mornings. This is a safe location for those who are looking to begin outdoor swimming or are wanting a convenient place to practise; swim coaching is available. There are three square courses of 400 metres, 750 metres and 1,500 metres. All swimmers must wear a brightly coloured swim cap, and non-wetsuit wearers must also have a tow float. The site offers everything a swimmer could need including hot showers, changing rooms and toilets. An on-site cafe can be found within the sports club and is a great stop to refuel after a refreshing swim. There are plenty of pubs and cafes in nearby Marlow and Little Marlow.

Access

Access via a wooden jetty (jumping/steps available). Level/ramped access around site; accessible changing rooms and toilets; ramped access to the water. Bus from Marlow Bottom stops at Westhorpe caravan park, two or three times a day; two kilometres to Marlow railway station via footpath to north of lakes. Free on-site parking.

HURLEY ISLAND, RIVER THAMES

51.5521, -0.8059 / Hurley, Berkshire / Swimming and paddling

Near the historic lock at Hurley, the River Thames swirls around several small islands; this was a spot beloved by Jerome K. Jerome for its beauty. Nowadays it's a favourite with swimmers as well as walkers and kayakers. The wooded river offers clean, refreshing water with plenty of shallow spots for splashing fun. Edged by grassy picnic spots, this is the perfect spot for messing about on the river, and kids big and small may be reluctant to pack up and go home. There is a tearoom by the lock, and plenty of places to grab an ice cream or something more substantial in Hurley, although you may be tempted to visit the historic Olde Bell pub, parts of which date back to 1135.

Access

Water accessed from sandy beaches. Buses depart four times a day to Maidenhead from Hurley High Street, a kilometre away. Parking at the Hurley Village car park, 700 metres away.

HILLINGDON SPORTS AND LEISURE COMPLEX

51.5510, -0.4673 / Gatting Way, Uxbridge, London, UB8 1ES / 03451 307324 / Swimming and paddling / *www.better.org.uk/leisure-centre/london/hillingdon/hillingdon-sports-lc*

Hillingdon's large, art deco lido closed in 1998, but in anticipation of the 2012 Olympics restoration began in 2007, and the unheated pool is now at the centre of a new health and fitness hub. Once known as Uxbridge Lido, this attractive pool sits near London's greener fringes. There are poolside sunloungers to hire, bubbling fountains and kids' splash pools as well as a bustling cafe. Whether you're a serious swimmer, a sun lover or a spectator, Hillingdon Sports & Leisure Complex offers something for everyone. You are advised to pre-book if you want to avoid the some-times-long queues outside the impressive, red-arched entrance.

Access

Level access to poolside; accessible toilets and changing rooms; manual hoist available. Uxbridge Underground station a kilometre away. Frequent U1 and U2 buses to West Drayton and Ruislip stop at College, adjacent to lido. On-site parking.

LIQUID LEISURE WINDSOR

51.4742, -0.5587 / Horton Road, Windsor, Berkshire, SL3 9HY / 01753 542500 / *windsor.liquidleisure.com/open-water-swimming*

Located in the beautiful Windsor area, just three kilometres from Windsor Castle and next door to the Queen Mother Reservoir, Liquid Leisure Windsor is a bustling water adventure venue. The lake is split into two sections, the southern of which is reserved for swimmers with two different routes available. The venue has excellent, modern changing rooms and showers and a cafe (you are not permitted

to bring your own food on-site). This is an adrenaline-packed venue with plenty of other opportunities for fun in the water, including ringo rides, inflatables, ninja challenge courses and a beach resort. For post-swim relaxation, you can enjoy the waterfront Lakeside Bar & Restaurant, which has been known to host an Oktoberfest.

Access

Access via grassy banks or floating pier. Sunnymeads railway station 800 metres away. On-site parking.

DUMSEY MEADOW

51.3897, -0.4795 / Chertsey, Surrey / Swimming and paddling

On the verge of a beautiful water meadow, this clean and peaceful stretch of the River Thames is perfect for a dip into the water. The river is easy to enter with lovely, sloping banks shel-tered by the occasional old trees that encircle the area. A popular place for visitors from the surrounding areas, in the summer months this is a hub for activity both in the water and on land. Picnics are popular, or for those wanting to stop for a meal the cosy Kingfisher pub can be found on the river's edge, 300 metres away from the meadow. You may want to avoid this swim spot in August, when the Chertsey and Shepperton Regatta takes place here, although you should watch out for passing boats at any time of year.

Access

Access via gentle, grassy banks. Water can be reached via Thames Path, which runs from Chertsey Bridge. Hourly buses on Chertsey Bridge Road, a few hundred metres away, to Addlestone and Sunbury; three kilometres to Chertsey railway station. Parking at Dumsey Meadow, off Chertsey Bridge Road.

OLD DEER PARK, RICHMOND. © SHUTTERSTOCK/BASPHOTO

SHEPPERTON OPEN WATER SWIM

51.3867, -0.4530 / Ferry Lane, Shepperton, Surrey, TW17 9LH / 07531 745133 / Swimming / *www. sheppertonopenwaterswim.co.uk*

Bordered by the River Thames, Shepperton Open Water Swim is loved for its sandy beaches, tree-fringed serenity and clear water. Swimmers of varying abilities are welcome, with two swim courses of 400 or 750 metres. Lifeguards patrol the water regularly and the site itself is home to all amenities that swimmers may need including changing rooms, showers and wetsuit rental. A small shop and cafe trailer are available on-site. Swimmers new to the lake will have to complete a short induction and a swim test to prove competency in open water; brightly coloured swim caps are compulsory. Swim sessions generally run from April to September, but the site has been trying out winter weekend swims. For

those wanting to enjoy a meal after their dip, the King's Head pub is located across the River Thames in Shepperton.

Access

Water accessed from gently sloping, sandy beach; ramp available. Accessible changing and toilet (at sailing club); cross grassed areas to reach water. Frequent buses to Sunbury via Shepperton (both with railway stations) from Chertsey Road near King's Head, 700 metres away; Shepperton railway station two kilometres away. Free on-site parking.

HAMPTON POOL

51.4182, -0.3582 / High Street, Hampton, London, TW12 2ST / 02082 551116 / Swimming and paddling / *www.hamptonpool.co.uk*

If you fancy a preprandial Christmas Day swim, Hampton Pool may be the spot for you. Nestled in the corner of Bushy Park, whatever the weather

this large, heated lido is open every day of the year. There is also a smaller children's pool. The lido offers swimming lessons, aqua aerobics and lifeguard courses. You can float under the stars at one of their popular moonlight swims or enjoy a poolside music concert in summer. If you don't fancy a full English at the Sun Deck Cafe, there's plenty of benches and grassy spots for a picnic. A two-kilometre stroll through Bushy Park, past the Diana Fountain, will take you to Hampton Court Palace if you want to make a day of your visit.

Access

Entry to water via ladders, shallow steps with handrails and slides. Level access to poolside; accessible changing rooms and toilets; hoist available. Approximately a kilometre from Hampton railway station. High frequency bus services from Kew to Hampton Court stop at lido. Limited on-site and street parking.

POOLS ON THE PARK

51.4651, -0.3062 / Old Deer Park, Twickenham Road, Richmond, London, TW9 2SF / 02037 722999 / Swimming / *www.richmond.gov.uk/ pools_on_the_park*

Tucked in the corner of Richmond's Old Deer Park, just down the road from Kew Gardens, you can discover Pools on the Park. The site has an indoor, twenty-five-metre pool, a learner pool and the thirty-three-metre outdoor pool on offer. The pools were built as part of a post-war commitment to improved community sporting facilities. Offering both spooky and festive swims, this heated pool is open all year around. In keeping with their green surroundings, the lido offers spacious lawns on which to lounge after your dip. There is a cafe on-site, but you could also enjoy one of Richmond's many pubs and cafes a short stroll away.

Access
Access via steps (across the shallow end) and ladders. Level access to poolside, accessible changing rooms and toilets; hoist and wet chair available. Less than a kilometre to Richmond Underground/ Overground/railway station. High-frequency 490 bus to Heathrow Airport terminates at Pools on the Park. Limited on-site parking and nearby pay-and-display Old Deer Park car park.

FINCHLEY LIDO

51.6045, -0.1718 / Great North Leisure Park, Chaplin Square, Finchley, London, N12 0GL / 02083 439830 / Swimming and paddling / *www.better.org.uk/ leisure-centre/london/barnet/ finchley-lido-leisure-centre/main-pool-finchley-lido-leisure-centre*

Next to the wooded Glebelands Local Nature Reserve, the narrow strip of Finchley Lido is nestled behind a modern leisure centre. The pool is only open in the summer – although there is an indoor alternative – and is closed in bad weather. There is an on-site cafe, and the leisure centre is part of an entertainment complex that offers plenty of restaurants. With its concrete surrounds and line of hard benches, this is not a place to picnic, but there is a shallow pool with stepped sides for those who want to lounge. This is perhaps not one of London's destination lidos, but is a precious resource for locals seeking an escape from the capital.

Access
Access via ladders; steps into small pool. Level access to pool; good accessibility provision in leisure centre, but no hoist for outside pool. Approximately two kilometres from West Finchley and Finchley Central Underground stations; high-frequency buses stop outside leisure centre. On-site parking.

PARK ROAD POOL

51.5829, -0.1300 / Park Road, London, N8 8JN / 02083 413567 / Swimming and paddling / *www.fusion-lifestyle.com/ centres/park-road-pools-fitness/ activities/lido*

Just a stone's throw away from London's leafy Highgate Wood, you'll find the fifty-metre-long Park Road Pool, fringed by yew trees. The site also has twenty-five-metre and learner pools, both indoor. The heated pool, recently extensively refurbished, is open all year round. In addition to the main pool, there's a generously sized toddlers' pool and plenty of poolside space to relax after your dip. One of London's earliest lidos, the pool will celebrate its centenary in 2029. There's an on-site cafe and plenty of historic pubs and other places to eat and drink nearby in Crouch End.

Access
Access via ladders and hand-railed steps. Level access to poolside; accessible changing rooms and toilets; no hoist or wet chair. High-frequency buses to Muswell Hill and Finsbury Park stop outside lido. Approximately a kilo-metre and a half to Hornsey railway station and Highgate Underground. On-site parking.

HAMPSTEAD HEATH BATHING PONDS.
© SHUTTERSTOCK/PHOTOCRITICAL

HAMPSTEAD HEATH BATHING PONDS

51.5607, -0.1660 / Hampstead Heath, London, NW3 1BP / Swimming / *www.cityoflondon. gov.uk/things-to-do/green-spaces/hampstead-heath*

In the green escape that is London's Hampstead Heath, you can enjoy a swim in one of the three Hampstead Heath Ponds, once reservoirs. A landmark legal ruling in 2005 established the right to swim in the ponds all year around; now the Men's (Highgate) and Women's (Kenwood) pools are open all year, but the mixed pool is closed during winter. Although lifeguarded, the ponds are deep and cold and can be tricky to get in and out of, so are only suitable for confident swimmers. There are cold showers and open air changing areas. These iconic lakes, a popular swim spot since Victorian times, are often busy in the summer and those seeking a post-dip picnic spot would be well

advised to leave the confines of the pool area and find somewhere shaded on the expansive Hampstead Heath.

Access
Access to water different for each pond: water accessed from piers or muddy banks. Hampstead Underground station just over a kilometre away; Hampstead Heath Overground station 800 metres away. Buses to London centre stop on Pond Street, just under a kilometre away. Paid parking at East Heath car park several hundred metres walk away, across parkland.

PARLIAMENT HILL LIDO

51.5563, -0.1510 / Parliament Hill Fields, Gospel Oak, London, NW5 1LT / 02073 323779 / Swimming and paddling / *parliamenthilllido.org*

From the imposing brick facade of the entrance, everything about Parliament Hill Lido is redolent of the golden age of lidos. The art deco pool is little changed from the 1930s although modernisation has forced some changes, such as the removal of the diving boards. The lido was the first outdoor pool in Britain to have a steel lining fitted to the tank. Open all year around, the pool is unheated, and an electronic display warns you just how cold the water will be as you arrive; there is a sauna to warm up in on winter days.

There's also an art deco pool fountain, toddlers' pool and a cafe for hot drinks and home-made food. There's plenty of paved space poolside, but if you want greenery you will have to head to the wide, grassy Hampstead Heath.

Access
Access via ladders and handrailed steps. Level access to poolside; accessible changing rooms and toilets; hoist available. Lido is across road from Gospel Oak railway station, where there are high-frequency buses to Archway and Brent Cross. On-site paid parking.

WEST RESERVOIR CENTRE

51.5671, -0.0919 / Green Lanes, Hackney, London, N4 2HA / 0208 4428116 / Swimming / *www.better.org.uk/ leisure-centre/london/hackney/ west-reservoir-centre*

With London's high-rises as your backdrop, you can enjoy a dip in the twenty-three acres of West Reservoir in Hackney's Woodberry Down. The site offers a 100-metre warm-up course, a 200-metre course and longer courses as the water warms up through the summer – swim sessions are available all year around. Sessions are for experienced swimmers only, and over-fourteens; swimmers must wear a red cap (which can be purchased from the centre). The centre also offers sailing and kayaking if you're not quite ready to get out of the water. The West Reservoir Centre has a number of amenities (and good accessible facilities), including changing rooms, showers and a cafe. The Coal House Cafe, found 450 metres away on the other side of the reservoir, is also a popular local spot for coffee and breakfasts.

Access
Water accessed from piers or water's pebbled edge. Frequent buses to London Bridge and Waterloo from Green Lanes, 150 metres away. On-site parking.

LONDON FIELDS LIDO

51.5426, -0.0614 / London Fields West Side, Hackney, London, E8 3EU / 02072 549038 / Swimming and paddling / *www.better.org.uk/ leisure-centre/london/hackney/ london-fields-lido*

London Fields is one of the capital's rescued lidos, and while the fifty-metre-long, floodlit pool may not be the best spot for a leisurely swim, it is a great example of how even historic lidos can be made accessible to everyone. The 1930s heated pool was closed in 1988, and the local community waged a twenty-year battle, facing down bulldozers and squatters who held raves in the empty tank, to finally

see it reopen in 2006. It was also extensively refurbished again in 2017. With plenty of poolside space as well as a cafe, you won't be short of options for a post-swim snack. The lido offers lane swimming but also a wider lane for social swimming. With plans afoot to add a learner pool (which should open by 2022), this is a resource for the whole community.

Access
Access via ladders, handrailed steps and handrailed slope. Level access to poolside; accessible toilets and chang-ing rooms; sloped access to water and hoist. London Fields Overground station on opposite side of London Fields park. Pay-and-display on-street parking near lido.

OASIS SPORTS CENTRE

51.5155, -0.1255 / 32 Endell Street, Covent Garden, London, WC2H 9AG / 02078 311804 / Swimming / *www.better.org.uk/ leisure-centre/london/camden/ oasis-sports-centre*

If you want to discover Theatreland's best-kept backstage secret, seek out the rooftop Oasis Sports Centre. Opposite the Shaftesbury Theatre, tucked behind Covent Garden's Craft Beer Company, you'll discover this blue haven. After your swim, you can enjoy a coffee on the wooden sun terraces. Open all year round, this heated

WEST RESERVOIR CENTRE. © *JULIAN OSLEY*

pool offers remarkable value for money for those seeking a different day out in the city. Although the pool lacks the charm of London's art deco lidos it is a historic site; there has been public bathing on the site since Turkish Baths opened here in the mid-eighteenth century. The pool really is in the heart of the city, within walking distance of Piccadilly Circus, Covent Garden, Leicester Square and Oxford Street, so post-dip you can take in a show, do a bit of shopping or have lunch in Chinatown.

Access
Access via ladders. Ramped access to poolside; accessible changing rooms and toilets; hoist available. Less than half a kilometre to both Covent Garden and Tottenham Court Road Underground stations; frequent buses to Putney Heath serve St Giles High Street, 300 metres away. Paid on-street parking, and Covent Garden car park 300 metres away.

TOOTING BEC LIDO. © *FLAVIO CENTOFANTI*

SERPENTINE LIDO

51.5047, -0.1690 / Hyde Park, London, W2 2UH /
07941 846566 / Swimming and paddling /
www.facebook.com/serpentinelido

Serpentine Lido is an ornamental lake in
London's Hyde Park, created in the 1730s by
the damming of the River Westbourne. The
Serpentine is home to one of the UK's oldest
swimming clubs, the Serpentine Swimming Club,
who take a dip here every morning between
5 and 9.30 a.m. The general public can swim
in the lido section of the Serpentine during its
summer opening; it opens at weekends in May
and daily from June to September. A sloping
beach provides access, and there is a paddling
pool for children. The Serpentine hosted the
swimming section of the triathlon during the
2012 Olympics, and also hosts open water
swimming events. If you don't mind sharing with
the lido's ducks and geese, the grassy banks are
perfect for a picnic, although you might choose
instead to head to the stylish lido cafe.

Access
Access via beach-style, sloped entry with
handrails and anti-slip maps and a jetty.
Level access to waterside. Hyde Park Corner,
Knightsbridge, Marble Arch and Lancaster
Gate Underground stations all within a
kilometre of swim spot. Pay-and-display
parking on outskirts of Hyde Park.

TOOTING BEC LIDO

51.4316, -0.1390 / Tooting Bec Road, London,
SW16 1RU / 02088 717198 / Swimming and
paddling / *www.placesleisure.org/centres/
tooting-bec-lido*

Ninety-one metres long and thirty metres wide,
the gigantic Tooting Bec Lido, resplendent with
a tiered, art deco fountain, is one of London's
finest surviving Edwardian lidos. The unheated
pool is open to the public during the summer
months and proves very popular, although
members of the South London Swimming Club
swim there year-round. When built, a condition
of construction was that it be concealed from
the common by an earthwork bank, and this
now hosts a green wall of trees around the
pool. This large pool is spacious enough to
accommodate lane swimmers and family fun
simultaneously, and there's plenty of poolside
space for a post-swim lounge. There's a
children's paddling pool and a lido cafe, as
well as the nearby Tooting Bec Common Cafe.

Access
Access via ladders. Level access to poolside;
accessible changing rooms and facilities; hoist
available. Streatham railway station a kilometre
away; frequent buses to Clapham Common,
Streatham and Sloane Square outside lido.
Limited on-site parking; pay-and-display
car park at Dr Johnson Avenue, less than a
kilometre away.

BROCKWELL LIDO. © FUSION LIFESTYLE

BROCKWELL LIDO

51.4532, -0.1062 / Brockwell Park, Dulwich Road, London, SE24 0PA / 02072 743088 / Swimming and paddling / *www.fusion-lifestyle.com/centres/brockwell-lido*

Affectionately nicknamed Brixton Beach, the large, art deco Brockwell Lido has had a precarious past, closing between 1990 and 1994 and 2001 and 2007, but the council-owned, Fusion-managed pool enjoys fierce local support, and now you can enjoy a cold-water swim at any time of year. In busy summer months, you may struggle to find a spot to lounge among London's most glamorous swimmers – police were called to control the queues on one particularly hot day in 2019. But, on cooler winter days, you can warm yourself up in the cedar wood sauna. The Lido Cafe is a popular brunch spot, so be prepared to wait for food.

Access

Entry to waters via shallow, handrailed steps and ladders. Level access to poolside; accessible changing rooms and toilets; hoist available. Herne Hill railway station 300 metres away; high-frequency buses to Westminster, Elephant and Castle and Peckham stop outside lido. Paid parking adjacent to lido.

CHARLTON LIDO AND LIFESTYLE CLUB

51.4752, 0.0391 / Hornfair Park, Shooters Hill Road, Greenwich, London, SE18 4LX / 02088 567389 / Swimming and paddling / *www.better.org.uk/leisure-centre/london/greenwich/charlton-lido*

On south London's suburban streets, in the shadow of high-rises, you'll discover one of the last of the capital's large, 1930s lidos, behind unassuming red-brick walls. Open all year round, it's the perfect spot for a winter swim, as steam wreathes the heated waters. The pool is subdivided to provide space for lane swimmers and those who want a more relaxed dip. The lido offers Swim Doctor sessions, for adults looking to improve on their swimming style. There is a shallow children's pool, although this is not always uncovered. After your swim, you can relax with a toastie at the roof terrace's cafe or stroll around the neighbouring Hornfair Park, named for the riotous three-day festival that used to be held in Charlton.

Access

Access via ladders and steps, with handrail. Level access to poolside, lift to roof terrace, accessible changing rooms and toilets; hoist available. High-frequency bus services to Lewisham and Woolwich stop outside lido. On-site parking and on-street parking.

TONBRIDGE SWIMMING POOL. © *TMACTIVE*

BECKENHAM PLACE PARK LAKE

51.4204, -0.0143 / Beckenham, London /
07736 930823 / *beckenhamplacepark.co.uk*

The 285-metre-long, aquifer-fed Beckenham Place Park Lake was London's first purpose-built swimming lake, opening in 2019, on the site of a former golf course. An incredibly popular spot, Beckenham Place Park Lake is ideal for families with older children (children under eight are not allowed to swim), and lifeguards patrol the water on canoes. The lake's water is consistently cool, and the shallows at the edge of the lake are perfect for paddling. The grounds of the 230-acre Beckenham Place Park are the greatest draw for swimmers: with sports facilities, ancient woodland, a sensory garden and an on-site cafe (which has public toilets nearby), this is an ideal place for a full day out.

Access

Access from sandy beach. Frequent bus to Elmers End and Woolwich stops by park gates; Beckenham Hill railway station, less than a kilometre away. Limited paid parking in park – park visitors are encouraged to arrive on foot, bike or by public transport.

DIVERS COVE

51.2521, -0.0721 / North Park Lane, Godstone, Surrey, RH9 8ND / *www.diverscove.co.uk*

Divers Cove offers open water swim sessions in the waters of a former sand extraction site, with 450- and 650-metre courses marked out. The venue offers great-value membership swims, but also allows non-members, including children over the age of seven, to take a dip in the vibrant waters. Due to the lake's varied biodiversity, the water becomes a beautiful turquoise colour in the summer, and with lush trees surrounding the lake it is easy to lose yourself in your surroundings. Wetsuits are required if the water temperature is less than 16 °C; bright swim caps are compulsory. You can enjoy a post-dip sauna session to warm up or visit the on-site cafe for a hot drink.

Access

Access via sandy and shingled beaches; handrails available. Regular buses to East Grinstead, Redhill and other local destinations on Waterhouse Lane, a kilometre away. On-site parking.

DIVERS COVE. © TOM BAKER

NEMES, HOLBOROUGH LAKES. © WWW.DRIVINGWITHDOGS.CO.UK

TONBRIDGE SWIMMING POOL

51.1961, 0.2718 / The Slade, Tonbridge, Kent,TN9 1HR / 01732 367449 / Swimming and paddling / www.tmactive.co.uk/locations/tonbridge-pool

🚆 🅿 ❌ 🚾 🛝 🆑 ♿

Built in 1910, Tonbridge was the UK's first heated lido, despite the objections of a local councillor who feared mixed bathing would damage the marriage prospects of girls who looked like 'wet terriers'. A major renovation in the 1990s saw the addition of an indoor pool, and you can now swim between the indoor and outdoor areas; there is also a learner pool and a shallow, beach-style area to enter the water. There is an on-site cafe, but also plenty of picnic benches if you want to bring your own food. Or, after your swim, you could enjoy your picnic in the extensive grounds of the ruined thirteenth-century castle, just across the road from the lido on the banks of the River Medway.

Access

Access via steps and ladders; also shallow, sloped, beach-style entry. Level access to poolside; accessible changing rooms and toilets; hoist to indoor fitness pool, which has swimming link to outdoor pool. Tonbridge railway station just over a kilometre away; frequent local bus services stop near castle. On-site pay-and-display parking.

NEMES DIVING AND WATER SPORTS ACADEMY, HOLBOROUGH LAKES

51.3343, 0.4404 / Holborough Lakes, Snodland, Kent, ME6 5GN / 07507 624911 / Swimming / nda-scuba.com

🚆 🅿 ❌ 🚾 🛝 ♿

Nemes Diving and Water Sports Academy is based at Holborough Lakes, an eleven-metre-deep former chalk quarry. Primarily a diving spot – underwater boat wrecks have been added for divers to explore – it also offers open water swimming sessions. There is a floating deep-water jetty, for those swimmers wanting to practise diving into the water. With lifeguards on standby and an on-site cafe for hot drinks and snacks, this is a great spot for a refreshing dip. The pretty lakes have a distinctive rocky shoreline that belie their urban location; there are plenty of restaurants, cafes and shops nearby in the rapidly developing local area for a post-swim meal. First-time swimmers must complete an induction.

Access

Entry into water via handrailed, concrete slipway, and floating jetty for diving. Frequent buses to Maidstone and Snodland on Holborough Road and Manley Boulevard, less than a kilometre away; Snodland railway station a kilometre and a half away. On-site parking.

THE STRAND POOL

51.3954, 0.5632 / Strand Approach Road, Gillingham, Kent, ME7 1TT / 01634 333927
Swimming and paddling / www.strandpool.info

The Strand Pool was built in 1896 on the mudflats of the Kent coast, on the estuary of the River Medway, and continues to use filtered saltwater from the river. Float along the lazy river that loops the main pool area, or cross a colourful bridge and slide down the trunk of a pink elephant into the lido if you want to make a splash. There is also a shallow toddlers' pool. Although run by the council, this curving, colourful pool owes much to the unwavering dedication of the Friends of the Strand Pool group. You can bring a picnic, lounge by the pool, and afterwards fit in a round of crazy golf or take a trip on the miniature railway. The pool offers free swims to local children and pensioners, through the Medway City Card scheme. The nearby Ship Inn can provide refreshments.

Access

Access via ladders, shallow steps and slides. Level access to the poolside; accessible changing rooms and toilets. Frequent buses to Gillingham centre and other local destinations on Pier Road, by lido entrance; Gillingham railway station a kilometre and a half away. On-site parking.

FAVERSHAM POOLS

51.3149, 0.8893 / Leslie Smith Drive, Faversham, Kent, ME13 8PW / 01795 532426 / Swimming and paddling / www.favershampools.com

At Faversham, you get three for the price of one – a heated main pool, a wild rapids splash pool and a toddlers' pool, complete with slides. There are also indoor pools. Keep an eye out for the ducks that like to visit the island in the middle of the wild rapids river. The deep end of the thirty-three-metre pool is often roped

WALPOLE BAY TIDAL POOL. © *AMANDA JEWELL*

off to allow for diving – Faversham is the only pool in the UK to have three diving boards: two springboards and a five-metre diving board. You can relax afterwards with sandwiches, soup or hot chocolate and cake at the Tides Cafe, or bring a picnic and enjoy the grassy parkland that surrounds the pools.

Access

Access via ladders and diving boards. Level access to poolside; accessible changing rooms and toilets; hoist available. Faversham railway station 500 metres away. Car park adjacent to lido.

FORDWICH, RIVER GREAT STOUR

51.2980, 1.1337 / Fordwich, Kent / Swimming and paddling

Near Fordwich, England's smallest town, you can enjoy a dip in the wildlife-rich waters of the River Great Stour. Riverside trees offer shade as they trail branches in the reedy, weedy water, and the river widens into a natural lake, perfect for a secluded swim. There are mooring platforms to enter the water from, as well as grassy banks, and footpaths follow the riverbanks on both sides. There are two riverside pubs in Fordwich if you fancy a post-swim lunch, and there are public toilets near Sturry railway station. This is a stretch of river popular with kayakers and stand-up paddleboarders so consider a bright swim cap.

Access

Access via grassy banks, with some reeds, and kayakers' mooring platforms. Fordwich well-served by frequent buses to Canterbury and other local destinations from Fordwich Road, a kilometre away; Sturry railway station, just over a kilometre away. Limited on-street parking in Fordwich, a kilometre from swim spot.

MARINE TERRACE TIDAL POOL

51.3876, 1.3735 / Margate, Kent / Swimming and paddling

Two tidal pools were built in Margate in the 1930s: one at Walpole Bay and the other at the centre of the town, on the golden sands in front of Marine Terrace. The town's lido was critically damaged in a winter storm in 1978, but the concrete-blocked tidal pools have weathered the storms. Although attempts have been made to designate Margate's smaller, shallower tidal pool as a boating lake, it remains a popular swim destination for locals. The pool has no facilities and no lifeguards – although the beach has some lifeguard coverage during the summer months. Although Margate's mechanical elephant (capable of speeds in excess of forty kilometres per hour) has long since disappeared from the seafront, this pool sits in the shadow of the Turner Contemporary art gallery and Margate's amusements. Walking a short distance into Margate provides a variety of refreshment options.

Access

Access via stone steps and ramp. Access to water via stone steps and ladder; sandy beach must be crossed. Less than a kilometre to Margate railway station; frequent buses to Ramsgate from Canterbury Road, 300 metres away. Paid car parks in town centre, less than a kilometre away.

WALPOLE BAY TIDAL POOL. © *AMANDA JEWELL*

WALPOLE BAY TIDAL POOL

51.3923, 1.4039 / Margate, Kent / Swimming and paddling

At low tide, the seaweedy walls of Walpole Bay Tidal Pool reveal themselves. It was built in 1937 because the large tidal range at Margate means that the sea recedes far into the distance at low tides. This pool, at its widest 170 by 140 metres, is almost four acres in size, and is a little over two metres deep at its seaward end. The beach provides a rocky natural floor for the pool. The pool is filled by not only seawater, but also freshwater springs that rise through the beach. The nearest public toilets are in the town centre, approximately a kilometre away, but there are plenty of nearby cafes to warm up at. The water at Walpole Bay is always refreshingly cold, and you should keep an eye out for the incoming tide and also for seals – one joined swimmers in the pool in 2019.

Access

Access via stone steps and ladders; no diving. Beach can be reached by steps or steep ramp; sandy beach must be crossed. Frequent buses from Margate centre to Ramsgate on Esplanade, less than a kilometre away; Margate railway station three kilometres away. Parking on Hodges Gap Promenade, adjacent to pool.

Central England

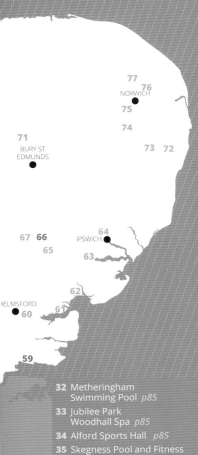

PETERBOROUGH LIDO. © *VIVACITY*

SYMONDS YAT. © *SHUTTERSTOCK/ANDREW ROSU*

SYMONDS YAT

51.8463, -2.6440 / Symonds Yat, Herefordshire / Swimming and paddling

On the River Wye, Symonds Yat is a secluded swimming spot just to the east of the eponymous small village. Loved by canoers and swimmers alike, this peaceful spot is surrounded by meadows and sandy bays which make entering the water simple. The current is gentle and shallows can be found near the banks, making this area suitable for swimmers of varying abilities. The surrounding meadows are perfect for relaxing after a dip in the water and there are plenty of spots to sit and enjoy a picnic. For visitors wanting a hot meal the village is home to the Ye Old Ferrie Inn, just 200 metres away.

Access

Access from sandy bays. Not easy to reach by public transport: 34 bus runs regularly from Ross-on-Wye to Monmouth and stops at Whitchurch, four and a half kilometres away. Paid parking and public toilets at Symonds Yat Rock car park, two kilometres away.

BACKNEY COMMON

51.9385, -2.6018 / Ross-on-Wye, Herefordshire / Swimming and paddling

Loved by swimmers for its beautiful surroundings and sandy beach, Backney Common is a pool on the River Wye. Located just over a kilometre west from the village of Brampton Abbotts, this spot is a great place to head for if you're looking for an untouched spot of nature. Currents can vary but are largely gentle and make for a relaxing swim downstream. A large, deep pool can be found near the beach, which is suitable for swimming without straying too far from the shore. The surrounding common is suited to picnics and the vast neighbouring meadows and fields are popular with walkers. Refreshments can be found at the Man of Ross pub in Ross-on-Wye.

Access

The common is access land; water accessed via sandy beach. Care should be taken to check strength of current before entering the water. Not easily accessed by public transport: 33 bus to Hereford stops several times a day on A49, six and a half kilometres away. Parking at Wilton Road car park, five kilometres away.

WILD SWIMMING. © SHUTTERSTOCK/LOIS GOBE

SELLACK BRIDGE

51.9488, -2.6345 / Ross-on-Wye, Herefordshire / Swimming and paddling

On a seven-kilometre stretch of swimmable water on the River Wye, Sellack Bridge is a serene spot to enjoy a swim. The historical footbridge which stretches across the river marks the best location to enter the water; beaches line the banks of the river and make entry into the water easy, and shallows which are suited to paddling and first-time swimmers can be found nearby. The current is gentle and the clean, cool water is great for swimmers of varying abilities. For those looking to explore the local area, this spot is loved by walkers due to its picturesque trails and wide, green spaces. There are no nearby restaurants or cafes to stop by for a meal, however venturing the eleven kilometres into Ross-on-Wye will provide a variety of refreshment options.

Access
Access via gravel beaches. Bus to Hereford stops a kilometre to the north at Village Hall stop once daily on weekends. Very limited parking roadside 350 metres south.

LUGG MEADOWS

52.0657, -2.6818 / Hereford, Herefordshire / Swimming and paddling

On a beautiful stretch of the winding River Lugg, Lugg Meadows can be found between the village of Lugwardine and Hereford. The gentle current is great for a relaxing dip into the clean water, and the surrounding gravel beaches allow access to the river. This stretch of the river spans around two kilometres, making longer swims possible, and the river can reach up to two metres in depth. The untouched, beautiful meadow which borders the river is an ideal spot for exploring after a dip in the water. For a bite to eat, the village of Lugwardine is home to the Crown and Anchor pub.

Access
Water accessed from gravel beaches. Regular buses throughout Hereford stop three and a half kilometres away; Hereford railway station three and a half kilometres from swim spot. Paid parking four kilometres away at Merton Meadow car park.

LEINTWARDINE BRIDGE. © *SHUTTERSTOCK/MARK ANDREW PHOTOGRAPHY*

DROITWICH SPA LIDO. © *GEORGE GRIFFITHS*

LEINTWARDINE BRIDGE

52.3597, -2.8780 / Leintwardine, Herefordshire /
Swimming and paddling

On the fringes of Leintwardine village,
Leintwardine Bridge is stunning location on
the River Teme. The small stretch of the river is
surrounded by woodland, rich nature and little
beaches. The spot is loved for its idyllic scenery
and calm water; the current is gentle near the
bridge and the water forms several deep pools
near the shore. Further upstream the water
becomes shallower and is perfect for paddling
or for those new to outdoor swimming. The
bridge is right next door to the Lion pub,
where you can enjoy some hearty food
after a dip in the water.

Access
Access from grassy banks or sandy beaches.
Lion bus stop 200 metres away; infrequent
services to Ludlow. Limited roadside parking
800 metres away, where A4113 intersects with
A4110.

HIGHLEY OUTDOOR SWIMMING POOL

52.4517, -2.3859 / Bridgnorth Road, Highley,
Shropshire, WV16 6JG / 01746 860000 /
Swimming and paddling / *haloleisure.org.uk/
highleyoutdoorpool*

In the heart of the Shropshire countryside,
Highley Outdoor Swimming Pool is located in
the town's Severn Centre. The twenty-five-
metre pool is heated to a warm 24 °C, with
ladders leading into the water. The lido offers
both adult and family sessions while it is open
from May to September. Facilities include
changing rooms, showers and lifeguards.
The pool is surrounded by vast, grassy areas
for relaxing after your swim, and an on-site
coffee stand can provide drinks and snacks.
On summer days this pool can become very
busy and pool time is limited via a colour-cod-
ed band system. A visit here can be combined
with a stroll in the Severn Valley Country Park,
followed by a meal at the Three Horseshoes pub.

Access
Access via ladder. From Recreation Ground
stop, bus leaves approximately every hour
to High Town. On-site parking at the Halo
Severn Centre.

UNIVERSITY OF WORCESTER LAKESIDE CAMPUS

52.2540, -2.2540 / Holt Heath, Worcester, Worcestershire, WR6 6NH / 01905 855000 / Swimming / *www.worcester.ac.uk/life/ campus-facilities/lakeside-campus*

Based on the official University of Worcester Lakeside Campus lake, this beautiful swim spot offers both beginners and experienced swimmers everything they need to enjoy a dip. A jetty and grassy banks allow entry to the water. The lake measures a kilometre and a half, and has a 600-metre circuit available for swimmers to follow between April and September (book online). Lifeguards are on hand and coaching sessions are available to any swimmer who wants to learn new skills. The facility itself has changing rooms and toilets, and for those looking for a snack and drink the Hill Top Cafe can be found 300 metres away.

Access

Access from grassy, sometimes muddy, banks and wooden pier. Regular buses to Worcester stop at Top Barn Farm, 350 metres south. On-site parking.

DROITWICH SPA LIDO

52.2659, -2.1450 / Worcester Road, Droitwich Spa, Worcestershire, WR9 8AA / 01905 799342 / Swimming and paddling / *www.riversfitness.co.uk/ droitwich-spa-lido*

Nestled near the centre of Droitwich Spa, Droitwich Spa Lido is one of the UK's last open-air, inland, saltwater lidos. The forty-metre pool has ramped access, a shallow end for younger visitors as well as deeper areas for swimming, and the surrounding trees provide a secluded feel. Heated to 24 °C, this is an ideal spot to visit in cool weather, however it should be noted that it can become busy in the summer months. The lido has changing rooms, toilets, showers, a wet play area and plenty of spaces

to relax after a dip in the water. Little Al's Kitchen provides on-site refreshments, or alternatively outside food is permitted poolside for a picnic.

Access

Access from steps; wheelchair access into the beach-style pool. Regular buses to Kidderminster, Bromsgrove and Birmingham from Queen Street stop, 250 metres away. Paid on-site parking.

THE OLD BATHING PLACE

52.1990, -1.6937 / Stratford-upon-Avon, Warwickshire / Swimming and paddling

Resting just outside historic Stratford-upon-Avon, the small stretch of the River Avon known as The Old Bathing Place is a fantastic spot to enjoy a dip. A small beach lines the shore of the river, making entry into the clean water easy and mud free. The water itself is shallow, meaning that even inexperienced outdoor swimmers will find this spot enjoyable. The surrounding field is perfect for picnics, and for visitors looking for food there is an abundance of restaurants and cafes available just over a kilometre away in the town centre. For those wanting to explore the area a little more during their trip, the Shakespeare's Birthplace museum lies a kilometre and a half away.

Access

Access via small beach. St Gregory's Road bus stop located 600 metres south, served approximately every half an hour to Stratford town centre. On-site parking.

ABBEY FIELDS SWIMMING POOL

52.3473, -1.5832 / Bridge Street, Kenilworth, Warwickshire, CV8 1BP / 01926 855478 / Swimming and paddling / www.everyoneactive.com/centre/abbey-fields-swimming-pool

CHASEWATER COUNTRY PARK. © SHUTTERSTOCK/DJAPHOTO

On the fringes of Kenilworth, this tree-fringed pool is an ideal spot for a day out. The lido, which has ladders into the water, is cool and clean with an adjoining paddling pool, with an adjoining paddling pool. Abbey Fields is usually open from late May to September, although it is currently closed with no clear plans for reopening. An indoor pool is also available and can be found inside the Abbey Fields Swimming Pool facility, as well as changing rooms, showers and toilets. The draw of this swim spot is its proximity to Kenilworth Castle. To round off your day, the Clarendon Arms pub can provide refreshments.

Access

Water accessed from ladders. Kenilworth train station, one kilometre; buses to Leamington Spa arrive approximately every fifteen minutes from Abbey Fields stop, 300 metres away. Parking available 250 metres away at Abbey Fields car park.

MIDLANDS OPEN WATER

52.5745, -1.6923 / Tamworth Road, Kingsbury, Warwickshire, B78 2HZ / 07399 776229 / Swimming / www.midlandsopenwater.com

Located to the south of Tamworth, Midlands Open Water is a family owned lake which prides itself on being completely natural and chemical free. Voted the best spot for open water swimming in the Midlands three years running, Midlands Open Water is perfect for both beginners and experienced swimmers thanks to its friendly atmosphere. A small, pebbly beach and grassy banks provide access into the clean water, which deepens gradually, and two circuits of 300 or 650 metres are available – swimmers must pay an annual

insurance fee before entering the water. With lush trees enshrouding the lake, this is an ideal place to unwind. Swimmers are encouraged to bring a picnic to enjoy by the lakeside, but alternatively the White Swan pub can provide refreshments.

Access

Access via pebbly beach and grassy banks. Regular buses to Tamworth call at Manor Farm stop, 350 metres away. On-site parking.

CLIFF LAKES WATER PARK

52.5822, -1.6954 / Tamworth Road, Cliff, Warwickshire, B78 2DL / 01827 872000 / Swimming / www.clifflakes.co.uk/swimming

In the heart of the Midlands, Cliff Lakes Water Park is a lake designed specifically with water-based activities in mind. Two courses of 250 and 750 metres are available to swimmers, and there are five fifty-metre lanes available from May to September – cold water swimming continues throughout the winter. Floating piers provide access to the water, and for those wanting to inject some excitement into their day, the site offers water sports including paddleboarding and wakeboarding. Facilities include toilets, changing rooms, showers and lifeguards, and brightly coloured swimming caps and wetsuits or tow floats are essential. The on-site Waterfront Ski Bar can provide some welcome refreshments after your swim.

Access

Water accessed from floating piers. Regular buses to Tamworth call at Manor Farm stop, 450 metres away. On-site parking.

DOSTHILL QUARRY

52.5965, -1.6893 / Church Road, Dosthill, Staffordshire, B77 1LU / 01827 281304 / Swimming / *dosthillquarry.com*

A former granite quarry, Dosthill Quarry is now a popular outdoor swimming location on the outskirts of Dosthill in Tamworth. A wooden pier and pebbly beach lead into the water of this site, which is open all year round. This spot has entertained swimmers since the 1930s, and as well as a 400-metre swimming course the site is also well known for scuba diving. Brave swimmers can often be seen jumping from a ten-foot natural cliff. The water which flooded the quarry came from a nearby freshwater spring, and as a result the swim spot is incredibly clean and clear, making it ideal for a refreshing dip. Facilities include a basic changing cabin, toilets, equipment rental and a small on-site cafe. A swim here can be combined with the Chapel to Chapel Walk, which takes you past Dosthill's historic Norman chapel.

Access

Accessible by wooden pier, gravelly shore or jumping from cliff. Buses to Tamworth leave the Fox Inn stop approximately every ten minutes. Tamworth railway station five kilometres away. On-site parking.

CHASEWATER OPEN WATER SWIMMING

52.6629, -1.9520 / Pool Road, Brownhills, Burntwood, Walsall, West Midlands, WS8 7NL / 07974 257086 / Swimming / *www.chaseopenwater.com*

Nestled in the centre of Chasewater Country Park, Chasewater Open Water Swimming is an expansive stretch of water and a hub for water-based activities. The refreshing, clean water is perfect for cooling down on hot summer days, or for learning the skills necessary to begin outdoor swimming from the various courses which cater to beginner to experienced swimmers. Toilets and changing rooms are available, and a shallow area can be found near the lake's edge – tow floats are necessary. For a full day out, Chasewater Country Park contains stunning nature trails and an abundance of deer. Plenty of spaces are available for a picnic, or alternatively the nearby Sidings Tearoom at Chasewater Railway allows visitors to enjoy their food while watching steam trains pass by.

Access

Access via sometimes muddy banks or wooden pier. Hourly buses to Brownhills from Garden Centre stop, 400 metres away. Parking available 400 metres away at Chasewater car park.

ALBRIGHTON SWIMMING POOL

52.6318, -2.2791 / Newhouse Lane, Albrighton, Shropshire, WV7 3QS / Swimming / *www.albrightonswimming.co.uk*

First opened in 1970, Albrighton Swimming Pool is a volunteer-run, heated swimming pool in the grounds of Albrighton Primary School. Fringed by trees, the pool has a private feel, but on sunny days the lido proves very popular. The water can be reached via ladders, and the site has lifeguards, changing rooms and toilets, perfect for a family day out during the summer season. For visitors wanting to stop for some food, the High Street is just 300 metres away and is home to a number of cafes and restaurants, including the Peckish cafe.

Access

Water accessed via ladders. Crown Inn bus stop 300 metres away; hourly buses to Telford. On-site parking.

ESSEX BRIDGE, RIVER TRENT

52.8006, -2.0090 / Great Haywood, Staffordshire / Swimming and paddling

Built in the sixteenth century by the Earl of Essex for Queen Elizabeth I, Essex Bridge remains to this day a popular location to enjoy the surrounding Staffordshire countryside. The River Trent here is clean, and although water depth can vary depending upon recent rainfall it is always deep enough for swimming. The current is gentle enough for inexperienced swimmers, with shallows for paddling near the riverbanks. For those wanting to explore some local history, 300 metres away rests Shugborough Hall, a seventeenth-century mansion house. The nearby village of Great Haywood is home to a number of pubs and bakeries where you can grab a bite to eat.

Access
Water accessed from grassy, gently sloping banks. Buses leave approximately every twenty minutes to Stafford and Lichfield from Clifford Arms stop, 200 metres away. Roadside parking in Great Haywood.

THREE SHIRES HEAD

53.2137, -1.9873 / Buxton, Derbyshire / Swimming, paddling and plunge pool

On the edge of the Peak District, Three Shires Head marks the intersection of three counties: Staffordshire, Derbyshire and Cheshire. Two bridges sit atop this collection of small waterfalls, gentle streams and shallow plunge pools, with easy access into the water from rock platforms and grassy banks. Wide, open countryside surrounding the area makes this a great spot for a family trip, with plenty of picnic spots on the rolling hillsides. For those looking to explore the local area, eight kilometres away sits the gritstone Lud's Church, reputedly where Robin Hood and Friar Tuck once spent the night. To complete your day out, the Crag Inn in Wildboarclough can provide well-deserved meals.

Access
Smooth rocks and grassy banks. 58 bus stops at Level Lane in Buxton on its way to Macclesfield several times a day; Buxton railway station nine and a half kilometres away. Lay-by parking at Three Shires Head parking, one and a half kilometres away.

MERMAID'S POOL

53.3948, -1.8894 / Hayfield, Derbyshire / Swimming and paddling

High on the slopes of the giant Kinder Scout, the twinkling eye of Mermaid's Pool is said to offer healing properties to all who swim there. The tarn is also reputedly home to a mermaid who only appears at Easter's midnight. The peaty water is always cool and often murky. The pool is a challenging five-kilometre hike from Hayfield, and you will need to cross boggy and pathless moorland; it is best enjoyed by determined walkers or fell runners who want to combine a day on the moors with a swim and perhaps lunch by the beautiful Kinder Downfall. Those who make the effort will be rewarded with expansive views of the Peak District's heathered moorland. The only facilities are in Hayfield or the nearby historic market town of Glossop, but there are toilets at Bowden Bridge car park.

Access
Edges of tarn are boggy and underwater hazards may be obscured. Accessible by following River Kinder through open countryside, or dropping down from Pennine Way. Frequent buses to Hayfield from Stockport, New Mills and Buxton; closest train station New Mills (five kilometres from Hayfield). Paid parking at Bowden Bridge, four kilometres away; limited road parking in Hayfield.

THREE SHIRES HEAD. © *JOHN COEFIELD*

SLIPPERY STONES. © *PATRICK COEFIELD*

SLIPPERY STONES

53.4546, -1.7472 / Bamford, Derbyshire / Swimming, paddling and plunge pool

Near the stone-arched packhorse bridge, Slippery Stones is a rocky paddling spot in the sparkling waters of the infant River Derwent. There is also a deep plunge pool, with just enough space for a swim – jump in (with caution) from the rocky ledge. The gorsy, green banks are perfect for a picnic. Sheffielders have fond memories of holiday afternoons at Slippery Stones, and it can be busy at week-ends and in summer, but under the shadow of the heathered Howden Moors it is the perfect spot for a quiet evening swim. Slippery Stones is also a great detour for those completing an on-foot or cycling circuit of the Ladybower, Derwent and Howden reservoirs. Food and hot drinks are available at Fairholmes cafe and the Ladybower Inn.

Access
Access via rocky ledges and grassy banks. Eight kilometres from Fairholmes car park; quickest cycling/walking route – cross dam at Fairholmes and follow east side of reservoir. Frequent summer buses from Sheffield to Fairholmes, reduced winter timetable. Car parking, bike hire and toilets at Fairholmes. Cars permitted on access road on weekdays, a kilometre and a half away; closed weekends/ during forestry work.

HATHERSAGE SWIMMING POOL

53.3286, -1.6531 / Oddfellows Road, Hathersage, Derbyshire, S32 1DU / 01433 650843 / Swimming / *www.hathersageswimmingpool.co.uk*

Dating from the early twentieth century, Hathersage Swimming Pool is a Peak District delight. Inside you'll find changing cubicles, showers and lifeguards during all swimming sessions. Once you're in the water, the twenty-eight-degree-heated, thirty-metre pool is perfect for lane swimming or relaxing with the family during a public session; there are grassy lawns to picnic on after a swim. Night sessions with live music are a particular treat, and on a clear day the views extend north to Stanage Edge. Booking is advisable, but on the right day you might find you have the pool all to yourself. The downstairs cafe serves everything from hot drinks and snacks to full meals and, of course, ice creams for the kids. A choice of cafes and pubs can be found in Hathersage.

Access
Access to the water via ladders. Lift to facilitate wheelchair access to pool area; hoist available. Hathersage railway station 300 metres away (connections to Sheffield and Manchester); Hathersage is well served by buses from Sheffield. Small on-site car park; large pay-and-display car park across the road.

CALVER WEIR. © @PEAKPIX)

FROGGATT BRIDGE

53.2811, -1.6362 / Froggatt, Derbyshire / Swimming and paddling

In the shadow of the Peak's gritstone edges, the River Derwent at Froggatt Bridge offers a gentle, tranquil swim spot. The wide, lazy bends of the wild-garlic-fringed river offer easy swimming and squelchy paddling near the muddy banks. Less than a kilometre upstream of the popular Calver Weir, the swim between the two spots is ideal for those looking for an easy evening glide. For those wanting a treat after their dip, it's a stiff, 500-metre hike up to the gastropub food at the eighteenth-century Chequers Inn. The Derwent Valley Heritage Way offers (generally) well-surfaced footpaths along the river between Grindleford and Calver, making it the ideal swim spot for a loop from Grindleford railway station (at Nether Padley) that takes in the gritstone edges of Froggatt and Curbar and returns via the riverbanks.

Access
Water accessed by gentle, muddy banks either side of the bridge. Hourly bus services to Sheffield, Bakewell (Buxton, Tideswell) from Stoke Bar stop, 500 metres away. Grindleford railway station four kilometres away. Very limited roadside parking by bridge and in village.

CALVER WEIR

53.2746, -1.6354 / Calver, Derbyshire / Swimming and paddling

Found near the peaceful village of Calver in the Peak District, the bridge by Calver Weir marks the start of a fantastic swim spot loved by local swimmers. Following the River Derwent south, this stretch of river is consistently deep, and its gentle current makes it ideal for a relaxing swim. The water remains cold all year round, and those seeking shallower water will find it downstream, away from the trees. Swimmers looking for an adrenaline rush can

jump from the nearby bridge, which proves a popular way to enter the water in the summer months. The nearby village is home to a number of places to stop for food, including the Bridge Inn.

Access
Water can be accessed from New Bridge near Calver Weir (A625) or from muddy banks. Footpaths by Derwent link Calver, Calver Weir and Grindleford. Hourly bus services to Sheffield, Bakewell (Buxton, Tideswell) from Crossroads stop, a kilometre away. Nearest train station at Grindleford, seven kilometres away. Limited roadside parking at Calver Weir and in Calver.

CHATSWORTH, RIVER DERWENT

53.2229, -1.6164 / Edensor, Derbyshire / Swimming and paddling

Chatsworth discourages swimming on the estate, but families still flock to the wide, gentle River Derwent as it flows through the parklands. With grassy banks, shady trees and sandy shallows to paddle in, the river is the perfect place to pass a sunny afternoon. The water is easily reached from the footpaths that pass through the estate; it is a short, downhill walk from the Calton Lees car park or can be accessed by following the river from Chatsworth House. There are refreshments available at

Chatsworth House, and at the garden centre at Calton Lees (where there are also toilets). You can also enjoy afternoon tea in the tea-rooms at Edensor, the village that one Duke of Devonshire had moved so that it didn't spoil his view. The nearby market town of Bakewell is a great post-swim destination if you want to treat yourself to the eponymous tart.

Access
Access via grassy, gently sloping banks; swim discretely out of sight of the house. 218 bus between Sheffield and Bakewell stops hourly at Chatsworth (less frequent in winter); other buses serve Chatsworth from Chesterfield, Buxton, Manchester and Matlock. Pay-and-display parking at Chatsworth and Calton Lees.

YOULGREAVE, RIVER BRADFORD

53.1732, -1.6854 / Youlgreave, Derbyshire / Swimming and paddling

Set on the Limestone Way, this section of the River Bradford in Youlgreave has been especially dammed and developed to permit outdoor swimming. This partially sheltered spot is great for kids, with grassy banks perfect for picnics and a nearby ice cream kiosk. The current is very gentle, and younger children will be able to paddle a little upstream.

There are pubs and cafes in the charming Peak District village of Youlgreave, and there are also public toilets on Holywell Lane. The narrow, winding streets of the village are not conducive to parking; you could incorporate a visit with the beautiful White Peak Walk, or alternatively Bakewell is approximately six kilometres away. Haddon Hall, home to Bess of Hardwick, and the Duke of Devonshire's Chatsworth House are close by if you want a day out exploring the Peak.

Access
Steep, stone-edged riversides; shallower entry points near weir. Dammed pool 200 metres along footpath links Brookleton and Holywell Lane. Buses leave every two hours during day from Youlgreave to Bakewell and Matlock (nearest train station). Limited parking on narrow village streets – please use car park on Coldwell End, just under a kilometre away.

NEW BATH HOTEL OPEN AIR POOL

53.1157, -1.5611 / New Bath Road, Matlock Bath, Derbyshire, DE4 3PX / 01629 340340 / Swimming / *newbathhotelandspa.com/open-air-pool*

Opened in 1934, the glamorous New Bath Hotel Open Air Pool – the only outdoor pool in England to be fed by geothermal springs – fell

YOULGREAVE. © *JOHN COEFIELD*

into disrepair when the hotel closed in 2013. It was rescued from dereliction and refurbished in 2019, and you can once again enjoy a swim in this beautiful pool under Matlock Bath – Queen Victoria visited the village as a teenager. The unheated pool, in the shadow of Matlock Bath's limestone cliffs, holds a steady temperature between 17 and 19 °C thanks to its subterranean-drawn waters. The pool, part of the hotel spa complex, is only open to swimmers over eighteen years old but may offer family swims during the holidays. You can treat yourself to afternoon tea on the terrace or a relaxing post-dip aromatherapy massage in the spa.

Access
Access to the pool via ladders. Frequent Sixes bus between Derby and Bakewell stops right outside the hotel; Matlock Bath train station a kilometre away. On-site parking.

HOOD PARK LIDO. © *CHRIS NETTEL*

ANCHOR CHURCH

52.8415, -1.4981 / Ingleby, Derbyshire / Swimming

In the heart of the Derbyshire countryside, Anchor Church is an inlet just off the River Trent. An area loved by visitors for its mysterious caves, partly natural but carved out to form a doorway and windows in the eighteenth century. Bordered by tall, sheer rocks on one bank and endless fields on the other, this is an atmospheric and unique swim spot. The force of the river which was responsible for carving out parts of the sandstone caves has fortunately nowadays calmed, and the gentle current is suitable for swimmers who enjoy a relaxing swim. For those who want deeper water, if you follow the river to the east, experienced swimmers can enter the challenging waters of the River Trent.

Access

Access via grassy banks. Can be accessed on foot by following the trail alongside the river. Difficult to reach via public transport: Ash Farm bus stop, just over a kilometre away, is served once daily by buses to Chellaston and Melbourne. Limited lay-by parking just under a kilometre away in Ingleby.

HOOD PARK LIDO

52.7491, -1.4711 / North Street, Ashby-de-la-Zouch, Leicestershire, LE65 1HU / 01530 412181 / Swimming and paddling / *www.everyoneactive. com/centre/hood-park-leisure-centre*

Refurbished in 2019, Hood Park Lido is a gem at the centre of the medieval town of Ashby-de-la-Zouch. As well as open-air laps of the pool, you can enjoy a game of squash, a gym session or even a drink at the bar at Hood Park Leisure Centre – there is also a cafe. There is a smaller pool for kids to enjoy next to the main thirty-by-ten-metre pool. After your dip, there are plenty of places to refresh yourself in Ashby's town centre, and you can explore the ruins of the fifteenth-century castle and timbered Elizabethan buildings on Market Street.

Access

Access to water via ladders and steps; pool offers wheelchair access, including easy-access steps and hoist. Good bus connections to Burton upon Trent, Loughborough and Coalville 300 metres away on Market Street; closest train station is Burton-on-Trent, fifteen kilometres away. On-site car park and pay-and-display parking in town centre.

WEST LAKE AT COLWICK COUNTRY PARK. © *CAMERON BONSER*

SPRING LAKES

52.8861, -1.2525 / Pasture Lane, Long Eaton,
Nottinghamshire, NG10 2FZ / 0115 9727788
Swimming and paddling / *www.springlakes.co.uk/
open-water-swimming*

Spring Lakes is a purpose-built water park,
converted from the former Trent Meadow
gravel pits and opened in 2019. You can
enjoy open water swimming all year round at
the spring-fed lakes, with lifeguards at every
session – swimmers have to pay a small annual
membership fee before their first swim, and
must wear brightly coloured caps. The lakes
also have a sandy beach, perfect for a paddle,
and you can try your hand at paddleboarding,
wakeboarding, pedaloes and bumper boats or
scramble over inflatable obstacles at the Aqua
Park. There is an on-site cafe as well as grassy
picnic areas, and nearby Long Eaton also has
plenty of refreshment choices.

Access

Access via gently sloping ramp and jetties.
Long Eaton railway station four kilometres
away; S16 bus between Wilsthorpe and Long
Eaton stops at Manor House Road, approximately a kilometre away. Free parking on-site.

WEST LAKE AT COLWICK COUNTRY PARK

52.9448, -1.0978 / Mile End Road, Colwick,
Nottinghamshire, NG4 2DW / 07813 965956 /
Swimming and paddling / *whollyhealthy.co.uk/
open-water-squad*

Colwick Country Park is home to the innovative
Nottingham City Open Water Swimming
Centre, and there are open water swim
sessions available to the general public all
year round run by WholeHealth. Although
swimmers must purchase an inexpensive
annual pass to swim here regularly, you can
enjoy two beginner or mindfulness sessions
before joining, depending on whether you
prefer a tranquil dip or laps around the clean
water. A swim in the tree-fringed West Lake in
the coral glow of the setting sun is the perfect
way to unwind after a busy day. The park is
frequently visited by a coffee van, if you want a
post-dip espresso or hot chocolate. There are
public toilets in the park, and plenty of walking
and cycling trails to explore.

Access

Access to water by shallow, grassy slopes;
concrete ramp into water for disabled access.
Netherfield railway station three kilometres
away; frequent buses from Nottingham stop
at racecourse neighbouring the lake. Parking
inside and outside park, some free.

JUBILEE PARK WOODHALL SPA. © *SARAH THELWALL*

BILLINGHAY POOL. © *BILLINGAY POOL*

STOKE BARDOLPH, RIVER TRENT

52.9727, -1.0372 / Stoke Bardolph, Nottinghamshire / Swimming and paddling

On the River Trent just north of the small village of Stoke Bardolph, this stretch of river is loved by swimmers for its easy access from multiple slipways. The wide river has a gentle current and is located just next door to the Stoke Bardolph Sewage Treatment Plant; local swimmers prefer the water upstream of the treatment plant, although the discharge meets Environment Agency standards. With its wide views of the vast fields on either side of the water, it is no wonder that this location can become busy during the warmer months, but it is a great spot to cool down on a summer's day. The river is overlooked by the popular Ferry Boat Inn, where you can enjoy a drink and a bite to eat while gazing out at the water.

Access

Access via slipways or grassy banks. Buses to Netherfield and Burton Joyce stop a few times a day at Stoke Lane bus stop, 200 metres away. Netherfield railway station four kilometres away. Roadside parking just beside swim spot.

BILLINGHAY AND DISTRICT COMMUNITY SWIMMING POOL

53.0829, -0.2812 / Fen Road, Billinghay, Lincolnshire, LN4 4HU / 07973 679234

Swimming / *www.facebook.com/Billinghay-And-District-Community-Swimming-Pool-251920804918415*

Billinghay's small pool is one of the UK's friendliest community-run pools, with a sand pit area for the kids, slides for children of all ages and a kiosk where you can buy bacon rolls and home-baked cakes. The heated pool is open from May to September, opening in the evenings and weekends during school term time and daily during the summer holidays. One unique experience that you could enjoy is the midnight swims, when the pool opens at 11 p.m. to allow you to float under starlit skies; your admission includes a free post-swim hot chocolate. Booking is not necessary but advised, particularly during the summer holidays and on sunny weekends. The Ship Inn rests a short walk away for a bite to eat.

Access

Access via slides and (sloping) ladders. Ramped access and accessible changing rooms; no hoist or easy stepped/sloped access to pool. Closest railway station is Ruskington, approximately ten kilometres away; occasional buses towards Sleaford connect Billinghay and Ruskington, nearest stop 500 metres away. On-site parking.

METHERINGHAM SWIMMING POOL

53.1381, -0.4062 / Prince's Street, Metheringham, Lincolnshire, LN4 3BX / Swimming / *www.megpool.org.uk*

Affectionately nicknamed 'Megpool', the tiny, community-run, heated Metheringham Swimming Pool is big on personality. As well as adult-only swims and mother and toddler sessions, you can join in on aqua Zumba and the season closes with doggy paddles. Adult-only swim sessions are not always life-guarded. You can enjoy a hot drink and sugary treat from the pool's tuck shop or treat yourself with lunch at one of Metheringham's four pubs. There is a grassy picnic area next to the pool, and non-swimmers do not have to pay admission fees. The pool is adjacent to a well-maintained play area and large, grassy playing fields.

Access
Access via ladder and a children's slide. Pool chair available; wheelchair friendly access to poolside and accessible changing facilities. Approximately a kilometre to Metheringham railway station, which is on Peterborough–Lincoln line. Frequent buses to Lincoln, Boston and Sleaford from Methodist Church stop, 400 metres away. On-street parking nearby.

JUBILEE PARK WOODHALL SPA

53.1554, -0.2220 / Stixwould Road, Woodhall Spa, Lincolnshire, LN10 6QH / 01526 353478 / Swimming and paddling / *www.jubileepark-woodhallspa.co.uk*

In the middle of the grassy lawns, play areas and pretty, ornamental gardens of Jubilee Park, you will find the tree-fringed, heated Jubilee Park Woodhall Spa. As well as the thirty-three-by-twelve-metre main pool, there is a twelve-by-twelve-metre paddling pool for the kids. Booking is advisable and necessary for their popular midnight swim sessions. You can warm up with a hot drink or burgers and hotdogs at the park's

cafe after your dip; the village is also well served by tearooms. If you want to make a proper holiday of it, there is a camping and caravan site in the park – you can take the opportunity to explore the Woodland Trust's Pinewoods, with its unique Kinema in the Woods.

Access
Access via ladder, steps and a children's slide. Poolside accessible to wheelchairs and electric scooters; easy-access steps into water and hoist available. Closest railway station is Boston, more than twenty kilometres away; hourly buses from Woodhall Spa to Boston. On-site car parking is free but donations are encouraged.

ALFORD SPORTS HALL

53.2580, 0.1831 / Hanby Lane, Alford, Lincolnshire, LN13 9BN / 01507 463867 / Swimming / *www.alfordsportshall.co.uk*

In the sleepy Lincolnshire Wolds village of Alford, with its five-sailed windmill, you can enjoy a dip in the open air pool at the community sports hall. The shared facilities are the result of collaboration between the council and John Spendluffe Technology College. Used by students during the day, since 2019 the pool has been open to the general public at evenings and weekends. At the heart of the village, this pool, with its covered poolside, also offers aquacise classes and swimming lessons for 'little fishes'. You'll find cafes and pubs in Alford, well known for its regular craft markets, or you might choose instead to enjoy a reasonably priced cream tea in the gardens of the seventeenth-century Manor House, also home to the Museum of Rural Life.

Access
Access via ladders. As a school swimming pool, facilities at the site – including for wheelchair access – are limited. Alford well served by buses from Skegness and Mablethorpe from Library stop, 700 metres away. On-site and nearby street parking.

BOURNE OUTDOOR SWIMMING POOL. © *BOURNE OUTDOOR SWIMMING POOL*

SKEGNESS POOL AND FITNESS SUITE

53.1426, 0.3449 / Grand Parade, Skegness, Lincolnshire, PE25 2UG / 01754 610675 / Swimming and paddling / *magnavitae.org/venue/ skegness-pool-fitness-suite*

In the shadow of Altitude44's high ropes course, this outdoor pool is a reminder that Skegness is still a magnet for holidaymakers seeking family fun by the seaside. There is also an inside pool with a water flume at the fitness centre. With poolside loungers and grassy lawns, Skegness Pool is the perfect spot for a family afternoon out, although the admission fees are higher than community-run lidos. You can enjoy a post-dip pizza from Cafe Magna, stroll to the sandy seafront just minutes away for an ice cream or visit the pier where you can try Laser Quest, bowling or an escape room.

Access

Access to water is via ladders, easy steps and a slide; accessible toilets and changing rooms, as well as wheelchair access to poolside. Skegness is a popular holiday destination and is well served by buses, coaches and trains (with services to Derby, Grantham and Nottingham). On-site pay-and-display car park.

HECKINGTON COMMUNITY SWIMMING POOL

52.9847, -0.2984 / Howell Road, Heckington, Lincolnshire, NG34 9RX / Swimming / *www.heckingtonpool.co.uk*

Tucked behind St Andrew's Church of England School, Heckington's little pool has a capacity of only twenty-eight, but despite being run entirely by volunteers this gem of a local pool offers a packed schedule of tots sessions, over-fifties social swims, inflatable sessions (with sharks and dolphins!),

aqua fit and adults-only as well as general swims. 'Glow' night sessions, barbecue dips and doggy sessions are among the more unusual swim options that the pool occasionally offers. For that post-swim ice-cream, the pool has a snack bar, and there are cafes, pubs and shops in the nearby village centre. Heckington is one of Lincolnshire's largest villages, and offers the fourteenth-century St Andrew's church, a railway museum and England's only surviving eight-sail windmill, with a tearoom where you can sample treats baked with flour from the mill's own supplies.

Access

Access via ladders (including sloped stepladder with handrail); wheelchair access to poolside and accessible toilets. Pool approximately a kilometre from Heckington railway station, with frequent services to Nottingham and Skegness. Infrequent buses to Sleaford from village centre. Nearby on-street parking.

RUTLAND WATER. © *SHUTTERSTOCK/NICOLA PULHAM*

BOURNE OUTDOOR SWIMMING POOL

52.7658, -0.3730 / Abbey Lawns, Abbey Road, Bourne, Lincolnshire, PE10 9EP / 01778 422063 / Swimming and paddling / *www.bourneoutdoor-swimmingpool.org*

Once a twelfth-century monks' fishing pond, Bourne Outdoor Swimming Pool celebrated its centenary in 2019. This unusual pool offers large grassy lawns, a children's play area, a toddlers' paddling pool and a fountain pool to splash in. It has undergone several refurbishments over the last century, including the introduction of heating in 1971, and more recently to improve the kitchen and accessible changing facilities. At forty-seven metres long, this is one of England's biggest outdoor pools. The pool is on the edge of the town centre, so there are plenty of places nearby to grab a hot drink, as well as an on-site snack bar. Adults can enjoy a child-free early morning swim here, and Friday night is under-fifteens Fun Night.

Access

Access by steps and ladders; pool area wheelchair accessible. Frequent buses from Bourne to Peterborough and Spalding; nearest stop 500 metres away. No on-site car park; nearby street parking and town centre car parks.

RUTLAND WATER BEACH

52.6629, -0.6151 / Sykes Lane, Oakham, Rutland, LE15 8QL / Swimming and paddling / *anglianwaterparks.co.uk/rutland-water-park/other-activities/beach*

Just outside of the picturesque village of Empingham, Rutland Water Beach is a vibrant swim spot full of activity. A sandy, 140-metre-long beach provides access to the reservoir's water, popular with families due to the shallows and deeper waters available. Two courses of 500 and 250 metres are available throughout the summer at the swim spot's weekly sessions; these popular sessions fill up quickly, so be sure to book. This bustling and busy location has lifeguards on duty, toilets and changing rooms and allows visitors to enjoy their own barbecues as long as they are raised above the ground. The water is surrounded by over 4,000 acres of beautiful countryside, which is full of walking and cycling trails as well as the Rutland Osprey Project. The Four Foxes cafe can be found just to the north of the beach.

Access

Access via sandy beach. Buses leave from Rutland Visitor Centre stop, 600 metres away, approximately every hour during the day to Oakham and Stamford. On-site parking.

SYWELL COUNTRY PARK. © *SHUTTERSTOCK/CONNOR ROY HAMILTON*

STANTON LAKES

52.5411, -1.2616 / Broughton Road, Stoney Stanton, Leicestershire, LE9 4JA / 01455 283043 / Swimming / *www.stantonlakes.co.uk/lake.aspx*

In the midst of Leicestershire's green farm fields, you can enjoy an open water swim in the tree-fringed Stanton Lakes. Supervised open water swimming sessions are available on Tuesday evenings and Sunday mornings between April and September; swimming is not permitted at other times. Introductory courses for open air swimming are also available, for both adults and juniors. The water is always refreshingly bracing so you may choose to wear a wetsuit; swimmers are strongly encouraged to wear a bright swimming cap. There is a restaurant at Stanton Lakes, the perfect place to indulge in a hearty post-dip Sunday roast, looking out over the water. There is also a caravan park if you want to stay and explore the area.

Access

Access to water via a gentle slope. Hard-topped/tarmac bridleway from Stoney Stanton to Stanton Lakes. Infrequent bus services to Hinckley and Leicester from Stoney Stanton, approximately a kilometre away. Closest railway station is Narborough, with good intercity services, five kilometres away. On-site parking.

COTTINGHAM, RIVER WELLAND

52.5102, -0.7676 / Cottingham, Northamptonshire / Swimming and paddling

As the River Welland flows under a bridge near the village of Cottingham, it forms a pool deep enough for a swim. A gravel beach leads into the pool, which is ideal for a relaxing dip, but water shallow enough for paddling can be found further downstream. The trees and tall reeds which frame your view from the water create a private feel, perfect for those looking for a secluded swim. The nearby village of Cottingham and neighbouring Middleton are home to a number of spots to pick up a filling meal, including the Spread Eagle pub.

Access

Water accessed from gravel beach or high, grassy banks. Bus services to Corby stop every ninety minutes at Middleton House Farm stop, just over a kilometre away. Limited roadside parking available two kilometres away in Cottingham.

PETERBOROUGH LIDO

52.5702, -0.2384 / Bishop's Road, Peterborough, Cambridgeshire, PE1 1YY / 01733 864761 / Swimming and paddling / *vivacity.org/sports-venues/peterborough-lido*

The art deco Peterborough Lido, with its two outdoor pools and paddling pool, retains many of its striking historical features, including its dramatic clock tower entrance. The heated pools have only been closed for one summer season (due to coronavirus in 2020) since their opening in 1936. With its midnight swims, aqua fit classes, solstice sunrise swims and movie screenings, there is something for everyone to enjoy. After your swim, you can relax with a coffee on the suntrap of the rooftop terraces. The lido is situated on the outskirts of the city near the Embankment, perfectly placed for a post-swim riverside walk.

Access

Entry to water via (handrailed) steps and ladders. Ramped access to poolside (not to rooftop terraces); accessible changing facilities; hoist available. Pool approximately a kilometre from Peterborough rail station. Easily reached on segregated cycleways from city centre. Large pay-and-display car park on-site.

OUNDLE, RIVER NENE

52.4888, -0.4619 / Oundle, Northamptonshire / Swimming

As the cows munch contentedly, you can enjoy a refreshing dip in the tranquil River Nene near the stone arches of Oundle's historic North Bridge. The kayakers' concrete pontoon provides a convenient way to get in and out. While you will usually be interrupted by nothing more than swans and moorhens, you are advised take a tow float and wear a brightly coloured swimming cap for the benefit of the occasional narrowboater or kayaker. There are plenty of independent cafes and pubs on Oundle's Georgian streets (and public toilets in the Co-op car park) although you might choose instead to refresh yourself at Nene Valley Brewery's Tap & Kitchen on the waterfront at the wharf.

Access

Access to water via a pontoon – you will need to lift yourself or climb out of water. No public right of way on opposite bank. Regular buses from Peterborough, with bus stops by swim spot. Nearby street parking and you are less than a kilometre from town centre.

HARPER'S BROOK, RIVER NENE

52.4228, -0.5081 / Aldwincle, Northamptonshire / Swimming and paddling

Surrounded by green fields, the tributary of Harper's Brook flows into the River Nene as it winds its way through Northamptonshire. The grassy, muddy slopes under the bridge make entering the water easy, and you can float up the deep water to join the River Nene – look out for views of Wadenhoe's church and the mound where Wadenhoe Castle once stood. Resting next to the bird-rich Titchmarsh Nature Reserve, this is a truly beautiful spot for a swim. Those looking for refreshments will have to travel five kilometres to Thrapston.

Access

Access via gently sloping, grassy riverbanks. Bus between Clapham and Peterborough stops once daily at Fox Inn, a kilometre away. No parking on-site, and you should not block the narrow bridge; limited roadside parking in Aldwincle, small car park at Titchmarsh Nature Reserve.

SYWELL COUNTRY PARK

52.2791, -0.7785 / Washbrook Lane, Ecton, Northampton, NN6 0QX / Swimming and paddling / www.northamptonshiresport.org/sywell-open-water-swimming

During the summer, you can swim in the sparklingly clean waters of this former drinking-water reservoir during organised open swim sessions on Wednesday evenings and Saturday mornings. The volunteer-run sessions are open to swimmers of all abilities and (accompanied) children over the age of eight, and have lifeguards, spotters and session leaders. Sywell Country Park has public toilets, play areas, a cafe and nature trails to explore. You must have a tow float to swim here if you do not wear a wetsuit, and should always wear a brightly coloured cap. Thanks to Northamptonshire Sport and Northants Tri Club, Sywell is the perfect place to enjoy a safe reservoir swim, and perhaps a waterside picnic afterwards.

Access

Access via grassy banks that give way to gritty mud on a shallow slope. Jetty and hoist (under construction in 2021) provide wheelchair access. Frequent bus services to the A4500 on outskirts of Ecton to Raunds, Corby, Kettering and Wellingborough, two kilometres away. Paid parking within park; charge in addition to swim fee.

RIVER GREAT OUSE NEAR BEDFORD. © *SHUTTERSTOCK/KEVINR4*

FELMERSHAM BRIDGE, RIVER GREAT OUSE

52.2102, -0.5517 / Felmersham, Bedfordshire / Swimming and paddling

On the outskirts of the eponymous village, the River Great Ouse forms a picturesque swim spot as it meanders under the arches of Felmersham Bridge. A mixture of shallows and deep water as well as a slow current make this an ideal spot for swimmers who want an easily accessible dip. As you float under the nineteenth-century bridge and gaze up at the trees which line the water, it is easy to lose yourself in the charming surroundings. After you climb out, there are plenty of spaces to settle down with a picnic. In warmer weather this area of the river can become surprisingly busy with both swimmers and fishermen. The Sun pub is just 350 metres away, and is great for grabbing a bite to eat in a welcoming atmosphere.

Access

Access from low, grassy banks. Buses leave approximately every hour to Bedford, 200 metres away at the Church stop. Limited lay-by parking just next to river.

PAVENHAM, RIVER GREAT OUSE

52.1864, -0.5533 / Pavenham, Bedfordshire / Swimming and paddling

As the River Great Ouse winds its way through Bedfordshire it forms a quiet stretch of water near Pavenham. Sloping, and sometimes muddy, grassy banks lead to the water's edge, and as you step into the deep water the river's slow yet strong current makes itself known. A rope swing can be found attached to one of the many overhanging willows – these trees provide a cooling canopy on a sunny afternoon. This stretch of the river is popular with fishermen so be sure to check the water before entering. A short swim takes you to the Pavenham Osier Beds, which in summer are dotted with meadow-rue, an uncommon wet-meadow flower. Swimmers can grab a bite to eat at the Cock pub in Pavenham.

Access

Grassy, sometimes muddy, banks lead into water. Infrequent buses to Bedford and Sharnbrook run from Weavers Lane stop, 300 metres away. Roadside parking on High Street in Pavenham.

OPEN WATER SWIMMING. © SHUTTERSTOCK/WOODYSPHOTOS

CLAPHAM, RIVER GREAT OUSE

52.1587, -0.4899 / Clapham, Bedfordshire / Swimming and paddling

Tucked away behind the residential streets of Clapham, this relatively unknown spot on the River Great Ouse is ideal for swimmers to enjoy a scenic swim. Characterised its by deep, flowing water, nature-rich landscape and easy-to-access location, this well-kept secret is a great stop for any passing swimmer. The river can be entered via a ford, where the water is at its shallowest, but as you travel further into the water it quickly deepens. Follow the river in either direction for views of neighbouring fields and wildlife from the Bromham Lake Local Nature Reserve – you may also spot a rope swing to the south of the ford. The river's edge is only a short walk away from the Horse and Groom pub, loved for its rich character, hearty meals and abundance of outdoor seating.

Access
Easy access from a ford. Buses run approximately every half an hour throughout the day to Bedford from the Swan stop. Roadside parking available twenty metres away on High Street.

BOX END PARK

52.1252, -0.5215 / Box End Road, Bedford, Bedfordshire, MK43 8RQ / 01234 846222 / Swimming and paddling / *www.boxendpark.com/open-water-swimming*

Just outside of of Bedford, Box End Park is a water sports and events centre which caters for experienced open water swimmers as well as those looking for coaching sessions. Centred around two spring-fed lakes, the calm and current-free waters are very clean and provide a feeling of wilderness without having to travel too far out of Bedford. You can also book other activities such as waterskiing, an inflatable aqua park and children's activity days, making this a great destination for all of the family. Swimmers must wear a brightly coloured cap and goggles. The on-site Corner 5 restaurant offers meals with panoramic views across the lake, and nearby Bedford offers plenty of other refreshment options.

Access
Access via grassy banks. Not easily accessible by public transport – Bedford railway station five and a half kilometres away. Free parking on-site.

OLNEY POOL. © WWW.NORTHAMPTONSHIREMUMSANDKIDS.CO.UK

OLNEY POOL

52.1550, -0.6927 / Olney, Buckinghamshire / Swimming and paddling

A historic swim spot on the River Great Ouse, Olney Pool rests on the edge of the picturesque market town of Olney. Curving, concrete steps lead into the water; the stony riverbed lies under around a metre of water, but as you move towards the centre of the river the water deepens to a depth suited to swimming. This is a popular spot for families with older children, and there is a rope swing just upstream. Framed by weeping willows, tall reeds and grassy fields, this encapsulates the beauty of the Buckinghamshire countryside. Olney has a variety of restaurants, cafes and pubs, but a picnic on the banks of the river would make for an idyllic afternoon.

Access
Easy access from gentle, grassy banks and concrete steps. Buses leave for Northampton hourly from High Street stop, 300 metres away. Parking available 700 metres away at Market Place car park.

WOBURN LIDO

51.9932, -0.6188 / Crawley Road, Woburn, Bedfordshire, MK17 9QG / 07517 461977 / Swimming / *woburnlido.weebly.com*

In the heart of the historic village, Woburn Lido was built as a gift for the villagers by the Duke of Bedford in 1911. This small pool, run by volunteers, has a picnic area and new changing rooms, built in 2015. The pool is heated, but in the winter the lido remains open for cold water swimming (swimmers over eighteen years old only). The kiosk sells basic swim supplies, as well as hot drinks, snacks and ice creams. Woburn has plenty to entertain visitors, including the Palladian Woburn Abbey, with its landscaped gardens, and Woburn Safari Park, with Go Ape on-site.

Access
Access into water via ladders and steps (shallow end). Level access to poolside; accessible toilets. Limited (daily) 47 bus service from Leighton Buzzard stops just outside the lido; Woburn Sands rail station approximately four kilometres away. Limited on-site parking.

EVERSHOLT SWIMMING POOL

51.9836, -0.5720 / Tyrells End, Eversholt, Bedfordshire, MK17 9DS / 01525 280515 / Swimming and paddling / *www.facebook.com/eversholtpool*

In the middle of Bedfordshire's green farmland, next to the village hall and cricket pitch, you can enjoy the small, sheltered and heated Eversholt Swimming Pool. There is a main pool, and dolphins leap across the floor of the semi-circle paddling pool. The pool was extensively refurbished in 2020, with a new liner and underwater lighting, ready for a grand re-opening in May 2021. Schoolchildren and season pass holders often taken priority, so you should check for public swimming sessions before you visit; with a maximum capacity of forty, you may find yourself queuing on sunny summer afternoons. Booking is advisable, although it may be difficult to contact the busy, volunteer-run pool. You can get snacks and hot drinks at the kiosk, or visit the nearby Green Man pub if you want lunch. Eversholt Swimming Pool is only five kilometres from Woburn Lido if you fancy a double dip.

Access
Access to water via ladders. No accessible changing area; accessible toilets. Eversholt is difficult to reach by public transport: occasional community-run Flittabus minibus service. Limited on-site parking; street parking in village.

WOBURN LIDO. © WOBURN LIDO

LANGFORD MILL, RIVER IVEL

52.0578, -0.2757 / Biggleswade, Bedfordshire / Swimming and paddling

On the edge of Langford, Langford Mill rests on a picturesque stretch of the River Ivel and is characterised by its convenient location and brisk current. The river can be followed in either direction: heading northwards taking you past forested areas and fisheries, and southwards by the pretty Henlow Common. A favourite of swimmers looking for a quick dip, the water here is shallow near the banks and grows deeper – swimmers should be wary of the fast current near the mill. This mainly residential area has a few grassy banks alongside the river suitable for a sit down and a picnic, and for visitors wanting a more substantial meal the nearest stop is the Langford Hideaway cafe.

Access
Easy access via shallow, grassy banks. Nearest bus stop at Lower School, connections to Hitchin several times a day. Arlesey rail station six kilometres away. Roadside parking just by swim spot.

LETCHWORTH OUTDOOR POOL

51.9847, -0.2240 / Norton Common, Icknield Way, Letchworth, Hertfordshire, SG6 4UF / 01462 684673 / Swimming and paddling
www.sll.co.uk/letchworth-outdoor-pool

Letchworth was developed as the world's first 'garden city', a settlement planned around its green, open spaces, designed to offer the best of urban living in a countryside environment. In a commitment to better living standards, Letchworth had an outdoor swimming pool from its creation, although today's heated, fifty-metre pool was built in the 1930s. At one colourful end, there is also a toddlers' pool for little swimmers. Toilets and changing rooms are available, and the lido runs adult-only and public swim sessions. Long a local family favourite, you can also try poolside yoga on the expansive lawns and in 2019, the pool, which closes over winter, had a very popular temporary ice rink. There is a cafe at the pool, and the nearby town centre provides a variety of refreshment options.

Access
Entry via easy-access steps and ladders. Steps between reception and poolside. Accessible toilets and changing facilities; portable hoist/pool chair. Less than a kilometre to Letchworth Garden City rail station; frequent bus from Stevenage stops directly outside pool. On-site parking.

WARE PRIORY LIDO. © *WARE PRIORY LIDO*

HITCHIN SWIMMING CENTRE

51.9529, -0.2814 / Fishponds Road, Hitchin, Hertfordshire, SG5 1HA / 01462 441646 / Swimming and paddling / *www.sll.co.uk/hitchin*

Travel back in time to the golden age of the lidos with a visit to the expansive, eight-lane lido at the Hitchin Swimming Centre; although opened in 1938, the pool was unheated until the 1960s. The fifty-metre lido, with wide lawns and plenty of paved poolside areas, is big enough to accommodate the crowds on all but the busiest sunny days. There is also a smaller children's pool/paddling area at this tree-fringed lido as well as a cafe, so you may find yourself whiling away the afternoon here. The centre is in the middle of the grassy parkland of Butts Close, once an archery ground, if you want a quieter spot for a picnic.

Access

Entry to water is via ladders/laddered steps; portable hoist may be available. Ramped access to poolside; accessible changing facilities. Centre well served by buses to Bedford; just over a kilometre to Hitchin rail station. Pay-and-display parking on-site.

HEMEL HEMPSTEAD OUTDOOR POOL

51.7460, -0.4774 / Park Road, Hemel Hempstead, Hertfordshire, HP1 1JS / 01442 507100 / Swimming and paddling / *everyoneactive.com/centre/hemel-hempstead-leisure-centre*

Part of the Everyone Active sports complex, Hemel Hempstead's outdoor pool is unusual because it runs from shallow to deep width-wise, rather than lengthwise. One advantage of this is that there are length-long graduated steps for easy access to the heated pool, and less confident swimmers and children can still swim lengths. There is a large, grassy lawn on which to sunbathe and a paddling pool with a fountain at its centre. There is an on-site cafe, but the pool is within easy walking distance of the town centre and the Marlowes Shopping Centre.

Access

Access to water via graduated steps along length of pool, and ladders. Accessible changing facilities, no hoist. Approximately one kilometre from Hemel Hempstead train station; buses to local area as well as Aylesbury and High Wycombe stop frequently outside leisure centre. Free on-site parking.

HITCHIN SWIMMING CENTRE. © *SARAH THELWALL*

WARE PRIORY LIDO

51.8114, -0.0369 / Priory Street, Ware, Hertford-shire, SG12 0DE / 01920 481563 / Swimming and paddling / *www.warepriorylido.co.uk*

If you want a swim with a view, the heated Ware Priory Lido – in the priory grounds, with views of the medieval priory – is a great choice. Painted fish swim under the waters on the sides of the main pool, and a giant octopus graces the floor of the small learner's pool. You can hire a sunlounger on the pool's lawns, enjoy the priory park's refreshment kiosk and rinse the chlorine off in the newly installed poolside showers (there are also indoor changing facilities and showers). The pool can get busy on a sunny day, so you are advised to arrive early if you don't want to stand in the queue for ages. The hedge-fringed pool is a short walk from Ware town centre, where there are plenty of cafes; you can also visit the spacious grotto, built into a chalk hillside in the eighteenth century by local poet John Scott.

Access
Entry to pool via steps. Accessible toilets and changing rooms, level access to pool. Lido is less than a kilometre from Ware rail station; frequent local bus services stop on nearby High Street, with connections to Stevenage and Hertford. Small on-site car park, and cycle parking.

REDRICKS OPEN WATER SWIMMING LAKE

51.7908, 0.1195 / Redricks Lane, Saw-bridgeworth, Hertfordshire, CM21 1RL / Swimming and paddling / *www.facebook.com/groups/300489263370967*

Located just north of Harlow, Redricks Open Water Swimming Lake is perfect for any swimmer wanting a welcoming and friendly experience. With a community of swimmers ready to offer advice and coaches to assist with learning new skills, this people-focused swim spot is great for those looking to enjoy their swim with other like-minded individuals. A soft, golden beach provides easy entry into the water, and the water's edge is dense with lush trees and vegetation. The water remains comfortably cool all year round so wetsuits are recommended, and for visitors wanting to try long-distance swimming, marker buoys help you keep track of your progress. The on-site Redricks Lake Cafe serves hot food and the surrounding area consists of rolling fields with plenty of space for picnics.

Access
Easy access from a sandy beach. Harlow Mill railway station two and a half kilometres away; frequent buses to between Harlow and Stanstead Airport just outside the station. Parking can be found across the River Stort at Town Park River Way car park.

WOODUP POOL. © SHUTTERSTOCK/RMC42

STUBBERS ADVENTURE CENTRE

51.5390, 0.2686 / Ockendon Road, Upminster, Essex, RM14 2TY / Swimming and paddling / *www.swimfortri.co.uk/stubbers*

On the fringes of Essex, Stubbers Adventure Centre is a collection of three lakes resting on the grounds of a former stately home. From April to September, swimmers can enjoy the tree-fringed lakes on one of several sessions throughout the week, and with sessions aimed at both newcomers and experienced swimmers there is something to please everyone. Lifeguards are on standby at the shores of the cold and deep lakes, which are accessed by jetties, grassy banks and small, sandy beaches. Swimmers must wear a wetsuit and brightly coloured cap, and also must purchase a Lakemate band before swimming. For those wanting to make a day of their trip, the lake hosts a variety of other activities including paddleboarding and laser tag. Alternatively, the beautifully restored Upminster Windmill is nearby. There are several cafes on-site for a drink and bite to eat.

Access
Access via jetties, grassy banks and small, sandy beaches. Bus stop 300 metres away with frequent connections to Romford. Upminster tube station (Overground, District and Hammersmith & City lines) three and a half kilometres away. On-site parking.

HADLEIGH PARK

51.5503, 0.5975 / Chapel Lane, Hadleigh, Essex, SS7 2PP / 01702 551072 / Swimming and paddling

Situated between Hadleigh and the Thames estuary, Hadleigh Park is home to a reservoir nestled in 500 acres of country park. Although the site is perhaps better known for hosting the mountain biking course of the 2012 Olympics, Hadleigh Park is a lovely place for a dip. A 400-metre swim course opens on Wednesday evenings and Saturday mornings, and visitors also have access to the venue's cycle trails, children's play areas and scenic walking trails. Toilets, hot showers and changing rooms are all on-site, and the nearby Hadleigh Castle is a great stop for those wanting to experience the remains of the once-imposing, thirteenth-century castle. An on-site cafe can provide drinks and snacks, or refreshment options can be found in Hadleigh.

Access
Access from floating pier or grassy banks. Accessible toilet, no hoist; many of the walking trails are wheelchair friendly. Regular buses to Rayleigh and Basildon stop at the Memorial stop, just under a kilometre away. On-site parking.

RIVER CHELMER, ULTING

51.7484, 0.6068 / Ulting, Essex / Swimming and paddling

With some of the cleanest water in the Essex area, this stretch of the River Chelmer is a beautiful place to swim while admiring the peaceful countryside. On the outskirts of the village of Ulting, for a prepared swimmer this is an idyllic spot for a day out. The water reaches up to two metres in depth, and can be followed in either direction for a peaceful dip. After your swim, the nearby Ulting Wick offers a picturesque stroll through its carefully maintained gardens. With very few stops nearby for food or supplies, a picnic will need to be packed by visitors, but the rolling fields surrounding the river making a comfortable spot for a rest.

Access

Grassy banks provide easy access – do not enter through the church grounds. Difficult to access via public transport: nearest bus services four kilometres away in Hatfield Peverel, with regular connections to Colchester. Limited roadside parking near Hoemill Bridge.

WOODUP POOL

51.7590, 0.8493 / Woodrolfe Road, Tollesbury, Maldon, Essex, CM9 8SE / Swimming and paddling / www.facebook.com/woodupool

The reed-fringed, tidal Woodup Pool is refilled with fresh seawater at the highest tides every ten days or so, and has been entertaining visitors since the early twentieth century. Concrete boundaries encircle the pool and there are wooden steps into the water, although there is also a sandy beach at the water's head. While the council provide Portaloos in the busiest summer months, there are few facilities here and no lifeguards, so swimmers should come prepared with all they need for their day out. The Loft Tea by the Sea cafe rests nearby.

Tucked away in a corner of Essex amid marinas and boatyards, it is easy to see why this spot has been charming visitors for generations.

Access

Access via sandy slopes and steps. Pool occasionally closed for kayaking events. Infrequent bus services (approximately every two hours) to Colchester and Maldon from Tollesbury Centre, just over a kilometre away. Parking at Woodrolfe Green car park, a kilometre away.

BRIGHTLINGSEA LIDO

51.8072, 1.0173 / Promenade Way, Brightlingsea, Essex, CO7 0HH / 01206 303067 / Swimming and paddling / www.brightlingsealido.org

Once a council-run pool, the unheated Brightlingsea Lido was rescued by the community in 2018. This bluest of pools, with a kink in its fifty-metre length, is really right beside the seaside; unfortunately damaged by a tidal surge, it underwent extensive refurbishment to reopen in summer 2021. Nearly a century after it was first built, the community charity that now runs it has visionary plans for the future. One welcome change already made is the expansion of the lido cafe, which will sell you a sausage sandwich or a hot drink. Brightlingsea Lido may yet prove to be the very best example of what an outdoor pool, abandoned by its council but beloved by its locals, can become. Whether you want to sit by the pool, swim long lengths or splash in the paddling pool, the lido is a great way to pass a summer's afternoon by the sea.

Access

Entry into pool via steps at shallow end. Ramped access to poolside; accessible changing facilities and toilets; future accessibility plans include a hoist. Frequent 62 bus from Colchester to Brightlingsea; good (largely) off-road cycle route to Colchester. Promenade car park and street parking nearby.

DEDHAM VALE. © *WWW.DRIVINGWITHDOGS.CO.UK*

BROOMHILL POOL. © *KLH ARCHITECTS*

DEDHAM VALE, RIVER STOUR

51.9595, 1.0198 / East Bergholt, Suffolk /
Swimming and paddling

If you're after a swim spot which allows you to bask on sunny banks and take in a bit of culture afterwards, the stretch of the River Stour in the Dedham Vale Area of Outstanding Natural Beauty is ideal. In the pretty hamlet of Flatford, the water reaches around two metres in depth as it flows under Fen Bridge, and can be followed in either direction for views of the historic vale. Grassy banks offer access into the water, which can be weedy, and although the water is fine to swim in care should be taken not to drink it. If your legs grow tired, rowboats can be hired from the nearby National Trust site. A short walk away lies Willy Lott's House, which featured in John Constable's iconic painting, *The Hay Wain*. Plenty of spaces for picnics are available, and the National Trust's Flatford Tearoom is on hand to provide refreshments.

Access
Access from grassy banks. Bus to Colchester stops a few times a day in East Bergholt, just over a kilometre away. On-site parking at National Trust's Flatford, 100 metres from the water.

BROOMHILL POOL

52.0683, 1.1410 / Sherrington Road, Ipswich, Suffolk, IP1 4HT / Swimming and paddling / *broomhillpooltrust.org*

Of all the 1930s lidos, Broomhill Pool in Ipswich was one of the finest, with its five-metre-deep diving pit, buffet cafe, water fountain, clock tower entrance, children's pool and grandstand. In its heyday thousands flocked here, both to swim and to watch diving displays, but in 2002 the council drained it for the last time. Still beloved by locals, the Save Broomhill Pool trust campaigned tirelessly, and in 2015 Fusion Lifestyle – restorer of Wycombe Rye and Brockwell lidos – secured lottery funding to reopen the lido with a new leisure facility beside it. Although it was expected to reopen in 2021, coronavirus has delayed, hopefully not permanently, its reopening. A generation of children have been denied the joy of floating under azure skies; let us hope that soon water-wrinkled feet will pad excitedly to the ice-cream stand, optimistic teenagers will bellyflop from diving boards and children of all ages will be able to splash under sunny skies.

Access
At the time of writing, the lido is being redeveloped and is not currently open. It was due to reopen in 2021.

GREAT CORNARD SWIMMING POOL

52.0254, 0.7493 / Head Lane, Great Cornard, Sudbury, Suffolk, CO10 0JU / 01787 374861 / Swimming / *www.gcsportscentre.co.uk*

Built next to the Thomas Gainsborough School, this outdoor pool is primarily for the students, but in the school summer holidays as well as in evenings and at weekends it opens for public use. It is part of a school and community leisure complex that includes a gym, climbing wall and sports courts. This is a pool built so that local children can learn to swim; it is functional, rather than scenic, and probably not the perfect spot if you want to spend the afternoon lounging poolside or picnicking, but if you want a quick dip in an outdoor pool at the heart of the community, it is worth a visit. There is a cafe in the leisure centre for a post-swim panini or hot chocolate.

Access

Access to water via ladders. Wheelchair access to poolside; accessible changing facilities. Frequent bus services from Colchester and Sudbury; closest train station Sudbury, approximately two kilometres away. Parking on-site.

GOSFIELD LAKE RESORT

51.9336, 0.5821 / Church Road, Gosfield, Halstead, Essex, CO9 1UD / 01787 475043 / Swimming / *gosfieldlake.co.uk*

Just west of Gosfield, Gosfield Lake Resort offers the opportunity to swim in the large, clean waters of Gosfield Lake. As the water, which is accessible from a pier, is never deeper than a metre and a half this is perfect for those new to open air swimming to build their confidence. As the lake is often reserved for waterskiing, those enjoying swimming at the lake must follow routes of up to 1,500 metres in designated sessions. An on-site restaurant, the Apple Tree, is a great stop for visitors who are after something to eat. A visit here can be combined with a scenic walk in the nearby Gosfield Sandpits, followed by a meal at the Tudor Kings Head pub.

Access

Access via grassy banks and muddy shallows. Buses to Halstead run every half an hour from Church Road stop, 800 metres from the lake. On-site parking.

CLARE SWIMMING CLUB/STOUR VALLEY COMMUNITY SCHOOL

52.0801, 0.5889 / Cavendish Road, Clare, Sudbury, Suffolk, CO10 8PJ / Swimming / *www.facebook.com/clareswimmingpool*

The on-site outdoor pool at Stour Valley Community School is used by students in term time, and is maintained and funded by the school. In summer, the lido is leased to Clare Swimming Club who oversee cheap afternoon and morning swim sessions, with lifeguards, for casual swimmers on weekdays, but not weekends. This is a functional pool, with a maximum capacity of forty, limited poolside space and basic facilities. No food or drink is allowed by the pool, although there is a small tuck shop for those in need of a post-swim sugar boost and cafes in the nearby village centre. This little, volunteer-run pool, nestled in a small village in the midst of Suffolk's green countryside, is probably not a day trip destination but offers a great community resource for locals.

Access

Access to the water via ladders. Approximately hourly bus services to Haverhill, Bury St Edmunds and Sudbury; no evening or Sunday services. Closest train station is Sudbury, fifteen kilometres away. On-site parking.

GRANTCHESTER MEADOWS, RIVER CAM

52.1785, 0.0994 / Grantchester, Cambridgeshire / Swimming and paddling

For around two kilometres, the River Cam provides plentiful opportunities to slide into the water as it meanders along Grantchester Meadows. From the Orchard Tea Garden to the bend in the river by Pembroke College Sports Ground, sloping, grassy banks lead to the cool water; upstream of Cambridge the riverbed can get muddy and the water can be occasionally reedy. With the river reaching up to two metres in depth swimmers can often be spotted jumping in, although take care to check water levels before plunging in. Grantchester village is just a short walk away, and here visitors can enjoy its thatched cottages or grab a bite to eat at the Red Lion pub, which is renowned for its cosy atmosphere.

Access

Access from grassy banks, which can be muddy. Frequent buses to Cambridge stop at Burnt Close stop, 800 metres away. Limited parking in the village; temporary/seasonal car park in a field on approach from Trumpington (Easter to late September, fine weekends and bank holidays).

JESUS GREEN LIDO

52.2130, 0.1233 / Chesterton Road, Cambridge, Cambridgeshire, CB4 3AX / 01223 302579 / Swimming / www.better.org. uk/leisure-centre/cambridge/ jesusgreenlido

Opened in 1923, this narrow, long and unheated lido stretches across the fields of Jesus Green, running by the side of the River Cam. The tree-fringed pool is one of Europe's longest, and was designed to mimic swimming on the nearby river. While the lido is open from May to September, one of the three lanes is reserved for 'fast' swimmers and diving is permitted in the middle section of the pool (the pool is deepest at its centre). For those over sixteen there is a sauna and sunbathing terrace, and there are plenty of picnic tables around the pool for all to enjoy. There is an on-site cafe and ice cream parlour, or alternatively there is an abundance of restaurants, cafes and pubs in Cambridge. If visiting with children, the Sheep's Green and Lammas Land learner pools also rest in the city.

Access

Access to water via ladders. Ramped access to poolside; accessible changing facilities and hoist available. Cambridge train station three kilometres away; frequent local buses from station. On-site cycle parking. No on-site parking; metered street parking across the river.

MILTON COUNTRY PARK

52.2372, 0.1626 / Cambridge Road, Milton, Cambridgeshire, CB24 6AZ / 01223 420060 / Swimming and paddling / www.miltoncountrypark.org/ows

Surrounded by lush greenery, Milton Country Park is a beautiful respite from the surrounding residential area. Todd's Pit is based just north of the park and is perfect for a swim in the clean water, recommended for competent swimmers, after exploring the trails which weave their way around the two lakes and the lush grounds. Look out for kingfishers and damselflies as you paddle round the 400-metre course. Whether you want to improve your cold water swimming in winter swimming sessions or just enjoy the scenery around you, the park is a convenient escape from the bustle of Cambridge. The on-site Grounds Cafe is a popular spot for visitors to grab a bite to eat, or benches are scattered around throughout the park for picnics.

Access

Muddy, sloping banks allow entry to water. Accessible toilets and footpaths, but no hoist to water. Citi 9 bus from Cambridge runs hourly and stops by Tesco a short distance from the park. Buses to park and ride site a kilometre and a half away run every ten minutes. Paid on-site parking.

GRANTCHESTER MEADOWS. © SHUTTERSTOCK/MARKOS LOIZOU

SANTON DOWNHAM, RIVER LITTLE OUSE

52.4530, 0.6859 / Santon Downham, Suffolk / Swimming and paddling

As it meanders through Suffolk, the Little Ouse river between Brandon and Thetford makes for a fantastic swimming location for both families and solo swimmers. This lovely area is characterised by a forested landscape and is dotted with picturesque villages. Although there are many spots for a swim along the river, the stretch on the outskirts of Santon Downham at the Saint Helen's picnic site proves popular. Here families can be found enjoying drinks and ice creams sold by on-site vendors and basking on the grassy banks which lead to the water. Swimming away from the picnic area unveils a tranquil stretch of the river, where your only company will be the endless fields and lush woodland. A journey into Thetford provides plenty of refreshment options.

Access

Easy access via grassy, sloping banks. 200/201 bus travels to Mildenhall a few times a day in Santon Downham, a kilometre away. Thetford rail station ten kilometres away. Parking available by the picnic grounds.

BECCLES LIDO

52.4577, 1.5598 / Puddingmoor, Beccles, Suffolk, NR34 9PL / 01502 713297 / Swimming and paddling / www.beccleslido.com

If outdoor swimming is all about fun in the sun, Beccles Lido is a great family destination with its poolside slide, diving board (into three-and-a-half-metre-deep water) and regular inflatable sessions. There is a well-stocked cafe and tree-fringed lawns, and also an adventure play area for kids. You get three for the price of one, with a large main pool, toddler pool and splash pool. The lido caters for all swimmers, with triathlon training, lane sessions and aquacise in addition to its family-friendly sessions. You can even arrive by the Big Dog Ferry or kayak to this riverside lido. Otherwise, you can enjoy a short stroll from Beccles town centre, which takes you past St Michael's Church, where Lord Nelson's parents were married; the climb to the top of the sixteenth-century Bell Tower offers you panoramic views of Norfolk's Broads.

Access

Entry to water via ladders, slide and diving board. Level and ramped access; accessible changing rooms and toilets; hoist available. Beccles rail station less than a kilometre away; Beccles well-served by frequent buses from Norwich, Lowestoft and Great Yarmouth. Cycle parking and boat mooring available next to lido. Disabled/motor-cycle parking on-site; pay car parks less than a kilometre away.

OUTNEY COMMON, RIVER WAVENEY. © *SHUTTERSTOCK/ EDWIN ROSIER*

OUTNEY COMMON, RIVER WAVENEY

52.4613, 1.4350 / Bungay, Suffolk / Swimming and paddling

The River Waveney was hailed by Roger Deakin in his classic *Waterlog: A Swimmer's Journey Through Britain* as one of his favourite rivers, and the three-kilometre stretch around Outney Common makes it easy to see why. The gentle water, which can reach up to two metres in depth, is popular with both swimmers and canoers alike. There are entry points all along the grassy riverbank, allowing you to easily bask in the surrounding greenery as you meander along the willow-fringed river. A visit here can be combined with a stop at the Norman Bungay Castle, and the nearby town of Bungay offers public toilets and a variety of cafes and pubs.

Access
Easy to access water from gentle, grassy banks. Green Dragon is the nearest bus stop 400 metres away, with frequent buses to Norwich. Plenty of parking at the Bungay car park, just under a kilometre away.

SHOTESHAM FORD, RIVER TAS

52.5472, 1.2816 / Newton Flotman, Norfolk / Swimming and paddling

Characterised by its overhanging willows and chestnut trees, Shotesham Ford is a shallow pool on the River Tas. The water in the middle of the pool is deep enough to swim in and the edges are great for younger family members to have a paddle. Just under two kilometres from the nearest village, Newton Flotman, this spot is relatively secluded and is rarely busy, except for on particularly hot days. With plenty of open spaces and picnic spots, prepared visitors can enjoy a tranquil day here. However, for those wanting to visit the village the Duke of Delhi restaurant can provide refreshments.

Access
Access to water via pebbled shallows. Frequent buses to Diss, Roydon and Norwich from Brick Kiln Lane stop, just under a kilometre away. Limited roadside parking in Newton Flotman and Shotesham.

ANDERSON'S MEADOW, RIVER WENSUM

52.6417, 1.2780 / Norwich, Norfolk / Swimming

In the heart of Norwich, Anderson's Meadow is an oasis for visitors to the bustling city. A slip-way provides access into the water of the River Wensum, found opposite the Eagle Canoe Club. While the meadow itself is very popular with local residents, the water is considerably less so: owing to the high current and low temperature it is important for swimmers to be confident outdoor swimmers before going for a dip. This area is perfect for visitors to the city looking to stop for a quick swim. Public toilets are 800 metres away in Wensum Park. Norwich Cathedral rests two and a half kilometres away, and for those wanting to grab a bite to eat the Gibraltar Gardens pub sits just across the river.

Access

Access via slipway opposite the Eagle Canoe Club. Buses throughout Norwich available 100 metres away at Heigham Street stop; Norwich rail station three kilometres away. Limited on-street parking on Swanton Road; Waterloo Park car park just over a kilometre away.

CAEN MEADOW, RIVER BURE

52.7049, 1.3968 / Wroxham, Norfolk / Swimming and paddling

On the edge of the Norfolk Broads, this stretch of the River Bure in Wroxham is accessed by a sandy shore and surrounded by a green meadow. The shallows which greet you as you wade in soon deepen slightly in the widest parts of the river. As you move through the cool water in this hidden gem of a swim spot, you may be able to see the Church of St Mary peeking out over the tops of the verdant trees. Swimmers should use brightly coloured caps and tow floats to make themselves visible to passing boats. Public toilets are available

in Hoveton. To extend your day out, the BeWILDerwood family adventure park is four kilometres away, and Wroxham offers a variety of pubs, cafes and restaurants.

Access

Entry into water from a gently sloping beach. Regular buses to Hoveton, Horning and Norwich from Keys Drive stop, 400 metres away. Nearest public parking is at Wroxham Broad public car park, two kilometres away.

LAMAS ON THE RIVER BURE

52.7599, 1.3256 / Buxton, Norfolk / Swimming and paddling

Near the village of Lamas, this stretch of the River Bure is a great spot to view the stunning Norfolk countryside while enjoying the clear water. Marshy banks give way to cool water, which can be weedy. For those looking for a quiet swim in an idyllic, rural setting need look no further than this spot, and as you float you can admire views of the nearby church and endless fields stretching far into the distance. The river has both deep and shallow areas depending upon entry point but is gentle enough for swimmers of varying ability. There are plenty of nearby locations for picnics, or for those who prefer to pick up a meal, neighbouring Buxton hosts a classic fish and chip shop as well as the popular Black Lion pub.

Access

Access via marshy banks which can be muddy; may be necessary to walk to find a suitable spot for entry. Nearest bus stop is Hautbois Road where the 210 runs regularly to Norwich; access footpath towards Oxnead by Buxton Mill. Parking by the railway station in Buxton, just under two kilometres away, and footpath access by Buxton Mill.

19
20
21
18
14 15   16
13   17
12
10 11
5   6   7 8
              9
        4
      3
    2
  1

22

27 29
  28 30

RIPON
●

23

26
25

YORK
●

24

LEEDS
●

HULL
●

SHEFFIELD
●

Yorkshire

JANET'S FOSS. © *LOUISE KIBLER, @VIEWSWITHLOU*

GADDINGS DAM. © @*LIVLEMOINE_*

GADDINGS DAM

53.6989, -2.0775 / Todmorden, West Yorkshire / Swimming and paddling

Set high on the vast, open moorland of the southern Pennines, Gaddings Dam is a large man-made dam, with a sandy beach which provides easy access into the water. Surrounded by a grassy bank and with nothing but sky and moorland beyond, Gaddings Dam offers spectacular panoramic views of the hills around it. Truly exposed to the elements, swimmers should take plenty of warm layers when enjoying England's highest beach. Waiting at the bottom of the hill is the Shepherd's Rest Inn, where you can find well-earned refreshments.

Access

Access via sandy beach. Bus stop for the T6 service outside the Shepherd's Rest Inn, a kilometre away, which comes several times a day; steep climb from here up to the dam. Roadside parking along Lumbutts Road, opposite the pub.

LUMB HOLE FALLS

53.7790, -2.0131 / Pecket Well or Hebden Bridge, West Yorkshire / Swimming, paddling and plunge pool

Tucked between hills along Crimsworth Dean Beck, Lumb Hole Falls is a small group of four waterfalls which feed into the same plunge pool. The far side of the pool consists of moss-covered stone walls, with some good platforms for jumping, providing the pool is deep enough at the time of your visit. Some rocks litter the bank close to the path, but access into the water is still easy, if a little muddy in wet weather. A swim here can be combined with a walk to Hardcastle Crags and Shackleton's Monument, enabling you to make the most of the panoramic views the Yorkshire countryside has to offer.

Access

Rocky banks provide access, can be quite muddy. A kilometre away is the Keighley Road Broad Shaw bus stop for the regular 594, 595 and Brontë Bus services to Hebden Bridge and Keighley. Lay-by along Old Road provides parking within 500 metres of the falls.

ILKLEY LIDO. © *SARAH THELWALL*

GOIT STOCK FALLS

53.8278, -1.8837 / Cullingworth, West Yorkshire / Swimming, paddling and plunge pool

Tumbling from a stone platform, Goit Stock Falls is a waterfall on Hallas Beck, hidden away in the woodland lining the river. Rocks around the edge of the pool serve as platforms for getting in and out of the water. This secluded spot is tucked away on the outskirts of Bradford, and can be combined with an exploration of the soothing woods on the Goitstock Woods and Harden Beck walk. Afterwards, you can find refreshments at the Fleece Inn or the George Hotel in Cullingworth.

Access
Access via a rocky ledge surrounding the water. 616, 619 and K17 Keighley Jets services stop at the Harden Lane Bents Lane bus stop in Wilsden, six kilometres away. Goit Stock Falls can be accessed by foot from Cullingworth. Roadside parking available on Hallas Lane at the junction with Greenside Lane, within a kilometre of the swim spot.

ILKLEY LIDO

53.9318, -1.8201 / Denton Road, Ilkley, West Yorkshire, LS29 0BZ / 01943 436201 / Swimming and paddling / *www.bradford.gov.uk/sport-and-activities/sports-centres-and-pools/ilkley-pool-and-lido*

Officially opened in May 1935 as part of the Silver Jubilee celebrations for King George V, Ilkley Lido is situated on the edge of one of West Yorkshire's prettiest traditional spa towns. With views of Ilkley's famous moorland, the lido's beautiful backdrop has established it as one of the most picturesque outdoor pools in the North of England. The lido is uniquely mushroom shaped and is approximately forty-five metres long and twelve metres wide. The circular part of the pool (approximately forty-six metres in diameter) slopes from paddling shallows to a depth of two metres in the 'stem' portion of the pool. There is also a water fountain in the middle of the lido. The pool is unheated and is a great place to visit if you need somewhere to cool off during the summer.

Access
Access via ramps, steps and ladders. Lido area wheelchair accessible; hoist available. Approximately three kilometres from the town's regular bus services to Skipton and Keighly, and rail services to Leeds. On-site parking.

SCALEBER FORCE. © @LYNDSEY_OUTDOORS

LOUP SCAR. © MARK OLDFIELD

SCALEBER FORCE

54.0588, -2.2450 / Settle, North Yorkshire / Swimming, paddling and plunge pool

Winding its way down a limestone staircase, Scaleber Force is an alluring waterfall and plunge pool. The shallow banks are a mixture of stone and mud, and although they may be slippery after wet weather they provide easy points to get into the pool. Entrenched in the peace of the gorge, a swim at this stunning spot can be incorporated into a walk from Settle to the waterfall, or you can detour to Warrendale Knotts and Hunter Bark, making the most of these majestic hills. Nearby Settle offers several options for refreshments, ranging from the Ye Old Naked Man Cafe to the Talbot Arms.

Access

Access via rocky, mossy and sometimes muddy banks, which can be slippery. Bus stop three kilometres away at the Market Place, regular services to Skipton. Roadside parking along High Hill Lane, within 200 metres of waterfall. Path down to the falls steep and narrow, and during periods of wet weather can be slippery.

JANET'S FOSS

54.0657, -2.1365 / Malham, North Yorkshire / Swimming, paddling and plunge pool

Tucked away in a wooded glen, Janet's Foss is a waterfall and plunge pool which links up with Gordale Beck. The trail leading down to the plunge pool makes for easy, direct access into the water, which grows deeper beneath the waterfall. Secluded and enveloped by the peace of the surrounding trees, this is a truly magical swim spot, with tales of a fairy queen living in the cave to the right of the swim spot. A dip here can be combined with the National Trust's walking trail from Malham village to the waterfall, or a visit to the Malham National Park Centre. You can find refreshments at the Old Barn Cafe or at the Secret Garden Bistro.

Access

Access via a gravel trail – muddy, pebbly sloping banks. Buses between Skipton and Malham (twice daily) can be caught one and a half kilometres from Janet's Foss. Limited parking available at lay-by beside bridge, Gordale Lane, 200 metres away; National Trust car park in Malham, two kilometres away. Take Gordale Lane to Janet's Foss.

GRASSINGTON WEIR

54.0679, -2.0038 / Grassington, North Yorkshire / Swimming, paddling and plunge pool

Situated beside a ruined mill-house, Grassington Weir is on a section of the River Wharfe, surrounded by the gorgeous landscape of the Yorkshire Dales National Park. The riverside common provides a grassy bank, enabling easy access into the water, and the slide beside the mill-house can inject your swim with some extra excitement. This swim spot is the perfect place for a family day out, or to cool off from one of the spectacular walks around the Grassington and Linton Falls area. However, the water is always cold, and look out for sudden drops underwater as well as varying currents. Nearby Grassington provides plenty of opportunities for refreshment, including the Cobblestones Cafe.

Access

Easy, grassy access to river from banks. Frequent bus services (to Skipton, Hebden, Buckden, Ilkley) call at Grassington National Park Centre, less than a kilometre away; also car parking at the centre. Follow Sedber Lane to reach footpath, go north along river.

LOUP SCAR

54.0518, -1.9545 / Burnsall, North Yorkshire / Swimming, paddling and plunge pool

A section of rapids on the River Wharfe, Loup Scar is home to a plunge pool walled by high, limestone cliffs. The sloping, grassy bank provides entry points to the shallower river pool upstream, from which you can also access the deeper plunge pool. During long hot spells the section between these two points may dry up, revealing the uneven, stony riverbed beneath. With the gorgeous open sky overhead, the high-sided hills and the tree-adorned rock face, this swim spot feels like its own little world, and you can find refreshments afterwards at the Wharfe View Cafe in the charming village of Burnsall.

Access

Grassy banks provide access to river pool upstream. Moderate downhill descent from the Dales Way path to river. Closest bus stop 800 metres away, at Red Lion Hotel, for 74A service from Ilkley twice daily on Mondays, Wednesdays and Fridays. Parking available on the road beside the church in Burnsall, 500 metres away.

RIVER WHARFE, APPLETREEWICK

54.0332, -1.9222 / Appletreewick, North Yorkshire / Swimming and paddling

Below the quiet, rural village of Appletreewick, this spot on the River Wharfe is nestled among the rolling Yorkshire hills. The mixture of grassy banks and shingle beach means there are plenty of options for easily accessing the water, which contains submerged rocks in places. With a rope swing on the far side and a natural log flume, this spot is great for family fun, and can be an excellent place to rest after exploring along the Dales Way, which runs by the river. A spot of food at the end of a day in the great outdoors can be found in Appletreewick at the Craven Arms pub or the New Inn.

Access

Shingle beach by water. 74A bus service stops twice daily on Mondays, Wednesdays and Fridays from Ilkley – stops at Craven Arms and New Inn. Limited roadside parking in Appletreewick village – if you are staying or dining at pubs, ask permission to park. Access to river via track opposite New Inn (not public right of way) or footpath next to Masons Campsite.

STAINFORTH FORCE. © *CHARLOTTE PLEASANTS*

STAINFORTH FORCE

54.0991, -2.2794 / Little Stainforth, North Yorkshire / Swimming, paddling and plunge pool

Situated between Stainforth and Little Stainforth, Stainforth Force comprises a series of falls and river pools along the River Ribble. Grassy banks and stone platforms make slipping into the water easy, although it may be a little peaty. The main falls are a short, easy walk from the bridge on the Dog Hill Brow road; the best swim spots are further downstream. A picturesque location for a picnic, a trip to Stainforth Force can be tied in with a visit to Catrigg Force as well as with one of the many walks around this part of the beautiful Yorkshire Dales National Park. There are public toilets in the car park at Stainforth. You can end the day with a meal at the Knights Table in Little Stainforth.

Access
Gentle, grassy slopes to enter water; large, often slippery stones. Stainforth (less than a kilometre away) served by Settle–Horton in Ribblesdale bus, approximately every two hours; railway stations at Settle and Horton. Paid parking available at Stainforth car park. Follow the Pennine Bridleway/A Dales High Way along river to reach falls.

CATRIGG FORCE

54.0993, -2.2587 / Stainforth, North Yorkshire / Swimming, paddling and plunge pool

A favourite of Edward Elgar, Catrigg Force is a waterfall and plunge pool overlooked by the impressive, monolithic stone walls of the gorge. The rocks lining the riverbed make for good stepping points to traverse from the path to the pool, although they may be slippery. The perfect place to cool off after walking through the surrounding hills, this hidden spot can be combined with a visit to Stainforth Force or the nearby Craven Lime Works, where you can discover the area's industrial heritage. You can find refreshments at the Craven Heifer Hotel in Stainforth; there are public toilets in Stainforth car park.

Access
Steep, slippery paths lead to water's edge. Stainforth (a kilometre and a half away) served by Settle–Horton in Ribblesdale bus, approximately every two hours; railway stations at Settle and Horton. Paid parking available at Stainforth car park. Follow Pennine Bridleway from Stainforth up Goat Scar Lane; turn left on footpath at wall corner.

IBBETH PERIL. © *GRAHAM DERBYSHIRE*

INGLETON WATERFALLS

54.1727, -2.4693 / Ingleton, North Yorkshire /
Swimming, paddling and plunge pool /
ingletonwaterfallstrail.co.uk

Nestled among the Yorkshire hills, Ingleton
Waterfalls tumbles from between two sheer
stone faces into a plunge pool below. The
stone steps and rocky ledge leading to the
water make the pool easily accessible. Although
overlooked by the gangway, this swim spot
provides a phenomenal view of the gorge
and surrounding hills, and can be reached as
part of the brilliant Ingleton Waterfalls Trail, a
seven-kilometre walking route which displays
the dynamic landscape of the Yorkshire Dales.
This is a popular tourist destination (there is an
entrance fee to pay), so you are unlikely to enjoy
this spot in solitude. You can grab a snack and
a drink to refresh yourself from the Falls Cafe
or from one of the many other cafes in Ingleton.

Access
Slippery, stony access to water; water shoes
strongly recommended. Approximately two
kilometres along Ingleton Waterfalls Trail
to best swim spots; trail well-surfaced but
includes large number of steps. Frequent
buses to Lancaster, Settle, Kirkby Lonsdale
from Ingleton, one kilometre from trailhead/
three kilometres from swim spot. Limited
parking at trailhead; paid car park in Ingleton.

IBBETH PERIL

54.2730, -2.3978 / Cowgill or Dent, South
Cumbria / Swimming, paddling and plunge pool

Supposedly the place where local witch Ibby
would drown unfortunate drunkards, Ibbeth
Peril is a waterfall and plunge pool located on
the River Dee. The shallow, mossy bank makes
accessing the water comfortable, however
swimmers should be aware that the pool can
rise quickly, and should only enter the adjoining cave in periods of sustained dry weather.
This secluded swim spot – surrounded by walls
of moss-covered rock – is the perfect place to
stop for a dip, and can be tied in with a walk
exploring the surrounding hills such as Aye
Gill Pike and Great Knoutberry Hill, or a visit
to nearby Dent Brewery.

Access
Access via shallow, mossy banks. Ibbeth Peril
three kilometres from Dent railway station.
Not easily accessible by bus: S1 bus comes to
Gibbs Hall, 500 metres from swim spot, a few
times a day on Saturdays. Parking 500 metres
from Ibbeth Peril, on the road from Dent to
Cowgill. Path and footbridge lead from the car
park, followed by a slight scramble to waterfall.

COTTER FORCE. © KEVIN WINTER, @KRWINTERPHOTOS

COTTER FORCE

54.3228, -2.2347 / Hawes, North Yorkshire / Swimming, paddling and plunge pool

Found on Cotterdale Beck, Cotter Force is a stepped waterfall with a deep plunge pool. The bank is soft and muddy, and once in the water you must wade over some stonier patches of riverbed towards the deeper water. This peaceful spot in the heart of the Yorkshire Dales National Park is near both Hardraw Force and Hawes National Park Centre, allowing you to make the most of the scenic countryside views. A variety of options for refreshments are also available in Hawes, from the Black Stag to Caffe Curva.

Access
Stony shallows follow soft and muddy banks. Regular buses to Leeds, Leyburn and North-allerton stop four kilometres away at Market Place stop in Hawes. Limited parking beside the A684, within 600 metres of waterfall; path to the swim spot is specially graded, making it suitable for wheelchair users.

HARDRAW FORCE

54.3195, -2.2019 / Hardraw, North Yorkshire / Swimming, paddling and plunge pool / *hardrawforce.com*

Hardraw Force is England's largest single-drop waterfall, with a serene plunge pool below. The stony edges to the pool provide platforms from which you can step into the water, although there may be shingle underfoot. Used as a filming location for *Robin Hood: Prince of Thieves*, this swim spot is truly spectacular, and you can discover more about its heritage and history at the Hardraw Force Heritage Centre, which is open during the summer months. The centre also has a tearoom where you can pick up snacks and a drink. Hardraw Force is on private land and is open daily, with an entry fee.

Access
Access via stony platforms. Nearest bus stop Penn Lane, for services to Hawes. Plenty of space for parking on the side of the road along Bellow Hill, less than a kilometre from Hardraw Force.

HARDRAW FORCE. © WWW.HARDRAWFORCE.COM   CAULDRON FALLS. © EMMA MARSHALL, @ELMPHOTOGRAPHY_27

AYSGARTH FALLS

54.2917, -1.9869 / Aysgarth, North Yorkshire /
Swimming, paddling and plunge pool

A series of waterfalls along the River Ure, Aysgarth Falls is surrounded by the beautiful foliage of the trees which line the riverbanks. The stony beach leads into the water at this wide stretch of the river, and this tranquil swim spot can perfectly slot in as part of a day out at the peaceful village of Aysgarth, where you can further explore the National Park Centre as well as visit the Aysgarth Edwardian Rock Garden. Refreshments are available at the park's Coppice Cafe, or at one of the other cafes in Aysgarth, such as Hamilton's Tearoom and Mill Race Teashop.

Access
Stone and shingle beaches. A kilometre away the 156, 856 and 875 bus services stop a few times a day in Aysgarth. Aysgarth Falls car park within 500 metres of the swim spot.

CAULDRON FALLS

54.2758, -1.9715 / West Burton, North Yorkshire /
Swimming, paddling and plunge pool

Known for its easy accessibility, Cauldron Falls is a waterfall and plunge pool on Weldon Beck. Smooth stone banks offer plenty of spots from which you can slip into the water. With impressive rock faces forming walls to the pool before opening up to the trees and sky beyond, it is no wonder that this location is popular with photographers. The waterfall's close proximity to West Burton means you can tie in a visit here with an exploration of the village, or as part of a day walk from West Burton to Aysgarth Falls. You can drop into the West Burton Village Shop and Tearoom for a well-earned drink and snack.

Access
Access via smooth stone platforms. 156 service runs to Post Office bus stop several times a day. Small car park for Cauldron Falls and some roadside parking along Front Nook, all within 200 metres of the waterfall.

HELL GILL

54.3665, -2.3303 / Aisgill, Cumbria / Swimming, paddling and plunge pool

Hell Gill is an impressive swim spot comprising a plunge pool, stream and waterfall, part of a deep gorge which Hell Gill runs through. Accessing the narrow gorge, which contains sheer rock walls and has a stony riverbed, requires scrambling skills and rope. Swimmers should be aware that this location can become dangerous in high water. Roughly a kilometre downstream the waterfall is accessible by walking down alongside the river and then turning back on yourself to walk up the gorge. Not for the faint-hearted, a swim here is a rare opportunity and a true reward for overcoming the challenge of Hell Gill's limited access. To cap it off, it can form part of a hike up to Wild Boar Fell, which boasts incredible panoramic views.

Access
Sheer rock walls – scrambling skills and a rope required. Not easily accessible by public transport: nearest bus stop at Wharton Road End for the S5 service, ten kilometres from gorge and seven kilometres from waterfall. Lay-by parking on the B6259 beside Aisgill Falls, two kilometres from gorge and a kilometre from waterfall.

WAIN WATH WATERFALL

54.4091, -2.1798 / Keld, North Yorkshire / Swimming, paddling and plunge pool

Tucked away beside the B6270, Wain Wath Force is a wide waterfall set beneath limestone cliffs and surrounded by lush, green foliage. The stony beach gives way to the shallows of the river (water shoes are recommended), and you can easily wade further in towards the plunge pool closer to the falls. Set slightly back from the river there is a grassy bank, ideal for picnics, and the shallow water upstream means the falling water warms quickly in hot weather. Close to Keld (where there are public toilets), a swim here can be combined with a visit to Currack, Kisdon and East Gill Force. There are cafes in Keld and Thwaite, and Tan Hill Inn, Britain's highest pub, is approximately six kilometres away.

Access
Easy access to shallow water via pebbly beach. Little White Bus runs daily services from Richmond to Keld, but some must be booked twenty-four hours in advance. Parking on lay-bys along the B6270 within a kilometre of waterfall.

HELL GILL. © @JENNYAITKENART

CATRAKE FORCE

54.4068, -2.1672 / Keld, North Yorkshire / Swimming, paddling and plunge pool

Concealed in the gorge below Keld, Catrake Force is a small waterfall with two drops on the River Swale. A shingle beach provides access into the river, and from here you can swim towards the waterfall, giving you a better view than from land. Surrounded by the peace of the trees and ivy-strewn, stone gorge wall, this secluded swim spot can be overlooked due to the popularity of nearby Kisdon Force and East Gill Force. These two waterfalls are close enough to visit after a dip at Catrake Force, and Keld's Resource Centre contains plenty of information about the area's rich heritage.

Access
Shingle beach. 831 bus stops in Keld once a day on its way from Middlesbrough to Kirkby

CATRAKE FORCE. © @MICHAELHOGGPHOTOGRAPHY

WAIN WATH WATERFALL. © @PEAKTORIAL

Lonsdale. Parking available at Keld car park, 200 metres away. To reach swim spot follow path downstream from the campsite to shingle beach.

KISDON FORCE

54.4039, -2.1567 / Keld, North Yorkshire / Swimming, paddling and plunge pool

Located on the River Swale, Kisdon Force is a series of waterfalls surrounded by a serene, wooded gorge. Stony banks make getting into the river relatively easy, though swimmers should watch their footing, and the stone platforms of the waterfall make excellent ledges for jumping into the plunge pool beneath. As the sun can struggle to reach the depths of the gorge, you should be prepared for cold water in this mesmerising location. Kisdon Force is an ideal stop along the Pennine Way, and nearby Keld offers both toilet facilities and a

Resource Centre with plenty of information about the heritage of the local area. The swim spot is approximately seven kilometres south of the Tan Hill Inn, the highest pub in Britain.

Access
Easy access points to the water, and rocky ledges to jump from. Little White Bus runs daily services from Richmond to Keld, but some must be booked twenty-four hours in advance. Parking available in Keld, just under a kilometre away. Kisdon Force is a short detour from Pennine Way footpath.

ELLERTON PARK

54.3779, -1.6102 / Ellerton Park, Scornton, Richmond, North Yorkshire, DL10 6AP / 07762 758878 / Swimming / *www.ellertonpark.com*

  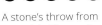

A stone's throw from Catterick, Ellerton Park is home to a sixty-acre lake

open to a variety of water sports. The jetty provides an easy place to slip into the water, however open water beginners are not permitted and all swimmers must wear wetsuits. Surrounded by open countryside, Ellerton is an excellent location for experienced open water swimmers looking for somewhere convenient and accessible to swim. Ellerton has an on-site shop for last minute kit purchases and wetsuit fitting. The Lakeside Country Cafe in Ellerton is a handy stop where you can grab food and drink, while Catterick also offers more substantial alternatives.

Access
Access via a jetty. The park is within a kilometre of the nearest bus stop at St Mary's Church in Bolton-on-Swale for 55 service from Northallerton, which stops a few times a day. On-site parking.

HELMSLEY OPEN AIR POOL. © *PAUL GOODWIN*

HELMSLEY OPEN AIR POOL

54.2509, -1.0642 / Baxton's Sprunt, Helmsley, North Yorkshire, YO62 5HT / 07512 262330 / Swimming / *www.helmsleyopenairpool.org*

Launched in 1969 by the Duke of Norfolk, Helmsley Open Air Pool is Yorkshire's only twenty-five-metre heated lido. Nestled in the heart of the countryside on the edge of the North York Moors National Park, the pool provides a holiday atmosphere for its visitors. The pool is open daily between 11:15 a.m. and 7 p.m., with open swim sessions, adult-only sessions and fun sessions throughout the day. The pool is also available for private hire sessions in the mornings and evenings. In 2018/2019, the lido underwent major restoration as part of the first phase of a long-term regeneration programme, which involved retiling the pool and re-turfing the grassed areas. There is a variety of refreshment choices in nearby Helmsley.

Access
Access via ladders. Lido area is wheelchair accessible; hoist available. Less than a kilometre from the nearest regular bus services to Scarborough and York. On-site parking.

ALLERTHORPE LAKELAND PARK

53.9037, -0.8136 / Melbourne Road, Allerthorpe, Pocklington, Yorkshire, YO42 4RL / 01759 301444 / Swimming / *www.allerthorpelakelandpark.co.uk*

Nestled in the Yorkshire countryside, Allerthorpe Lakeland Park is home to a man-made, weed-free lake which, during summer, can reach 28 °C. With sessions set aside specifically for open water swimming as well as a designated transition point for entering and exiting the lake, Allerthorpe is a great destination for experienced open water swimmers and newcomers alike. The lake is also home to plenty of other family friendly, bookable activities, such as canoeing and paddleboarding, and has an on-site cafe.

Access
Access via a designated transition area. Allerthorpe Lakeland Park four kilometres from bus services in Pocklington, which run regularly to York. On-site car park.

ALLERTHORPE LAKELAND PARK. © *ALLERTHORPE LAKELAND PARK*

WYKEHAM LAKES

54.2250, -0.4848 / Long Causeway Road, Wykeham, Scarborough, Yorshire, YO13 9QU / 01723 865052 / Swimming / *www.northyorkshire-waterpark.co.uk*

Run by the North Yorkshire Water Park, Wykeham Lakes is a vast area of open water, perfect for those looking for a designated open water swim circuit, whether for training or for fun. A shingle beach slopes into the lake, and with an average summer temperature of 18 °C, Wykeham is an excellent place to get out into the water while enjoying the scenery of the Yorkshire countryside. All swimmers must wear wetsuits and use tow floats, which are available to hire, and there are plenty of other activities to get involved with too, from cycling to kayaking. Afterwards you can refresh yourself in the park's cafe.

Access

Shingle beach. Regular 128 bus service to Helmsley stops three kilometres away at Hutton Buscel. On-site car park.

ALPAMARE WATER PARK

54.2960, -0.4137 / North Bay, 28 Burniston Road, Scarborough, North Yorkshire, YO12 6PH / 01723 861431 / Swimming and paddling / *www.alpamare.co.uk*

Alpamare is one of the UK's largest water parks. Based in Scarborough, the alpine-themed water park boasts both indoor and outdoor sections, and is perfect for anyone seeking adventure, fun or relaxation. Alpamare features an outdoor garden pool, which is heated to 28 °C. The lido features built-in jacuzzis, bubble recliners and whirlpool baths. There is also an infinity pool, which is heated to 35 °C and rests alongside a bar and restaurant. The infinity pool is filled with healing iodine water known for its special therapeutic properties. With fantastic views of the North Sea, the outdoor pools at Alpamare are ideal for anyone seeking a bit of relaxation.

Access

Access to both the outdoor garden pool and infinity pool via steps; hoist available. Two and a half kilometres away from Scarborough railway station. Direct bus service to the water park from Scarborough park and ride on Seamer Road. On-site parking.

RIVER ESK, LEALHOLM. © *MIKE POLLARD*

MALLYAN SPOUT WATERFALL.
© *@ANTONIASLATERPHOTOGRAPHY*

LEALHOLM, RIVER ESK

54.4583, -0.8253 / Lealholm, North Yorkshire / Swimming and paddling

Twisting through the idyllic village of Lealholm, this section of the River Esk is the perfect place to swim on a sunny afternoon in the cool shade of the trees. The grassy common provides a soft bank for getting in and out of the water, as well as an excellent spot for a picnic. The section by the bridge is shallow and ideal for paddling, while the peaceful, deeper water upstream is more suited to swimming. Conveniently in the centre of the village, this spot is within easy reach of the Shepherds Hall Tearooms, the Board Inn and Stepping Stones Bakery.

Access
Access via grassy banks. Public transport within easy reach: 95 bus stops every half an hour at the Primary School stop, 200 metres away. Lealholm railway station within 300 metres. Parking on road opposite Lealholm village shop, less than 100 metres away.

MALLYAN SPOUT WATERFALL

54.3976, -0.7320 / Goathland, North Yorkshire / Swimming and paddling

Nestled among trees and ferns, Mallyan Spout is a waterfall beside the River Esk. Access to the river is a slight scramble over rocky banks, where you can enter the shallower section of water in full view of the spout, or move along the river to some of the deeper pools, remaining mindful of the boulders lining the riverbed. Surrounded by the calmness of the woods and bracken, this is the perfect place not only for water bathing, but also forest bathing. Mallyan Spout can be tied into a day walk to Thomason Foss, as well as a visit to picturesque Goathland, where you can also find refreshments at the Goathland Tearooms.

Access
Scramble over rocky banks. Easily accessible by public transport: 840 Coastliner Service stops hourly at the Mallyan Spout Hotel bus stop, 700 metres away. Car park in Goathland on Beck Hole Road, a kilometre and a half away.

THOMASON FOSS. © *SHUTTERSTOCK/MARK BULMER*

THOMASON FOSS

54.4082, -0.7282 / Goathland, North Yorkshire / Swimming, paddling and plunge pool

Hidden away on Eller Beck, Thomason Foss is an idyllic waterfall surrounded by trees and high-sided rock walls, strewn with vines and moss. The boulders littering the entrance to the plunge pool mean swimmers should watch their footing as they approach the water, but the tranquillity of this woodland waterfall makes it worth the scramble. With plenty of points to picnic, as well as walking routes to discover the outstanding beauty of the area around Beck Hole, Thomason Foss is a must for wild swimmers. You can find refreshments at the Birch Hall Inn in Beck Hole, or at the Goathland Tearooms a little further down the road. There are public toilets in Goathland.

Access
Rocky scramble, followed by shallow access from large boulders. Do not jump from rocky ledge. 840 Coastliner bus (Leeds–Whitby, several daily services) stops at Goathland; also stop on North Yorkshire Moors Railway, approximately a kilometre away. Easiest access via grassy, steep footpath across bridge from Birch Hall Inn; footpath can also be followed north from Goathland. Parking on Beck Hole Road near the pub.

FALLING FOSS

54.4190, -0.6329 / Littlebeck, North Yorkshire / Swimming, paddling and plunge pool

Sequestered among breathtaking Yorkshire woodland, Falling Foss is an enchanting waterfall and plunge pool. An excellent spot for swimming or paddling, the shingle beach leads into the water, though the shallows may be a little stony underfoot. You can further explore the magnificent forested gorge on the May Beck and Falling Foss walking route, and perfectly placed by the waterfall is the Falling Foss Tea Garden, which is open from April to September for well-deserved refreshments in a stunning setting.

Access
Easy access via shingle beach. Closest bus stop five kilometres away at Fylingthorpe Road End, for frequent services from Whitby and Middlesbrough. Parking available to side of Foss Lane, close to the start of the path. Path through the gorge is an easier route to waterfall; alternative a bit of a scramble.

CARLISLE

NEWCASTLE
UPON TYNE

49

DURHAM

MIDDLESBROUGH

45 46 47

56

55
54 53

51
50

52

43
42

37   41

33   36   40

34   39
35   38

28
27 29   32
16 26 22   30 31
15 18 21
14 17 20 25
19   24
13   23
12

KENDAL

11

10

LANCASTER

9

8

7
6
5
LIVERPOOL   MANCHESTER
2

3 4

1

44

48

122

Northern England

DERWENT WATER AND CAT BELLS. © SHUTTERSTOCK/PHILMACDPHOTO

MARBURY PARK SWIMMING CLUB OUTDOOR POOL. © *DAVID HUGHES*

NANTWICH SWIMMING POOL

53.0700, -2.5242 / Wall Lane, Nantwich, Cheshire, CW5 5LS / 01270 685590 / Swimming / *www.everybody.org.uk/locations/nantwich*

The heated Nantwich Swimming Pool is one of the last brine pools left in inland Britain. With its sunloungers and sun-drenched grassy area, this gives a holiday feel to its visitors. This popular site, open on weekdays from May to September, also hosts an indoor pool for colder weather as well as a separate teaching pool and indoor gym. Toilets are available in the attached leisure centre. Conveniently located near the centre of pretty town of Nantwich, a swim here can be followed by a visit to Barony Park. Snacks are available to buy on-site from a kiosk and picnics with non-alcoholic refreshments are welcome. Alternatively, Nantwich has no shortage of local restaurants and cafes.

Access

Access via ladders. Buses to Newcastle upon Tyne and Crewe stop regularly at the Frog & Ferret, less than a kilometre away. Nantwich railway station a kilometre away; direct services to Manchester and Cardiff. On-site parking.

LIVERPOOL WATER SPORTS CENTRE

53.3927, -2.9858 / 110 Mariners Wharf, Queens Dock, Liverpool, Merseyside, L3 4DG / 01517 089322 / Swimming / *www.liverpoolwa-tersports.org.uk*

The charity-run Liverpool Water Sports Centre is an outdoor swimming and water sports hub in the city's historic Queen's Dock. Open seven days a week between Easter and the end of September and five days throughout the winter, the centre aims to make water sports accessible for all. Open water swimming is available in organised sessions, and for those wanting to try something new they offer a range of activities, from powerboating and paddleboarding to obstacle courses and kayaking. Swimmers must wear a brightly coloured cap, and goggles are recommended. Ideal for those wanting to have a dip in the heart of a bustling city, a swim can be followed by a trip to Liverpool's Cavern Club, or one of the city's many pubs, cafes and restaurants. There is also an on-site coffee bar.

Access

Access via steps and jetty; a Wheelyboat can take wheelchair users on to water. 4 and 4A buses run regularly throughout Liverpool from Queen's Dock stop, 130 metres away; Liverpool Lime Street railway station just under three kilometres away. On-site parking.

PICK MERE. © SHUTTERSTOCK/SUE BARTON PHOTOGRAPHY

MARBURY PARK SWIMMING CLUB OUTDOOR POOL

53.2835, -2.5252 / Comberbach, Cheshire, CW9 6AT / 01606 77893 / Swimming and paddling / *www.marburyparkswimmingclub.co.uk*

Sheltered by the lush woodland of Marbury Country Park near Northwich, Marbury Park Swimming Club Outdoor Pool is one of Cheshire's most alluring outdoor pools. Ladders lead into the unheated pool, which has rested within Marbury Country Park since the 1930s. The lido features two diving boards as well as a children's paddling pool and numerous picnic tables around the grounds, and is also available for private hire while it is open from May until August. Nestled between numerous lakes and stunning lawned gardens, this is a great place to get into the water while enjoying the scenery of the expansive Northwich Woodlands. This popular lido fills up quickly, and although it does sell day tickets priority is given to membership holders. A small shop at the entrance can provide snacks and drinks for visitors while the Spinner & Bergamot pub is nearby.

Access
Access via ladders and diving boards. Bus to Warrington stops several times a day less than a kilometre away at Cogshall Lane; Northwich railway station three and a half kilometres away. On-site parking.

PICK MERE

53.2884, -2.4739 / Pickmere, Cheshire / Swimming and paddling

Once home to a popular fairground, Pick Mere lake is now best known as a hidden gem just north of Northwich. The lake is characterised by its crystal-clear water and beautiful seasonal wild flower blooms, although swimming shoes are recommended due to the silty lakebed and sudden drop in depth. Despite the signs which discourage swimming the popularity of this swim spot has endured, and swimmers can often be seen slipping into the lake from its jetty and grassy banks. The surrounding area is perfect for the prepared picnicker with grassy, flat banks surrounding the water. You can pick up a hot drink from the community-run Turton Pavilion, which is open on Sundays, and the Red Lion pub in Pickmere can provide more substantial meals.

Access
Access via jetty, pebbly beaches and grassy banks. Less than a kilometre away 89 bus to Knutsford stops several times a day; Northwich railway station four and a half kilometres away. Very limited on-site parking.

DOCK 9. © SHUTTERSTOCK/MOUNTAINTREKS

SALE WATER PARK

53.4315, -2.2997 / Rifle Road, Sale, Cheshire, M33 2LX / 01619 051100 / Swimming / *www.visitmanchester.com/things-to-see-and-do/sale-water-park-p144111*

Situated between the River Mersey and the M60, Sale Water Park was created after materials such as gravel were taken from the area for the construction of the motorway. The result is an expansive area of open water set within a 152-acre park, designed specifically for swimming and water sports. From April to September swimmers can enjoy the six open water swimming sessions that are run a week, while taking in the beauty of the surrounding Chorlton Ees Nature Reserve. For the adventurous there is no shortage of bookable activities, from jet-skiing to kayaking, and the site is equipped with toilets, changing rooms and wetsuit hire. Designed to be an oasis in a largely metropolitan area, Sale Water Park is a wonderful chance to swim in a unique body of water and explore riverside walks along the Mersey Valley. Food and drinks are available on-site from the Boathouse.

Access

Access via jetties and sloping beaches. Some riverside paths suitable for wheelchair users, but water itself not wheelchair accessible. Nearest bus stop a kilometre and a half away at the Tennis Club stop, regular 18 bus to Manchester Airport. Tram stop 800 metres away. On-site parking.

USWIM DOCK 9

53.4719, -2.2951 / Dock 9, Salford Quays, Greater Manchester, M50 3AZ / 07871 268289 / Swimming / *www.uswimopen-water.com/salford-quays*

Tucked away in the middle of Salford, Uswim Dock 9 is a unique swim spot and opportunity to swim in the clear, clean Salford Quays. Jetties, steps and ladders lead to the water, which is marked with lanes between 450 metres and a kilometre long. Open on Wednesday evenings and weekend mornings, and with arctic water training available in colder months, this is ideal for beginners wanting to learn all the skills needed for outdoor swimming as well as those wanting a quick dip without having to travel out of the city. Toilets and lifeguards are available. With MediaCityUK overlooking the water and central Manchester a short journey away, this is a great place to ignite a love of outdoor swimming without having to travel out of the city. There is a variety of choices for refreshments surrounding the water.

Access

Access via ladders, steps and jetties. Nearest bus stop twenty metres away, regular buses throughout Manchester; tram stop across the bridge at MediaCityUK. Paid parking in Waterside car park in Quayside MediaCityUK; free roadside parking less than a kilometre away on Ohio Avenue.

SALFORD WATER SPORTS CENTRE

53.4706, -2.2893 / 15 The Quays Road, Salford Quays, Greater Manchester, M50 3SQ / 01617 780109 / Swimming / *salfordwatersports.com*

Located in Ontario Basin in the centre of Salford, Salford Water Sports Centre is an ideal place to escape the bustle of the city. Open Monday, Tuesday and Thursday evenings as well as Sunday mornings, the centre offers swim sessions as well as open water swimming coaching, catering from beginners to seasoned swimmers. Lanes up to 500 metres are available; wetsuits are recommended and brightly coloured caps essential. Children must be over eight years old to attend a swimming session. The centre has lifeguards on hand, wetsuit rental, toilets and changing rooms. For those wanting an adventure, water sports from paddleboarding and sailing to windsurfing are on offer. With plentiful opportunities for refreshments on your doorstep, this is a great way to discover an unseen side of the city.

Access

Waterside platform and ladder. Accessible toilets and changing rooms available but no hoist. Nearest bus stop is Winnipeg Quay located immediately outside the centre, regular buses throughout Salford and Manchester. On-site parking.

BLACKPOOL WAKE PARK

53.8006, -2.9587 / Ream Hills Farm, Weeton, Lancashire, PR4 3NJ / 01253 836543 / Swimming and paddling / *www.blackpoolwakepark.co.uk*

Blackpool Wake Park is a ten-acre, spring-fed lake on the fringes of Blackpool. Specific areas are designated for swimmers and are supervised by lifeguards and coaches. Swimmers must swim with a partner or have a spotter, and wetsuits are compulsory. This is a popular spot for families with older children as the park has various other activities available, including paddleboarding, kayaking

and a challenging wakeboarding obstacle course. The park has toilets and changing rooms and the on-site cafe offers hot food and drinks. Nearby Blackpool provides a variety of refreshment choices, from pubs and cafes to takeaways. Blackpool Wake Park is not open to swimming sessions in 2021.

Access

Access via flat, grassy banks. Eagle and Child bus stop a kilometre and a half away in Weeton for regular services to Blackpool, or Clifton Road, four kilometres away, served by regular buses throughout Blackpool. On-site parking.

LAKE BURWAIN

53.8733, -2.1827 / Reedymoor Lane, Colne, Lancashire, BB8 7LJ / 07970 427520 / Swimming / *www.facebook.com/swimlakeburwain*

Sitting next to the village of Foulridge, Lake Burwain is a man-made lake created in the nineteenth century. A jetty provides access to the water, which is deep and fringed by trees. Within easy reach of nearby Foulridge and Colne, this is a great spot for those who would like a reliable outdoor swimming location or want to try it out for the first time under the watch of life-guards. Open water swimming on Lake Burwain is run by the Pendle Triathlon Club from May to September, with swim sessions on Thursdays evenings and Sunday mornings. Amenities offered to swimmers include showers and changing rooms. In colder weather the water temperature can be surprisingly low and care should be taken for those inexperienced with cold weather. Food and drink can be found in Foulridge at the Hare and Hounds Inn, or there is plenty of choice in Colne.

Access

Access via jetty. Buses to Burnley stop a kilometre away at Causeway stop in Foulridge approximately every half an hour; Colne railway station two and a half kilometres away. On-site parking.

FELL FOOT PARK. © *IAN WILDING*

CAPERNWRAY DIVING CENTRE

54.1372, -2.7231 / Jackdaw Quarry, Capernwray Road, Carnforth, Lancashire, LA6 1AD / 01524 735132 / Swimming and paddling / *www.dive-site.co.uk*

Resting in the open fields on the edge of Carnforth, Capernwray Diving Centre boasts the second cleanest recreational bathing water in the UK. A jetty and concrete slipways provide access to the crystal-clear water, which has several underwater attractions to spot. Open throughout the year with both swimming and diving facilities available, Capernwray prides itself on being able to provide an exciting and unique experience, with carefully curated underwater caves and an abundance of friendly fish. The site offers toilets and changing rooms. For a full day out, a swim here can be combined with a trip to nearby Leighton Hall. An on-site restaurant can provide food for hungry guests, and the Canal Turn pub in Carnforth offers refreshments.

Access

Jetty and concrete slipways. Regular buses to Lancaster a kilometre and a half away at Capernwray Church; Carnforth railway station four kilometres away. On-site parking.

FELL FOOT PARK

54.2746, -2.9536 / Newby Bridge, Windermere, Cumbria, LA12 8N / 01539 531273 / Swimming and paddling / *www.nationaltrust.org.uk/fell-foot*

Located on the southernmost tip of Windermere as the water meets the River Leven, Fell Foot Park is a great spot to enjoy swimming amidst stunning views. Owned by the National Trust and open every day from 10 a.m. to 5 p.m. (reduced hours in winter), Fell Foot Park offers easy access via a ramp into water just out of reach of boaters. The park's Active Base offers heated flooring, changing rooms, toilets and hot showers. Playgrounds and open green spaces dot the surrounding area, making it perfect for keeping younger family members entertained. For a full day out, the Windermere Ferry can be caught just under four kilometres away at Lakeside, and Wray Castle is seventeen kilometres away. The nearby Boathouse Cafe is a great spot for grabbing a bite to eat while enjoying the views of the lake.

Access

Access via ramp. Accessible toilets and pathway available. 6 bus to Windermere stops a few times a day at Gummers How Turn stop, 150 metres away. On-site parking – entry tickets are inclusive of parking.

ULPHA BRIDGE

54.3264, -3.2369 / Ulpha or Duddon Bridge, Cumbria / Swimming and paddling

In a small hamlet tucked away in the Cumbrian countryside, Ulpha Bridge is the middle of a popular stretch of the River Duddon. The spot is known for its clear, cold water, grassy riverside and bridge. Home to the historic ruins of the Duddon Iron Furnace just across the river, Ulpha Bridge is a spot which allows you to immerse yourself in the past. A popular place for visitors from the local area, in the summer months this stretch of the River Duddon becomes a hub for new and experienced swimmers alike. The Old Kings Head in nearby Broughton in Furness provides opportunity to enjoy a good meal and refreshing drink.

Access

Water easily accessible via grassy banks. Not easily accessible by public transport: Green Road railway station eleven kilometres away, with connections to Carlisle. Roadside parking available on both sides of the bridge.

DEVOKE WATER

54.3612, -3.2909 / Eskdale, Cumbria / Swimming and paddling

The Lake District's largest tarn, Devoke Water provides swimmers with the chance to swim in rougher waters. Over a kilometre in length, the size of the tarn means it can experience more extreme weather and choppier waters than others in the area; swimmers should keep this in mind, especially when temperatures begin to drop in the winter months. However, this bucolic location can provide a serene backdrop to a beautiful sunset, and a remote challenge for experienced swimmers. The ruin of an old boathouse sitting at the water's shore is not only a popular spot for photographers, but an accessible place to enter the water from. A circuit around the picturesque lake can

be enjoyed after your swim, and the Boot Inn can offer a bite to eat to round off your day.

Access

Access via shallow, rocky banks. Tourist steam train connects to Ravenglass from the Eskdale Green station, six kilometres away. Parking at Devoke Water parking, just over a kilometre from the water.

GILL FORCE

54.3900, -3.2663 / Boot, Cumbria / Swimming, paddling and plunge pool

Gill Force is a small, picturesque gorge on the River Esk. Characterised by its emerald water, this stunning little spot is a wonderful place for swimmers who want to enjoy endless rolling countryside. The shade of the surrounding mossy trees leads to an oasis of rocks circling the pool. Water levels can be changeable, however, so make sure to check local weather before your trip. With plenty of space for a picnic, this spot is ideal for a bit of tranquillity. A trip here can be combined with a stop to see Stanley Ghyll Force, an impressive and much-photographed waterfall. Refreshments can be found in the Boot Inn.

Access

Access via mossy, rocky platforms; rocks can become slippery when wet. Tourist steam train stops a kilometre away on its way through local stops. Bus service runs through Boot but must be pre-booked. Limited roadside parking near Hardknott Roman fort, and further down road on Wrynose Pass.

BURNMOOR TARN. © *SHUTTERSTOCK/ELAINE251*

BURNMOOR TARN

54.4253, -3.2638 / Boot, Cumbria / Swimming and paddling

In the shadow of Scafell Pike and Illgill Head, Burnmoor Tarn is a beautiful, entirely natural tarn located high up in the Lake District. Although this is not the easiest spot to get to, it is a journey worth making for swimmers after calm waters and astonishing views. Grassy banks and rocks dot the entrance to the water, and the gentle surrounding area is more than suitable for relaxing with a packed lunch after your swim. In this isolated part of the Lake District, it may feel as if you are the only person in the world. Wasdale Head provides opportunity for refreshments at the Wasdale Head Inn, or alternatively the Boot Inn in Boot is a good stop for food and drink.

Access

Access via grassy banks. Difficult to access, with challenging navigation, often wet underfoot; an uphill walk of three kilometres from Boot, or a five-kilometre walk from Wasdale Head. Not easily accessible by public transport: tourist steam train connects to Ravenglass from the Eskdale Green station, seven kilometres away. Parking four kilometres away at Wasdale Head car park.

OVERBECK BRIDGE

54.4493, -3.2846 / Wasdale Head, Cumbria / Swimming and paddling

As Over Beck flows into the expansive Wast Water, Overbeck Bridge provides a stunning place for a dip. Although there are several entrances to the lake, Overbeck Bridge is favoured due to its gently sloping beach, leading to water which is known for its quartz-rich, gravelly lakebed and cold, crystal-clear depths. As you swim out into England's deepest lake, with views of Hollow Stones and Scafell Pike before you, it is easy to see why Wast Water is known as one of the Lake District's most iconic scenes. A swim here can be combined with a challenging walk around the lake, where you can take in the stark, awe-inspiring views of the surrounding valley. The nearest village is Nether Wasdale which offers refreshments at the Screes Inn and Strands Inn, which have their own microbrewery.

Access

Gentle, sloping and sometimes rocky beaches lead to water. Not easily accessible by public transport: nearest bus twenty kilometres away in Elterwater, which runs to Kendal and Ambleside a few times a day; Seascale railway station sixteen kilometres away. Small car park on-site; Wasdale Head car park just under two kilometres away.

BIRKS BRIDGE, RIVER DUDDON. © @alwaysswimmingwild

BIRKS BRIDGE, RIVER DUDDON

54.3838, -3.1806 / Seathwaite, Cumbria / Swimming and plunge pool

Birks Bridge is a beautiful, shaded patch of stream running under an eighteenth-century stone packhorse bridge. The surrounding rocks create a steep path to the water, which is crystal-clear but may become swollen after rainfall. With a waterfall upstream and smooth rocks under the bridge, worn away by years of erosion, this spot is a relatively unknown piece of natural beauty and history. A swim here through the deep water allows you to enjoy one of the Lake District's magnificent and relatively untouched scenes. For those wanting to explore the local area further, the Old Man of Coniston sits nearby and presents a challenging but rewarding walk. Alternatively, the second-century Hardknott Roman fort is located three kilometres away. The Newfield Inn in Seathwaite can provide refreshments.

Access
Steep, rocky banks. Not easily accessible by public transport. Limited roadside parking 100 metres from swim spot.

TONGUE POT

54.4236, -3.1908 / Boot, Cumbria / Swimming and paddling

Regarded as one of the most beautiful swimming spots in Britain, Tongue Pot is a clear pool lined with sheer rock faces, steep grassy banks and an enchanting waterfall. In the heart of the Lake District, the spot is characterised by its emerald water, which swimmers often jump into, and is overlooked by Hard Knott. Set beneath a packhorse bridge, a swim here is well worth the considerable walk to reach it, and with the ruins of Hardknott Roman fort nearby, this spot has the feel of being cut off from the rest of the world. Finding refreshments requires a walk of seven kilometres to the Boot Inn.

Access
Access via pebbled beach or jumping from surrounding rocks. Four-kilometre walk from foot of Hardknott Pass. Tourist steam train passes through Boot (seven kilometres away), connecting to Ravenglass. Bus from Kendal to Ambleside stops in Elterwater several times a day, ten kilometres away. Limited roadside parking near Hardknott Roman fort, and further down road about four kilometres away.

CONISTON WATER

54.3719, -3.0544 / Coniston, Cumbria / Swimming and paddling

In the shadow of the Old Man of Coniston, Coniston Water is an impressive and popular spot for a swim. At the head of the lake, Monk Coniston car park provides both public toilets and a calmer place to enter the water, via a narrow stone beach away from areas of higher boating traffic. The calm and tranquil water grows deeper quite quickly. Stretching for over five miles, Coniston Water provides breathtaking views no matter the time of year, with hoards of wild garlic in spring and falling leaves in autumn. For those wanting to join in with other water-based activities, Coniston Boating Centre on the lake's edge allows day hire for their motorboats, kayaks and paddleboards. Food and drink can be found at the Coniston Inn, 800 metres away.

Access
Pebbled beach. Bus to Kendal and Ambleside stop several times a day at Crown Inn, just under two kilometres away. Paid on-site parking.

HOLME FELL LAKE

54.4010, -3.0547 / Coniston, Cumbria / Swimming

A former reservoir, Holme Fell Lake is tucked away three kilometres south of Little

Langdale. Accessible by a walk of a kilometre from Hodge Close Quarry, this little lake's scenic views are a great reward for visitors. Grassy banks and rocks slope into the water, which is lined with lush trees. With relatively shallow waters which warm up in the summer, this is a great spot for families, and feels like one of the Lake District's hidden gems. After your swim you can summit Holme Fell, with its beautiful, far-reaching views down to Coniston. The High Park Tea Garden in Little Langdale can provide snacks and drinks.

Access
Access via grassy banks. Four and a half kilometres away, bus from Kendal to Ambleside stops several times a day at Holly How Youth Hostel. Parking just over one kilometre away near Low Tilberthwaite.

SLATER'S BRIDGE POOL

54.4188, -3.0623 / Little Langdale, Cumbria / Swimming and paddling

Situated just upstream of an ancient pedestrian bridge, Slater's Bridge Pool is a pool on the River Brathay. This clear, deep pool is perfect for a refreshing dip, with verdant green grass surrounding the area ideal for picnics. The water towards the bridge becomes gradually shallower and is a perfect paddling depth for younger children. Public toilets are three kilometres

CONISTON WATER. © SHUTTERSTOCK/CATSTYECAM

away in Elterwater. This is a great place to relax after a walk, and can be combined with treks up Lingmoor Fell. Refreshments can be found in the High Park Tea Garden in Little Langdale, before continuing your exploration of this beautiful area.

Access
Access via grassy banks. Regular buses to Ambleside and Kendal stop at Britannia Inn in Elterwater during the week, four and a half kilometres away. Parking three kilometres away at Blea Tarn car park.

BLEA TARN

54.4292, -3.0908 / Elterwater, Cumbria / Swimming and paddling

At the head of the Langdale Valley, Blea Tarn rests in the shadows of the Langdale Pikes. The water is accessed by a pebbly beach, and the tall trees and dramatic scenery make this spot loved by

photographers and swimmers alike. Blea Tarn is a designated Site of Specific Scientific Interest, and the water is so still you almost won't want to disturb the picturesque reflections of the surrounding scenery. This smaller tarn can be reached on a well-surfaced, compacted stone path so is more accessible, and more popular, than many wild swim spots. There is plenty of space to stretch out with a picnic after your swim, but the Britannia Inn in Elterwater can also provide refreshments.

Access
Access via pebbly beach. Three-kilometre walk through Langdale Valley from Little Langdale. Regular buses to Ambleside and Kendal stop at Britannia Inn in Elterwater, four and a half kilometres away. Car park just 100 metres away.

MILLERGROUND, WINDERMERE

54.3805, -2.9222 / Windermere, Cumbria / Swimming

Millerground is a popular swimming spot on Windermere. The water here (particularly between the two jetties) is quite shallow, but grows significantly deeper towards the end of the jetties, where you can sometimes see swimmers jumping into the water. Millerground and neighbouring Rayrigg Meadow are popular locations for

families and can get quite busy during the weekend, especially on warm days. There are few facilities on-site, however a short distance away Rayrigg Meadow provides accessible toilets, a play area and a wheelchair-accessible path to the lake. A swim here can be combined with a trip to Hill Top, formerly Beatrix Potter's house and now a museum dedicated to the beloved author. The nearby town of Windermere has plenty of choice for refreshments.

Access
Entry via pebbly beach. Wheelchair-accessible path to the shore a few hundred metres away at Rayrigg Meadow. Rayrigg Meadow bus stop 300 metres away, served four times a day by bus to Penrith; Windermere railway station just over a kilometre away. Paid parking available at Rayrigg Meadow car park, 300 metres away.

WRAY CASTLE, WINDERMERE

54.3990, -2.9623 / Ambleside, Cumbria / Swimming and paddling

Situated on the picturesque shores below Wray Castle, this spot is renowned for its stunning views across Windermere and the surrounding mountains. A pebbly beach slopes gently into the moss-green water, which with its surrounding heather offers

MILLERGROUND, WINDERMERE. © *KEVIN STAFFORD*

awe-inspiring views. There are spacious, grassy banks ideal for picnicking on, making this a great place for a family day out and perfect for anyone looking for a swim in a beautiful location. Once you've dipped your toes in the water, a visit to nineteenth-century Wray Castle can complete your day out. Hot drinks and baked snacks can be found at Wray Castle's pop-up cafe, which also has toilets, or alternatively the Outgate Inn is four kilometres away.

Access
Shingle beach. Access to the shore via a path leading down from the castle. Wray Castle Road End bus stop, two kilometres away, served approximately every hour by the 505 between Kendal and Coniston. Paid parking on-site in National Trust Wray Castle car park.

SPRINKLING TARN. © *ANYWHEREWEROAM.COM*

LOUGHRIGG TARN

54.4295, -3.0096 / Skelwith Bridge, Cumbria /
Swimming and paddling

Loughrigg Tarn is a small tarn just north of the popular Windermere. Gently sloping grassy banks lead to the water, which is relatively warm, and although this spot can get quite busy it has a feeling of seclusion. This natural lake is surrounding by views of the Langdale Pikes, with open, grassy spaces by the water perfect for picnics. On a sunny day, it will feel as if you have stepped straight into a postcard. A trip here can be followed by a visit to Ambleside Roman fort, believed to have been built under Hadrian's rule. Nearby Ambleside provides plenty of opportunities for refreshment, from cafes to pubs and takeaways.

Access
Easy access via grassy banks. Bus to Dungeon Ghyll stops just over a kilometre away at Foulstep Crossroads several times a day. Roadside parking a kilometre away on B5343, just outside the Skelwith Bridge Hotel.

SPRINKLING TARN

54.4709, -3.1943 / Wasdale Head, Cumbria /
Swimming and paddling

Overlooked by Scafell Pike, Sprinkling Tarn sits high up in this popular area of the Lake District. Surrounded by grassy slopes, this spot is often frequented by walkers due to its astonishing views and remote location. Accessing the tarn requires a walk across rugged and mountainous routes, but it is worth the trek: it would be difficult not to find the view of the mountains awe-inspiring. With deep, cold water and a large island sitting on the north side, this is a great place to cool off for those returning from climbing Scafell Pike or other surrounding summits. Refreshments can be found at the Wasdale Head Inn.

Access
Easy access to water with flat, grassy banks. Only accessible by strenuous, five-kilometre hike from Wasdale Head or Seathwaite. Difficult to reach via public transport: regular buses to Keswick run from Seatoller National Trust car park, seven kilometres away. Parking just under five kilometres away at Wasdale Head car park.

BLACKMOSS POT. © *MICHAEL GRAHAM*

BLACKMOSS POT

54.4918, -3.1329 / Stonethwaite, Cumbria /
Swimming and plunge pool

Encircled by sheer rock faces, this popular pool is a must visit for those wanting to enjoy outstanding views and crisp, cold water. There are shallows from which the water can be entered downstream, but it is possible to jump in from the high rocks. The deepest parts of the water stretch for about fifty metres downstream, and there are many other swimmable pools further up Langstrath Beck. Swimmers should be aware of the upstream current under the falls, which can be dangerous. For those wanting to relax in the surrounding area, open, grassy fields and flat rocks make for a great spot to sit and picnic after swimming. Located below Sergeant's Crag in the heart of the Lake District, a visit here can form part of a hike from Stonethwaite, where visitors can park and grab a meal at the Langstrath Country Inn.

Access
Access via jumping from tall rocks, or entering shallows downstream. On foot, Blackmoss Pot around two and a half kilometres from Stonethwaite. Regular bus to Keswick runs from Seatoller National Trust car park, seven kilometres away, where there is also parking.

GALLENY FORCE

54.5080, -3.1247 / Stonethwaite, Cumbria /
Swimming, paddling and plunge pool

The Galleny Force waterfall, based near the centre of the Lake District, comprises of two sets of pools with a waterfall at the head. Grassy banks and sometimes steep rocks allow you to climb into the water. Also known as the Fairy Glen, this spot, easily reached on foot, offers a shaded swim. With more popular swimming spots based around the top of the river near Borrowdale, the pools further down are sometimes quieter. If you're wanting to extend your swim, the equally popular Blackmoss Pot is two kilometres south. The Langstrath Country Inn can provide some well-deserved refreshments, or alternatively the Flock-In Tearoom lies in Rosthwaite.

Access
Grassy banks and sloping, sometimes steep, rocks. Frequent buses to Keswick stop two kilometres away at Longthwaite road end. Paid parking three kilometres away off B5289 by the Scafell Hotel.

RYDAL BOWER. © *SUE STAFFORD*

EASEDALE TARN

54.4692, -3.0659 / Grasmere, Cumbria / Swimming

With dramatic views and bracingly cold water, Easedale Tarn is one of the Lake District's best-loved wild swim spots. Grassy banks lead to the gentle water, which deepens quickly but grows shallow enough near the centre for you to stand on a small rock. The grassy banks are ideal for picnics, or for reclining after a swim or a walk in one of the nearby trails. Easedale Tarn has something to delight everyone, and in the clear water it is easy to feel connected to the stunning nature around you. The track towards Easedale Tarn from Grasmere passes by numerous pools, and your day can be rounded off with some of the town's unique gingerbread, from the Grasmere Gingerbread Shop. For more substantial refreshments, head to the Jumble Room or the Inn at Grasmere.

Access
Access via sloping, grassy banks and rocks. From Grasmere Youth Hostel, follow signs to Easedale Tarn up rocky and sometimes uneven path. Regular buses to Kendal and Bowness-on-Windermere stop just over three kilometres away in Grasmere. Paid parking three and a half kilometres away in Grasmere, at Red Bank car park.

RYDAL BOWER

54.4597, -2.9784 / Rydal, Cumbria / Swimming and plunge pool

Hidden deep in the woods, Rydal Bower is a patch of the River Rothay with a waterfall which looks as though it has stepped straight out of a fairy tale. Grassy banks slope to the deep water, which is hidden in a cleft between rock walls and has a mystical feel to it. Often overlooked by tourists for more popular spots such as Buckstones Jum, visitors may find themselves having this little hidden gem all to themselves. Encircled by rowan trees, this spot is perfect for a secluded dip in the crisp Lake District water. After your swim you can stop in at Rydal Cave, an impressive cavern formed as a result of slate quarrying. Refreshments can be found at the Glen Rothay Hotel and Badger Bar.

Access
Access via grassy banks and rock walls. On foot, access from a trail (sometimes rough) signposted from the road. Regular buses to Grasmere and Kendal stop two kilometres away at Church for Rydal Mount. Pelter Bridge car park two kilometres away, or White Moss car park three kilometres away.

BUCKSTONES JUM

54.4610, -2.9788 / Rydal, Cumbria / Swimming, paddling and plunge pool

On Rydal Beck, Buckstones Jum is a plunge pool fringed by a pebbled beach. The stone slabs lining the water and waterfall make this a picturesque spot for a dip, and a great place for families with older children to enjoy. The deep pool will be bracingly cold on a cool day, but with the sun shining and blue skies above you it will be difficult not to be in awe of the Lake District's beauty. A trip here can be integrated with a visit to Rydal Mount, the former home of William Wordsworth. Rydal offers a choice of places to eat and drink, including the Glen Rothay Hotel and Badger Bar.

EASEDALE TARN. © *SHUTTERSTOCK/GEORGE GREEN*

Access

Pebble beach. Follow steep, muddy paths up beck from Rydal Hall. Regular buses to Grasmere and Kendal stop two kilometres away at Church for Rydal Mount. Pelter Bridge car park two kilometres away, or White Moss car park three kilometres away.

BROTHERS WATER

54.5052, -2.9271 / Hartsop, Cumbria / Swimming and paddling

Nestled at the bottom of the Dovedale and Hartsop valleys, Brothers Water is a small lake loved by swimmers for the incredible views it offers of the surrounding areas. A shingle beach allows you to enter the water with ease. The clear, still water is shallow and fairly cold, with water tumbling down straight from the fells. Underfoot the lakebed is rocky, with weedy patches. Designated as a Site of Specific Scientific Interest, the lake hosts a variety of bird species as well as an endangered freshwater fish, the schelly – swimmers should swim here in autumn or winter, rather than nesting season, and avoid the southern shore. For those looking for a bite to eat, the Brotherswater Inn is located a kilometre and a half from the water's edge.

Access

Shingle beach and grassy patches lead to water. Bus to Windermere stops at Hartsop

Hall campsite a few times a day. Parking at Cow Bridge car park, a kilometre away.

LOWESWATER

54.5795, -3.3563 / Loweswater, Cumbria / Swimming and paddling

In the north-western corner of the Lake District, Loweswater is a secluded and quiet lake. A small beach leads into the water, and the gravelly lakebed deepens gradually. Swimmers should watch out for blue-green algae blooms, particularly in the summer months, but these are becoming increasingly infrequent. Holme Wood shrouds the lake's edge, offering an enchanting view as you move through the cool water. You are unlikely to encounter many other swimmers here; this tranquil spot captures why the Lake District has inspired its visitors for generations. Following Holme Beck upstream, visitors can find the Holme Force, a hidden waterfall tucked away among the woodland. Food and drink can be found a kilometre and a half away at the Kirkstile Inn.

Access

Pebbled beaches lead to water. 77/77A bus runs from Keswick to Brackenthwaite from Easter to October. Loweswater car park less than a kilometre from the lake.

BUTTERMERE. © SHUTTERSTOCK/STEPHEN BRIDGER

CRUMMOCK WATER

54.5462, -3.2889 / Buttermere, Cumbria / Swimming and paddling

One of the Lake District's lesser-visited lakes, Crummock Water is for swimmers who prefer to avoid the crowds. This beautiful, calm expanse of water is nestled between Grasmoor and Mellbreak and has multiple shingle beaches for swimmers to easily enter the water. Crummock Water shares the dramatic views of neighbouring Buttermere, yet a fraction of the visitors, meaning you may have chance to enjoy a peaceful swim in the cool water. The surrounding grassy areas provide spaces for scenic picnics, and although there are no facilities nearby, a kilometre away at Buttermere there are paid public toilets and the Syke Farm Tearoom.

Access
Access via shingle beach. Buses to Keswick and Lorton

stop several times a day in Buttermere, a kilometre from water's edge. Parking available 600 metres away in Buttermere on B5289.

BUTTERMERE

54.5260, -3.2533 / Buttermere, Cumbria / Swimming and paddling

In the western Lake District, Buttermere is a small lake owned by the National Trust. Much-loved by swimmers and walkers alike for its scenic views and relatively flat trails, Buttermere is fed from streams running down from the surrounding fells, meaning it is cool all year round despite its relative shallowness (maximum depth of twenty-eight metres). Grassy banks lead to the water, which is rocky underfoot – water shoes are recommended. As you swim further out High Stile rests beside the lake, and although the resulting view is magnificent, it also attracts lots of visitors – entering the lake at Horse Close will prove a more secluded spot. A popular photo opportunity is the famous Lone Tree on Buttermere's edge, often photographed at sunset, which forms a striking silhouette against the surrounding landscape. The nearby village of Buttermere has public toilets, and refreshments can be found at the Croft House Farm Cafe and the village pub.

Access
Access via grassy banks – rocky underfoot, water shoes recommended. Court Hotel stop in Buttermere served by 77/77A buses to Keswick (Easter to October). Paid parking two kilometres away at Gatesgarth Farm car park.

DERWENT WATER

54.5954, -3.1416 / Keswick, Cumbria / Swimming and paddling

With the tourist hotspot of Keswick resting just beside it, Derwent Water is a bustling lake with heaps of charm. The clear, gentle water is accessible by a sloping, shingle beach, and as you swim out you encounter stunning views of Cat Bells, Maiden Moor and Skiddaw. Several piers along the shoreline are favoured by swimmers, although you should watch out for boats making their way across the water. Derwent Isle lies 150 metres from the shore, and swimming around the island makes for a delightful dip. There are public toilets in the Lakeside car park. For a full day out, motor and rowing boats can be hired, and Keswick hosts the Puzzling Place optical illusion attraction as well as plenty of choice for refreshments.

Access
Sloping, shingle beach. Regular buses to Kendal, Penrith and Windermere from

DERWENT WATER. © *REBECCA WALES*

Greta Bank stop, a kilometre away. Paid parking 300 metres away.

BASSENTHWAITE

54.6620, -3.2135 / Bassenthwaite, Cumbria / Swimming and paddling

Located in the north Lake District, Scarness Bay on Bassenthwaite Lake has the feel of a secret spot despite the bustling holiday park nearby. With warmer and shallower waters than other lakes, Scarness Bay is a favourite for swimmers. A small pier and stony shore provide easy access to the water, which is soft underfoot with a few boulders. The meadow and, in spring, wild garlic that fringe the water gives this a mystical feel. A trip here can be incorporated into a visit to Mirehouse & Gardens, a manor house which features a manuscript collection from the many writers inspired by the area. The Sun Inn in Bassenthwaite offers refreshments along with picturesque views of the surrounding landscape.

Access

Stony beach and pier leading to water. Buses to Keswick and Penrith stop a few times a day along A591. Small lay-by on approach to Bassenthwaite Lakeside Lodges.

SHAP SWIMMING POOL

54.5286, -2.6736 / Gayle Avenue, Shap, Cumbria, CA10 3NS / 07512 466172 / Swimming and paddling / www.shapswimming-pool.co.uk

Shap Swimming Pool is the UK's highest open air heated swimming pool (275 metres above sea level). The volunteer-run facility, which is heated to 26 °C, boasts a kids' pool, picnic tables and a small shop to provide visitors with refreshments, making it an ideal place for a family day out. The pool is accessed via steps and ladders, and opens daily between May and September, offering adult-only, children's and general swim sessions, all lifeguard supervised. Located in the centre of the Shap village, the pool is surrounded by the beautiful Memorial Park for those wanting to relax after their swim. For visitors wanting to add in some sightseeing, the National Trust site of Keld Chapel sits just over two kilometres away. The Kings Arms in Shap can provide a bite to eat.

Access

Access via steps and ladders. Accessible toilets and changing facilities; pool area wheelchair accessible, but no hoist. Bus services to Kendal stop on Tuesdays and Thursdays at Greyhound Hotel, less than a kilometre away. On-site parking.

KAILPOT CRAG

54.5762, -2.8732 / Pooley Bridge, Cumbria / Swimming

Kailpot Crag is nestled among the forested banks of Ullswater in the Lake District. A high crag offers the chance to jump into the deep, clear water, but there is also a shingle beach. With ancient, gnarled trees framing the approach to the water, this is an atmospheric place for a picnic after your swim, and you can watch boats glide gently past on their way to the Howtown Pier landing. Kailpot Crag inspires a childlike joy, and as you watch the sunset from the west-facing swim spot it showcases the beauty of the Lake District. Refreshments can be found in Pooley Bridge, at the Pooley Bridge Inn.

Access
Water accessed by steep, rocky descent or precision cliffside jump. Bus to Penrith stops several times a day nine kilometres away at Bus Shelter stop. Limited lay-by parking five kilometres away on road approaching Ullswater Yacht Club – alternatively, park in Pooley Bridge and catch ferry across Ullswater to Howtown Pier landing, two kilometres from swim spot.

ASKHAM OUTDOOR SWIMMING POOL

54.6063, -2.7548 / Askham, Cumbria, CA10 2PF / 01931 712999 / Swimming and paddling / www.askhamandhelton.co.uk/swimming-pool-2

Askham Outdoor Swimming Pool is a heated, twenty-metre pool nestled in the picturesque Cumbrian village of Askham. Surrounded by a versatile green space, the lido comes equipped with on-site showers, a children's paddling pool and toilets as well as a kiosk for purchasing a variety of refreshments. Open from May to October, this volunteer-run pool is an ideal family day out. Qualified lifeguards are on duty and barbecue hire is available for those

wanting to make the most of sunny days. For a full day out, the spectacular Lowther Castle & Gardens are two kilometres away, and the pool is based just next door to the Queen's Head pub.

Access
Access via ladders. Accessible toilets available in neighbouring village hall. Fellrunner 111 travels between local areas, including Penrith, with nearest stop located 100 metres away outside Askham Stores; driven by volunteers and runs infrequently throughout the week. Penrith North Lakes railway station eight kilometres away. On-site parking.

GREYSTOKE POOL

54.6692, -2.8668 / Church Road, Greystoke, Cumbria, CA11 0TW / Swimming and paddling / www.greystokepool.org.uk

On the edge of the Lake District National Park, Greystoke Pool lies in the heart of the village it is named for. The volunteer-run lido has ladders into the water, which is heated to 27 °C. With lifeguards, slides, a toddler pool, toilets, changing rooms and showers, this space is perfect for spending a day relaxing poolside, or enjoying the adjoining playing field and park. Open from May to September, the lido offers adult-only (members only) as well as general swimming sessions. The towering Greystoke Castle, which dates back to the twelfth century, stands just 800 metres from the pool and is a popular spot for those visiting the village. An on-site cafe, which was extensively furnished along with the changing rooms in 2020, can provide visitors with hot drinks and snacks or alternatively the Boot and Shoe Inn lies under 200 metres away.

Access
Pool accessible by ladder. Difficult to reach via public transport: community Fellrunner bus runs once a week. Penrith North Lakes railway station eight kilometres away. On-site parking in clearly signposted car park.

GREYSTOKE POOL. © GREYSTOKE POOL

HUNSONBY SWIMMING POOL

54.7122, -2.6517 / Hunsonby, Cumbria, CA10 1PN / 01768 881381 / Swimming / *www.facebook.com/ Hunsonby-Swimming-Club*

Based in the small village of Hunsonby, the volunteer-run Hunsonby Swimming Pool is a popular spot for the local community. Nestled between the Lake District and the North Pennines, this is a rewarding and quieter alternative to other pools in the area. As well as toilets, changing rooms and a children's paddling pool, the heated lido features a small cafe to provide a variety of hot and cold snacks. Open from May to September, the pool has a relaxed feel and is a great place to unwind. A trip here can be combined with a visit to the Long Meg and her Daughters stone circle, the largest stone circle in Cumbria. The Shepherds Inn in Langwathby can provide drinks and hearty meals. Hunsonby Swimming Pool is not open to swimming sessions in 2021.

Access
Access via ladders. Not easily accessible by public transport: bus to Penrith runs once a day on Tuesdays. Langwathby railway station three kilometres away. On-site parking.

LAZONBY SWIMMING POOL

54.7525, -2.6976 / Lazonby, Penrith, Cumbria, CA10 1BL / 01768 898346 / Swimming and paddling / *www.lazonbypool.co.uk*

Lying next to the River Eden, the volunteer-run Lazonby Swimming Pool rests on the edge of the rural Cumbrian village of Lazonby. Heated to a toasty 26 °C, the seventeen-metre pool has a team of fully qualified lifeguards as well as a playground, picnic area, showers and an adjoining campsite. Families are more than welcome, with both a toddler pool and an abundance of pool toys and floats available. Events run while the lido is open from May to September, and can provide the opportunity for visitors to learn a new water-based skill such as kayaking or water polo. Just under two kilometres from the pool, the ruins of Kirkoswald Castle rests in Cumbria's lovely local landscape. Snacks are available to buy from the on-site kiosk, or the nearby Midland Hotel can provide refreshments.

Access
Ladders lead into water. Lazonby and Kirkoswald railway station 600 metres away. 134 bus stops once a day on Wednesdays at the Church stop. On-site parking.

EGGLESTONE ABBEY BRIDGE. © *NATALIJA VEREBA*

EGGLESTONE ABBEY BRIDGE

54.5296, -1.8994 / Barnard Castle, County Durham / Swimming and paddling

Situated near the elegant ruins of Egglestone Abbey, Egglestone Abbey Bridge crosses the tree-lined River Tees. The banks are formed of stone blocks, serving as perfect platforms for jumping or sliding into the river, with points downstream better suited for the scramble out. While the mild current directly beneath the bridge makes it unsuitable for children or weaker swimmers, there are shallower areas for paddling further upstream. During sunny spells, the water is warm despite the shelter of the bridge and lush greenery of the trees. Nearby Barnard Castle offers a variety of choices for refreshments, from cafes and tearooms to pubs and takeaways.

Access

Access via stone platforms. Can be accessed by following the signed Teesdale Way footpath, followed by a scramble. Bus service from Barnard Castle stops approximately five times a day, less than 100 metres away. Free parking at Egglestone Abbey, half a kilometre up the road.

NORTH EAST WAKE PARK

54.5777, -1.4358 / Bishopton Lake, Bishopton, Stockton, Cleveland, County Durham, TS21 1EY / 07492 693602 / Swimming and paddling / *www.northeastwakepark.co.uk*

Surrounded by rolling countryside, the lake at North East Wake Park is available for open water swimming training during specific sessions. Open throughout the week in the summer season, the park provides facilities such as toilets, showers, changing rooms and lifeguards. Swimmers are encouraged to come in pairs or be prepared with a tow float, wetsuit and swim cap if swimming solo. North East Wake Park is also home to wakeboarding facilities and an adventure-packed aqua park, and a day of water sport fun here can be followed up with a meal at the Blue Bell Inn, just along the road in Bishopton.

Access

Pebbly beach leading to water. Not easily accessible by public transport: 952 service from Trimdon Colliery stops at Messines Lane once a day, five kilometres away. On-site car park, located besides Surf Store.

PRESTON PARK

54.5340, -1.3364 / Yarm Road, Eaglescliffe, Stockton-on-Tees, County Durham, TS18 3RH / 01642 527375 / Swimming and paddling / *prestonparkmuseum.co.uk*

Winding through Eaglescliffe, Middlesbrough and Stockton-on-Tees, the River Tees is surrounded by a diverse mixture of urban and natural landscapes which meet in harmony at Preston Park. With a slipway and pontoon, accessing the deep water of the river is easy and the perfect way to escape the bustle of town without needing to venture far. Open throughout the week from 6 a.m. to 9 p.m. in summer, and 7 a.m. to 5 p.m. in winter, the Park is also home to a museum, cafe and gardens. Combining a trip here with the nearby Bowesfield Nature Reserve makes this swim spot an excellent destination for a complete day out.

Access

Access via slipway and pontoon. Bus services from Stockton regularly stop less than a kilometre away; railway services run to Eaglescliffe railway station, just over a kilometre away. On-site car park.

WILKINSON LAKE

54.5745, -1.2316 / Middlesbrough, North Yorkshire / Swimming and paddling

Tucked away in the heart of Middlesbrough, Wilkinson Lake is a tranquil, fifty-metre-wide swim spot located in a small area of parkland. The man-made, rocky bank offers easy access into the water, or alternatively you can slip in from the concrete lip of the circular plaza. The banks on the far side make this the perfect place to inject a little wild into your swim, and it can easily be integrated with a visit to the Bottle of Notes, which overlooks the lake, as well as the Institute of Modern Art. There is plenty of choice for refreshments in Middlesbrough.

Access

Access via rocky bank or concrete platform. Easily accessed through public transport: variety of bus services to Middlesbrough and Guisborough stop at Albert Road stop. Paid parking at MIMA car park, a couple of hundred metres away.

STANHOPE OPEN AIR POOL. © *SARAH THELWALL*

HALTWHISTLE SWIMMING & LEISURE CENTRE. © *SARAH THELWALL*

STANHOPE OPEN AIR POOL

54.7483, -2.0140 / Castle Park, Stanhope, County Durham, DL13 2LU / 01388 528466 / Swimming / *www.stanhopepool.co.uk*

Founded as a community charity project in 1974, Stanhope Open Air Pool is nestled among the north Pennine hills in the charming market town of Stanhope. A stone's throw from the River Wear, the pool is surrounded by the lush trees which line the riverbank. Open from 10.00 a.m. to 7.30 p.m. throughout the week from May to September, both cold and heated water sessions are available here, with the water reaching 27 °C. Twenty-five metres long and thirteen metres wide, the pool has a springboard and a smaller children's pool with a slide. An on-site sauna can be privately booked. The picnic benches and cafe make Stanhope the perfect destination for a family day out.

Access
Water accessible by ladders only; pool area wheelchair accessible, but no hoist. Less than a kilometre away, Newtown House bus stop served by frequent buses to Cowshill and Rookhope. On-site parking; alternatively parking by Stanhope Castle or at lay-by on the B6278 – cross the river via stepping stones to reach the pool.

LYONS LAKE, HETTON LYONS COUNTRY PARK

54.8233, -1.4422 / Downs Pit Lane, Hetton-le-Hole, Tyne and Wear, DH5 0RH / 01915 266684 / Swimming / *www.facebook.com/hettonlyonscountrypark*

Found among the vast array of woodland, grassland and lakes at Hetton Lyons Country Park is Lyons Lake, managed by Springboard Adventure. A small beach area enables easy access into the water. Surrounded by the relaxing greenery of the park, this is a great place to swim as a part of organised sessions, run by groups such as Tri-It Coaching. With picnic tables and plenty to explore, a swim in the lake can be incorporated with a day out adventuring, with the variety of refreshment options of Hetton-le-Hole right on your doorstep.

Access
Sandy beach leads to water. 35 and 35A services from Low Moorsley stop at Caroline Street bus stop every few hours, less than a kilometre away. Two free car parks on-site.

FEATHERSTONE, RIVER SOUTH TYNE

54.9426, -2.5139 / Haltwhistle, Northumberland / Swimming and paddling

In view of the majestic Featherstone Castle, the Featherstone section of the River South Tyne offers sandy beaches along its banks. Ranging from deeper water mid-river to paddle-friendly shallows, this beautiful and serene location is perfect for family fun and swimmers alike. A visit here can be combined with the National Trust's Featherstone Castle and Lambley Viaduct walk, and you can find refreshments at the Wallace Arms in Rowfoot, or at one of the several outlets in Haltwhistle.

Access
Sandy beach leads to water. 681 Tyndale Links bus from Haltwhistle stops twice daily two kilo- metres away, at the Village Hall stop in Rowfoot. Parking in lay-bys along the road beside the river on approach to Featherstone Castle, a few hundred metres from the swim spot, or at Featherstone Park car park, a kilometre and a half away.

HALTWHISTLE SWIMMING & LEISURE CENTRE

54.9711, -2.4662 / Greencroft, Haltwhistle, Northumberland, NE49 9DW / 01434 320727 / Swimming and paddling / *www.haltwhistlelei-sure.co.uk*

Located in the heart of Hadrian's Wall Country, Haltwhistle Swimming & Leisure Centre offers three outdoor pools suitable for swimmers of all ages and abilities. Open from mid-April to early September, the site features a twen-ty-five-metre main pool, a smaller learner pool for less confident swimmers and a paddling pool for toddlers and babies. All three pools are heated to 28 °C and are supervised by qualified lifeguards. The centre's entry fee gives visitors unlimited all-day use of the pools, adventure

play area and picnic area. After a fun family day out, there is a cafe on-site for refreshments.

Access
Access to main pool via ladders and a flume, and to learner pool via steps, a ladder and a slide. Lido area wheelchair accessible. Nearest frequent bus and rail services to Hexham and Newcastle less than a kilometre away. On-site parking.

CHESTERS RUINS

55.0241, -2.1368 / Chollerford, Northumberland / Swimming and paddling

Sandwiching the River North Tyne are the ancient Roman ruins of Chesters Fort and Chesters Bridge, surrounded by a mixture of woods and open farmland. Shallow and with grassy banks, the Chesters section of the River North Tyne is easy to enter, with deeper pools available downstream. This historic and bewitching location lends itself to an explo-ration of Chesters Roman fort and Chesters Bridge Abutment, run by English Heritage, or Brunton Turret further along Hadrian's Wall. Nearby Chollerford also provides refreshment opportunities at the Riverside Kitchen.

Access
Access via grassy banks. Recreation Ground bus stop a kilometre away for 680 Tyndale Links from Hexham; in summer AD122 stops regularly outside Chesters Roman Fort and Museum. Parking available a kilometre and a half away at lay-by on Front Street (A6079), beside starting point for the walk to Brunton Turret – take footpath down from Chollerford Bridge on Low Brunton side.

LINHOPE SPOUT. © *LUCY HOLMES, KIDS OF THE WILD*

HARBOTTLE LAKE

55.3329, -2.1303 / Harbottle, Northumberland /
Swimming

Watched over by the Drake Stone and
surrounded by a mixture of open moorland
and woodland, Harbottle Lake is a tarn infused
with mystical atmosphere. The grassy banks
make it easy to slip into the water and enjoy
this secluded spot, rich with Druid heritage.
From here you can walk to the ancient Drake
Stone, providing a breathtaking panoramic, as
well as an exploration of the ruins of Harbottle
Castle, which boasts stunning views of the
surrounding valley. You can find refreshments
at the Star Inn in Harbottle, or travel a little
further up the road to the Rose and Thistle
Inn in Alwinton.

Access
Access via grassy banks. 16A and 16B services
stop at First School bus stop twice daily on
Tuesdays, Thursdays and Saturdays. Parking
at Harbottle Forestry England West Wood car
park, on left shortly after the Harbottle Castle
car park if driving from Harbottle, roughly a
kilometre from the lake.

SHILLMOOR, RIVER COQUET

55.3696, -2.2098 / Alwinton or Harbottle,
Northumberland / Swimming and paddling

Twisting through the Cheviot Hills, the River
Coquet is home to a series of river pools near
the Shillmoor farmstead. The banks are a
mixture of soft, grassy beds and small, stony
beaches, from which you can slip or step into
the water. The depth of the pools may vary,
and in some places the riverbed is dotted
with small boulders. With the nearest village,
Alwinton, roughly seven kilometres away,
Shillmoor offers the chance to swim in an undisturbed location, surrounded by a timeless,
striking landscape. A swim here is the perfect
activity to pair with a walk from Shillmoor over
Green Side and Lords Seat to Usway Burn.
The Rose and Thistle Inn in Alwinton can offer
well-deserved refreshments.

Access
Grassy banks and stony beaches. Not easily
accessible by public transport: 16A and 16B
services stop twice daily on Tuesdays, Thursdays
and Saturdays at Phone Box stop in Alwinton,
seven kilometres away. Small car park off
riverside road on approach to Poppy's
Cottage, less than 100 metres away.

UNION CHAIN BRIDGE. © *JIM GIBSON PHOTOGRAPHY*

LINHOPE SPOUT

55.4478, -2.0671 / Ingram, Northumberland / Swimming, paddling and plunge pool

Located on the Linhope Estate, Linhope Spout is a waterfall and plunge pool in a wooded area of the moorland. Its bank is rocky and mossy, with access points for both slipping and jumping into the water. A peaceful and idyllic spot for swimming, it is a perfect way to cool off after the picturesque walk from Hartside. It is also within reach of the National Park Visitor Centre in Ingram, where you can get a cup of tea or a snack in the cafe, as well as try out the Woodland Walk.

Access
Rocky, mossy bank. Access on foot via mixture of stone and grassy tracks which may be steep at times. Access by public transport limited: closest bus stop over eleven kilometres away at Jubilee Hall for services from Wooler, which stop several times a day. Parking two and a half kilometres away, along verge before Hartside Farm; keep access to the gates clear.

UNION CHAIN BRIDGE

55.7539, -2.1070 / Horncliffe, Northumberland / Swimming

On the Scottish–English border, Union Chain Bridge crosses the River Tweed in a stunning area of grass and woodland. Its sloped, grassy banks offer easy spots to get into the water. In this beautiful, wide section of the river it is possible to swim across the border, however swimmers should be conscious of the strong current and should swim against it. The Chain Bridge Honey Farm and Cafe Bus are nearby, although refreshments can also be found at the Fishers Arms in nearby Horncliffe.

Access
Sloped, grassy banks. Accessing the river requires crossing a stone stile set into the wall beside the lifebuoy. 67 bus from Berwick-upon-Tweed stops twice daily a kilometre away in Kelso. Parking available 200 metres away along the verge shortly after Chain Bridge House Bed and Breakfast.

BANGOR

47 48 49
46 45 50
44 43
41 42 51
40 39 38
37 36
35
34

33

32
31
30
29
28
27

ABERYSTWYTH

26 25
23

24

22
20
21

19

2

18

1

17

3 89

16
15

11

4 5
6

10

12

13

14

SWANSEA

7

NEWPORT

CARDIFF

Wales

GLASLYN. © SHUTTERSTOCK/ALEXANDRA GLEN

LLYN Y FAN FACH. © *JOHN COEFIELD*

LLYS-Y-FRÂN RESERVOIR

51.8842, -4.8514 / Clarbeston Road, Pembroke-shire, SA63 4RR / Swimming / *llys-y-fran.co.uk*

Unlike English water companies, Welsh Water has been exploring pioneering approaches to safe reservoir swimming, and after trialling open water sessions at Llandegfedd it is now planning to run open swim sessions at Llys-y-frân. This reservoir is already a popular water sports centre, with new, purpose-built facilities including changing facilities, toilets and a cafe. There are plenty of spots for picnics, picturesque walks and an adventure playground. The site achieved accreditation as a safe swim venue in March 2021, so open water swimming should commence later in the year. Open swimming is also being trialled at Llandegfedd Reservoir, and under considera-tion at other reservoirs such as Llyn Brenig.

Access
Swimming given green light in March 2021 and access arrangements still being finalised at time of going to print, but the reservoir has a new purpose-built activities hub with accessi-ble facilities. Poorly served by public transport: Clarbeston Road railway station six kilometres away, where there are also infrequent buses between Haverfordwest and Wiston. On-site parking.

LOWER TEIFI GORGE

52.0558, -4.6306 / Cilgerran, Ceredigion / Swimming

Walled by trees, the Lower Teifi Gorge section of the Afon Teifi is tucked below a gorgeous, grassy slope and has a small, wooden jetty which provides the perfect point to slip into the serene water. This is a calm, sheltered spot and from here you can swim up past the forested banks to the historic ruins of Cilgerran Castle. After your visit to the Norman keep, this swim spot is great to combine with an exploration of the Teifi Marshes Nature Reserve, home to some of Wales's best wetland sites, and you can find a hot drink and snack at the Glasshouse Cafe.

Access
Entry to water via grassy slopes and wooden jetty. Cardiff Arms bus stop, 500 metres away, served by buses to Cardigan approximately five times a day. Cilgerran Lower car park (with public toilets) fifty metres from jetty.

LLYN Y FAN FACH

51.8831, -3.7397 / Llangadog, Carmarthenshire / **Swimming and paddling**

Nestled beneath Black Mountain in the Brecon Beacons National Park, Llyn y Fan Fach is a lake with breathtaking sunset views.

With a wide, stony beach, there are plenty of points from which you can ease yourself into the cool but refreshing water. The legendary home of a nymph known as the Lady of the Lake, Llyn y Fan Fach is great to combine with a hike up and along the Black Mountain, where you will find captivating panoramas of this timeless landscape. There are no facilities nearby, so be sure to pack a drink and bite to eat.

Access

Access via stony beach. Lake is on Beacons Way, which can be followed up from Llyn y Fan Fach car park on grit trail and tarmac, with steep inclines. Poorly served by public transport: closest train station in Llangadog, sixteen kilometres away. Llyn y Fan Fach car park two kilometres away.

HENRHYD FALLS

51.7942, -3.6632 / Coelbren, Powys / Swimming and plunge pool

Nestled in a forested gorge, Henrhyd Falls is the highest waterfall in South Wales, cascading from a spectacular ninety-foot outcrop into a sheltered plunge pool below. Boulders lining the banks of the river approaching the waterfall require a slight scramble to get over, and from here you can walk across the shallow riverbed to the plunge pool. The surface beneath the water comprises a mixture of shingle and larger stones, so swimming shoes are advisable. Once in the cool water, bask in the glory of the moss- and lichen-covered stone, as well as the view of the gorge stretching before you. Afterwards, grab a snack and drink at the Coelbren Welfare Hall Tearooms, or alternatively at the Prices Arms.

Access

Access to water over boulders. Follow marked, sometimes steep and slippery, waterfall path. Frequent local bus services to Dyffryn Cellwen, Ystradgynlais and Neath stop at Moriah Chapel

SGWD GWLADYS. © SHUTTERSTOCK/RICHARD WHITCOMBE

stop, 500 metres away. Designated car park at Henrhyd Falls.

SGWD GWLADYS

51.7713, -3.6006 / Pontneddfechan, Powys / Swimming and plunge pool

Gushing from a natural stone amphitheatre, Sgwd Gwladys is a majestic waterfall with a wide, open plunge pool, perfect for swimming and soaking up the atmosphere of this stunning swim spot. A large, pebbled beach makes wading in and out of the chilly water easy, and you can swim up beneath the overhanging ledge to stand behind the waterfall. This unique swim can easily be combined with a dip in the nearby Horseshoe Falls and a relaxing woodland walk along the Elidir Trail, or head slightly further afield to Sychryd Waterfall a little way beyond Pontneddfechan. You can find a hearty meal at the Angel Hotel (there are public toilets just next door) or the Dinas Inn.

Access

Entry to water via mossy banks – stony under-foot. Follow footpath along river from Waterfalls Centre, opposite Angel Hotel, nearly two kilo-metres. Parking and buses (a few per day to Neath and Morfa Glas) from Angel Hotel.

THE OUTDOOR SWIMMING GUIDE

HORSESHOE FALLS

51.7746, -3.5923 / Pontneddfechan, Powys / Swimming and plunge pool

Tumbling through a wooded gorge in the Brecon Beacons National Park, Horseshoe Falls is a series of small, beguiling waterfalls and deep plunge pools along the Afon Neath. Moss-laden banks form shallow steps into the tranquil water which can be a little stony underfoot. This serene swim spot, surrounded by the lush greenery of the trees and bracken, can easily be tied in with a visit to nearby Sgwd Gwladys and to Dinas Rock in Pontneddfechan, where you can also find refreshments at the Old White Horse Inn. Toilets are also available at the car park across from the Angel Hotel.

Access
Entry to water via mossy banks – stony under-foot. Follow footpath along river from Water-falls Centre, opposite Angel Hotel, for two and half kilometres. Parking and buses (a few per day to Neath and Morfa Glas) from Angel Hotel.

LIDO PONTY

51.6017, -3.3389 / Ynysangharad War Memorial Park, Pontypridd, CF37 4PE / 0300 004 0000 Swimming and paddling / *www.rctcbc.gov.uk/EN/Resident/SportsandLeisure/Lido/Home.aspx*

Devastated by flooding in February 2020, the recently refurbished National Lido of Wales, Lido Ponty, is home to a twenty-five-metre main pool, an activity pool and a splash pool, all of which are heated to 28 °C and under lifeguard supervision. Located in Pontypridd, this Grade-II listed lido was originally con-structed in 1927 and new additions include a state-of-the-art visitor centre, the Waterside Cafe and a play area. Open on weekdays in term times and daily at weekends and during school holidays, and with no admission charges for those under sixteen, Lido Ponty is a must-visit for families and swimming

HORSESHOE FALLS. © SHUTTERSTOCK/LEIGHTON COLLINS

enthusiasts in the area. To extend your day out, Ynysangharad Park lies just outside the lido, and a variety of refreshment options are available in Pontypridd.

Access
Entry to water via ladders. Level access to poolside, accessible changing areas and toilets; hoist and wet chair available. Pontypridd railway station 500 metres away; well-served by local bus services, within 500 metres of lido. No on-site parking; Gas Road car park 500 metres away.

LLYN CWM LLWCH

51.8881, -3.4517 / Brecon, Powys / Swimming

In the shadow of Pen y Fan, Llyn Cwm Llwch is a modest mountain lake with spectacular views of the peaks above. Grassy banks provide easy points from which you can step into the shallower water, however as the lakebed can be rocky, water-friendly shoes are advised. Within easy reach of Corn Du, this is an excellent swim to combine with a walk up to the peaks above and experience the breathtaking panoramic views of the surrounding landscape. You can find a warming drink and snack afterwards at Garnwant Visitor Centre.

LIDO PONTY. © THE NATIONAL LIDO OF WALES, LIDO PONTY/RHONDDA CYNON TAF COUNCIL

LLYN CWM LLWCH. © SHUTTERSTOCK/ RICHARD WHITCOMBE

Access

Access to water via grassy banks. Follow Beacons Way over Corn Du, then footpath; trail sometimes uneven and steep. Storey Arms bus stop, three kilometres away, served by the T4 TrawsCymru line from Newtown and Llandrindod Wells a few times a day. Pont ar Daf car park four kilometres away.

PEN Y FAN

51.8970, -3.4167 / Brecon, Powys / Swimming and plunge pool

Snug between the hills of the Brecon Beacons and with a view of Pen y Fan towering above, this section of the Nant Sere is home to a series of small waterfalls and plunge pools with cushioned, grassy banks leading to the water. Surrounded by the calming green and purple hues of the heather and the hills, this is a mesmerising and remote swim and can be tied in as part of a packed day of hillwalking to Cribyn, Pen y Fan and Corn Du. Reward yourself afterwards with a hearty meal at the Brecon Tap.

Access

Entry to water via grassy banks. Swim spot is 500 metres downhill from footpath over Cribyn and Pen y Fan. Nearest public transport in Brecon, six kilometres away, for regular buses to Cardiff and Swansea. Parking two kilometres away at Cwm Gwdi car park.

PARC BRYN BACH

51.7830, -3.2727 / Merthyr Road, Tredegar, Blaenau Gwent, NP22 3AY / 01495 355920
parcbrynbach.co.uk

Weed-free open water swims are available at Parc Bryn Bach on Wednesday and Saturday mornings. In the midst of this pleasant, wooded parkland, a landscape reclaimed from open-cast mining, you can swim a 450-metre circuit. Swimmers must wear a wetsuit and brightly coloured swim cap. The park is an outdoor adventure hub, with kayaking, climbing and foot golf also available. If you're after a bite to eat, there is a cafe on-site and the Nags Head pub rests opposite the park entrance.

Access

Entry to water via slipway. Accessible changing rooms and toilets available. Buses to Tredegar stop a few times a day at park entrance. On-site parking.

CRICKHOWELL BRIDGE

51.8567, -3.1416 / Crickhowell, Powys / Swimming and paddling

Built in the eighteenth century in place of a medieval bridge, Crickhowell Bridge crosses the Afon Usk and is home to a large river pool as well as shallower pools which are ideal for paddling. A sloping, grassy bank down to a concrete platform serves as an easy point from which you can slip into the water, and further along the riverbank on the other side of the weir (which you should not swim too close to) are pebbled beaches. This is a great place to swim with views of the bridge and river stretching into the distance on either side. Head to the Bridge End Inn afterwards for a drink and meal overlooking the water.

Access
Entry to water from concrete platform and pebbly beaches; footpath on eastern side of river. Less than a kilometre to Crickhowell centre, well-served by buses to Builth Wells, Abergavenny, Brecon and other local destinations. On-street parking.

PEN-FFORD-GOCH POND (KEEPER'S POND)

51.7906, -3.0821 / Blaenavon, Monmouthshire / Swimming

Located in the countryside of South Wales, Pen-fford-goch

Pond, also known as Keeper's Pond, is a large lake which enjoys extensive, infinity-pool-style views into the valley beyond. Grassy banks form soft points from which you can slip into the water, as well as cushioned places to climb out. Expect company at this man-made lake, once used for powering local iron forges but now popular with local swimmers. You could also pay a visit to the Big Pit National Coal Museum or Garn Lakes Local Nature Reserve in Blaenavon, where you can find refreshments at the Heritage Tearooms.

Access
Entry from grassy, reedy banks. Frequent bus services from Blaenavon to Newport (Casnewydd), three kilometres away. Pond car park, off B4246, fifty metres away.

THE BRYN

51.7794, -2.9701 / The Bryn, Monmouthshire / Swimming and paddling

Tucked away just beside the A40, The Bryn is a small village a few hundred metres north of one of the Afon Usk's wide, tranquil meanders. The curving, shingle beach along this stretch provides access into the river pool for both swimming and paddling, and with lush, green fields in every direction, this is the perfect place for a family picnic and swim on a summer's day.

Take the time to explore some of the area's picturesque walking trails, and afterwards head to the Gardeners Kitchen in Llanellen for some refreshments.

Access
Entry to water via grassy banks. Frequent buses to Monmouth and Abergavenny from the Bryn village, a kilometre away. Roadside parking available along the main street in The Bryn, a kilometre away.

USK ISLAND

51.7064, -2.9080 / Usk, Pembrokeshire / Swimming and paddling

Situated in the middle of the Afon Usk, Usk Island is a modest shingle island which can be reached from an entry point on the bank next to Usk Island car park, where there are also toilet facilities. The water is deeper beneath the bridge and in the summer sun the river warms to a pleasant temperature. This is an excellent spot for a refreshing dip and a picnic, and you can take the time to discover more about Usk's history at the Usk Rural Life Museum. Alternatively, the captivating ruins of Usk Castle overlook the town. You can find fresh takeaway snacks at the Parsons Bakery, or something more substantial at one of Usk's many pubs.

PEN-FFORDD-GOCH POND. © *JOHN COEFIELD*

Access

Entry to water via shingle beaches. Usk centre less than a kilometre away, well served by buses to Newport (Casnewydd), Pontypool and Monmouth. Parking fifty metres away at Usk Island car park.

TREGATE BRIDGE

51.8520, -2.7603 / St Maughans Green, Monmouthshire / Swimming and paddling

Surrounded by the green countryside of the Welsh–English border, Tregate Bridge crosses the tranquil waters of the Afon Monnow. The sloping, muddy bank offers a tree-sheltered spot from which you can slip into the river pool, which has slightly shallower sections closer to the bank that are ideal for paddling. With soft, grassy fields above the riverbank, this is the perfect spot to relax and cool off on a hot day with a picnic. You can tie in a

visit up to Skenfrith Castle, or alternatively Rockfield Castle on the way to Monmouth, where you can find a variety of refreshment options.

Access

Entry to water via sloping, muddy banks. Difficult to reach by public transport: closest buses three kilometres away in Welsh Newton, to Hereford and Monmouth. Limited roadside parking in St Maughans Green, less than a kilometre away.

SKENFRITH CASTLE

51.8785, -2.7895 / Skenfrith, Monmouthshire / Swimming and paddling

In the charming village of Skenfrith, Skenfrith Castle is a medieval ruin managed by the National Trust, located next to a section of the Afon Monnow with river pools ideal for swimming. Sloping, muddy banks lead into the water, although some scrambling

may be required, and from further along the river you can enjoy views looking back on the castle. You can take the time to explore the castle and immerse yourself in the region's past, and afterwards treat yourself to a bite to eat at the Bell restaurant.

Access

Entry to water via steep, muddy banks. Difficult to reach by public transport: bus to Hereford stops once daily in Broad Oak, three kilometres away. Roadside Castle car park 200 metres away.

LLANTHONY PRIORY. © *JOHN COEFIELD*

BUGLE BRIDGE

51.9398, -3.0336 / Llanthony, Monmouthshire / Swimming

Bugle Bridge is a short, stone bridge which crosses the Afon Honddu as it flows through the Welsh countryside. Grassy, sloped banks lead down to the water, where there is a river pool shaded by overhanging trees. There is also a walled segment of the bank, from which you can jump into the river, however swimmers should always check the water depth before doing so. With an open field behind, this is a perfect location for a picnic, and you can take the time to explore the idyllic village of Llanthony, home to the ruins of Llanthony Priory (where toilet facilities are available) and the Half Moon Inn, where you can find a light lunch or a heartier meal.

Access

Access via grassy banks and walled edges. Follow road from village. Poorly served by public transport: nearest buses ten kilometres away in Pandy. Car park by Llanthony Priory (with toilets), a kilometre away.

THE WARREN

52.0757, -3.1370 / Hay-on-Wye, Powys / Swimming and paddling

On the outskirts of Hay-on-Wye, The Warren is a riverside meadow with a long, shingle beach offering easy access for both paddling and swimming in the winding waters of the Afon Wye. Shaded by the trees which line the bank, this section of the river hosts shallower waters below the bend and deeper waters above it, making it an ideal spot for swimmers of varying abilities to enjoy. With the peace of the meadow behind, this is a great location to relax in the sun and can be tied in with an exploration of the charming market town, including Hay Castle. Stop for a drink at Cafe Hay or the Granary or treat yourself to a meal at one of the town's many pubs and bars.

Access

Entry to water via shingle beach. Hay town centre a kilometre away (follow footpath along river), well served by buses to Hereford and Brecon. The Warren has parking area at the end of a rough track off Gipsy Castle Lane, less than 300 metres from the riverbank.

PENDDOL ROCKS

52.1580, -3.4160 / Builth Wells, Powys / Swimming

Winding past Builth Wells, Penddol Rocks is a section of the Afon Wye with sandy bays and a small gorge. Shingle and sandy beach areas to rocky ledges provide access to the water. The river deepens quickly here due to potholes along the riverbed and is not advised for weaker swimmers or for swimming after periods of heavy rainfall. With clear water and trees overhanging the bank, this spot in the midst of the Welsh countryside is great to combine with an exploration of the pretty town of Builth Wells. There are a variety of refreshment options nearby such as the Cwtch Cafe or the Cosy Corner Cafe, and public toilets can be found in Groe car park.

Access

Access via sandy beaches; take caution of currents. Follow river to reach Builth Wells (south) or Builth Road (north). Builth Road railway station a kilometre and a half away, centre of Builth Wells two kilometres away. Parking available in Groe car park in Builth Wells.

WASHPOOL

52.1361, -3.6680 / Llanwrtyd Wells, Powys / Swimming and paddling

Located on the Afon Irfon, Washpool is a wide river pool at the mouth of a short gorge with a wall of trees towering above on the far bank. The grassy banks provide access, while a gravel track offers an alternative for wading into the water, the depth of which varies throughout the pool. With the convenience of a nearby bench, this is the perfect stop for a dip and a picnic in the sun. You can head up to the flora-rich Vicarage Meadows Nature Reserve in Abergwesyn to make a day of your visit, and afterwards drop in at Caffi Sosban in Llanwrtyd Wells for a drink and a snack.

Access

Access via grassy banks, gravel slipway. Follow (wheelchair-friendly) track from car park, or roads/footpaths from Llanwrtyd Wells, for five kilometres. Railway station and buses to Builth Wells in Llanwrtyd Wells, five kilometres away. On-site parking.

YSTRADFFIN (JUNCTION POOL)

52.1044, -3.7864 / Rhandirmwyn, Carmarthenshire / Swimming

Flowing past the RSPB Gwenffrwd/Dinas Nature Reserve, the Afon Towy splits into a fork at Ystradffin, where it is surrounded by the lush foliage of a forested gorge. At the point of the junction is a river pool, with rocky banks which provide good platforms for slipping into the water in this mesmerising spot, although you should be careful after periods of heavy rainfall. This location can easily be tied in with a day at the neighbouring nature reserve, which is brimming with wildlife and home to a legendary cave where Twm Siôn Cati is said to have hidden from the authorities. Picnic benches are located nearby for you to enjoy views of this atmospheric reserve while you eat.

Access

Entry into water via grassy banks. Follow path along river from Ystradffin. Difficult to reach via public transport: Llanwrtyd Wells railway station ten kilometres away. Small car at RSPB Gwenffrwd–Dinas Nature Reserve, a kilometre away.

WOLF'S LEAP

52.1802, -3.6966 / Llanwrtyd Wells, Powys / Swimming and paddling

Sandwiched between the glorious green hills of Abergwesyn Common and the Nant Irfon National Nature Reserve, Wolf's Leap is a series of deep pools along the Afon Irfon which run into a narrow gorge. Rocky outcrops into the river form solid platforms from which you can lower yourself into the water. With the open sky above, this is an idyllic location where you can lie back and dry beneath the sun or head for a walk along the river. Refreshments can be found in Llandovery at the West End Cafe or the Owl's Nest Tearoom Diner.

Access
Access to water via rocky shelves. Difficult to reach by public transport: railway station and buses to Builth Wells in Llanwrtyd Wells, eleven kilometres away. Limited roadside parking for Nant Irfon National Nature Reserve, a kilometre away.

LLYN EGNANT

52.2922, -3.7716 / Pontrhydfendigaid, Ceredigion / Swimming

In the west of the 'green desert' of the Cambrian Mountains, Llyn Egnant is a large lake at the far end of the Teifi Pools cluster. Grassy banks provide easy access

into the shallower water, which shelves off quickly. Due to the altitude of these pools, Llyn Egnant and its neighbours can be particularly cold, so a wetsuit is recommended for enjoying this exposed and exhilarating swim spot, as well as a thermos of hot drink and a snack to refuel. Make the most of this expansive landscape by walking some of the trails around the other Teifi Pools, experiencing the raw beauty Wales has to offer.

Access
Access via grassy banks; requires uphill walk on grit tracks or bridleways. Difficult to reach via public transport: closest bus stop, Teifi Inn, seven kilometres away, for buses to Aberystwyth. Limited roadside parking in Pontrhydfendigaid, nine kilometres away.

PONT MARTEG

52.3316, -3.5396 / Rhayader, Powys / Swimming and paddling

With the River Marteg Nature Reserve to one side and a forested valley to the other, Pont Marteg crosses the Afon Marteg where it meets the Afon Wye. Grassy banks lead into the Wye, where there are river pools of various depths, making this an ideal, shady location for a swim or for paddling on a summer's day. With both the River Marteg Nature Reserve and the Gilfach Nature Reserve in

easy reach, this is the perfect swim spot to tie into a day of outdoor adventure, experiencing all the wildlife the area has to offer. The Roadside Delight takeaway van offers snacks and hot drinks.

Access
Entry to river via grassy banks. Bus stops by Pont Marteg, services to Llandrindod Wells, Aberystwyth and Shrewsbury a few times a day. Large lay-by parking by bridge.

HAFOD ESTATE

52.3411, -3.8106 / Pont-rhyd-y-groes, Ceredigion / Swimming and paddling

Meandering through the Hafod Estate, the Afon Ystwyth contains wide river pools with pleasant, still water – perfect for a soothing swim. A shingle beach along the grass-lined bank provides access for a swim or for paddling in the river, which may be a little stony underfoot. With a picnic bench overlooking the water, this location is great for a lunch stop and can easily be combined with further exploration of the Hafod Estate, with waterfall trails through woodland as well as an impressive walled garden. You can find a drink and a snack afterwards at the Cwtch Tearoom in Pont-rhyd-y-groes.

Access
Entry to water via shingle beach. Infrequent buses from Aberystwyth stop at

Penffynnon Hall in Pont-rhyd-y-groes, four kilometres away. National Cycle Route 81 passes through Hafod Estate. Parking is available at the Hafod Estate car park, two kilometres away.

RHEIDOL VALE, AFON RHEIDOL

52.3860, -3.8688 / Devil's Bridge, Powys / Swimming and paddling

Coursing through the Rheidol Vale, the Afon Rheidol is home to a series of small waterfalls and river pools, perfect for paddling and swimming. The shingle beach provides access into the water as well as a beautiful location for a post-swim picnic, making it a tranquil spot for a family day out. Surrounded by the lush greenery of the vale, a dip here can form part of a day adventuring along the many cycle tracks and woodland walks the area has to offer, as well as the charming Vale of Rheidol Railway. The nearest refreshments can be found in Devil's Bridge.

Access
Access via shingle beaches. Less than 100 metres to Rhiwfron on heritage Vale of Rheidol Railway. Limited roadside parking by swim spot.

LLYN CAU. © SHUTTERSTOCK/JHMIMAGING

LLYN MWYNGIL

52.6675, -3.9037 / Corris, Gwynedd / Swimming

Stretching out below Cadair Idris, Llyn Mwyngil is a long, rectangular lake with a short, concrete slipway on the south-western bank. With tree-covered hills and mountains surrounding the lake on all sides, not only is this swim spot picturesque, but with its extensive views along the lake it is also sheltered from the wind. This location is great to tie in with a visit to the Centre for Alternative Technology in Machynlleth or at the Cors Dyfi Nature Reserve. If you like starting the day with a swim, why not treat yourself to a hot breakfast or lunch at the Ty'n y Cornel Hotel afterwards.

Access
Access via concrete slipways or grassy banks. Bus stop by waterside, four or five daily to Tywyn, Dolgellau and other local destinations. Parking in roadside lay-bys.

LLYN CAU

52.6942, -3.8987 / Minffordd, Gwynedd / Swimming

In the shadow Cadair Idris, Llyn Cau is a vast lake with dramatic views of the mountain rising above it. Grassy banks provide cushioned points for accessing the cool, clear waters, which can warm a little in the sunshine but may still be provide a bit of a shock when you first dip your toes in. With awe-inspiring views of the glacial valley, this remarkable swim spot is the perfect way to connect with the landscape and soak in the atmosphere after the hike up. A rewarding cup of tea and piece of cake can be found afterwards at the Tŷ Te Cadair Tearoom in Minffordd, and toilets are available at the Dôl Idris car park.

Access
Entry to water via grassy banks and stony beaches. Follow Minffordd Path up towards Cadair Idris, which involves steep inclines and uneven ground. T2 bus (Aberystwyth to Bangor) stops at least every two hours at Minffordd, two and a half kilometres away – free at weekends. Paid parking at Dôl Idris Car Park, two and half kilometres away.

LLYN Y GADAIR. © *SHUTTERSTOCK/NICHOLAS BILLINGTON*

LLYN Y GADAIR

52.7037, -3.9126 / Minffordd, Gwynedd / Swimming

Snug against the curved, rock basin of Cadair Idris, Llyn y Gadair is a large, oval lake with a small beach area, making entering and exiting the chilly, revitalising water quick and easy. A wetsuit is recommended for enjoying the water here, where the world seems to drop away beyond the slopes at the lake's northern shore. This awe-inspiring swim can be combined with a hike up the Minffordd Path to Penygader, as well as a dip in the neighbouring Llyn Gafr. Be sure to take a thermos of hot drink with you, as well as a snack to refuel.

Access

Entry via shingle beach and rocky shore. Follow Minffordd Path. T2 bus (Aberystwyth to Bangor) stops at least every two hours near Minffordd, four kilometres away. Parking (and toilets) at Ty-nant, two kilometres away.

LLYN GAFR

52.7097, -3.9115 / Minffordd, Gwynedd / Swimming

In the shadow of Cadair Idris, Llyn Gafr is a mountain lake, slightly smaller than its neighbour Llyn y Gadair. A small beach area provides easy access for wading into the chilly water. With breathtaking views of the mountain ahead and stunning panoramas of the surrounding hills, this is an excellent swim spot to combine with a hike up to the neighbouring peak. As there are no nearby facilities, take plenty of warm layers as well as a hot drink and bite to eat for once you leave the water.

Access

Entry via small, shingly beach. Follow Minffordd Path. T2 bus (Aberystwyth to Bangor) stops at least every two hours near Minffordd, five kilometres away. Parking (and toilets) at Ty-nant, a kilometre and a and half away.

PONT LLANELLTYD

52.7562, -3.8999 / Llanelltyd, Gwynedd / Swimming and paddling

Crossing the Afon Mawddach, Pont Llanelltyd is a five-arched, eighteenth-century bridge, near which there are several large, shingle beaches providing access into the river pools, as well as perfect places for a family picnic. Surrounded by the lush greenery of the Welsh countryside, this is a serene swim-spot whether you're a hardy swimmer or looking for somewhere to cool off on a hot day. Drop in at the elegant ruins of Cymer Abbey, where you can connect with Llanelltyd's heritage, and either end the day with a meal at Mawddach Napoletana Pizza restaurant or head down to Dolgellau where you can find a variety of cafe options.

Access

Access via shingle beaches. T2 bus stops (for Bangor and Aberystwyth), 500 metres away in Llanelltyd. Parking near bridge, or road parking.

RHAEADR MAWDDACH

52.8301, -3.8779 / Bronaber, Gwynedd / Swimming and plunge pool

Plunging from a rocky outcrop into a deep pool below, Rhaeadr Mawddach is located in the forested gorge of the Coed-y-Brenin Forest Park. This dramatic swim spot has blocky stone banks, which serve as ideal platforms for launching into the refreshing water. Be wary of turbulence if water levels are high or rising fast. After your dip you could explore one of the many bike trails weaving throughout the park, or you could spend the day rambling among the trees, as well as visiting the nearby falls of Pistyll Cain. Grab a snack and drink afterwards back at the Coed y Brenin Visitor Centre cafe, where toilets and shower facilities are also available.

Access

Entry into water from rocky ledges. Trails through forest and by river; popular mountain biking spot. Coed y Brenin bus stop served by T2 TrawsCymru services between Bangor and Aberystwyth, two and a half kilometres away. Coed-y-Brenin Forest Park car park (with toilets), two and a half kilometres away.

LLYN TEGID

52.8760, -3.6339 / Y Bala, Gwynedd / Swimming

The largest natural lake in Wales, Llyn Tegid is a vast body of water with beautifully clear depths. The curving, shingle beach provides an easy entry and exit point as well as a great spot for paddling, making this an ideal location for a family day out. You can enjoy the deep, revitalising water from the foreshore, but swimming is not permitted from boats. With the convenience of nearby toilets at the Llangower Station car park, you can easily spend a day beside the water and enjoy a trip on the Bala Lake Railway before heading up to Y Bala for a hot drink or meal at one of the town's cafes and restaurants .

Access

Entry to water is via shingle beaches. Llangower Station, adjacent to swim spot, for Bala Lake Railway (where there is also parking). Station Road bus stop is roughly a kilometre and half away, for the T3 TrawsCymru service from Barmouth, Wrexham and Ruabon.

LLYN EIDDEW-BACH

52.8899, -4.0145 / Eisingrug, Gwynedd / Swimming

In the northern segment of the Coed-y-Brenin Forest Park, Llyn Eiddew-bach is a modest tarn encompassed by the lush, green slopes and impressive scenery of the Rhinogs. This remote pool has grassy banks which serve as entry points into the lake, and swimmers can enjoy views of the scenery before them as they bask in the refreshing water. A dip here can easily be tied in with a walk to Bryn Cader Faner, where the Bronze Age cairn can be found. Afterwards, head to Penrhyndeudraeth for a warming vegan meal at the Eating Gorilla.

Access

Entry to water via grassy banks and cliff jumping. Follow tracks and footpaths, often uneven, to lakeside, approximately two kilometres from road end. Tygwyn railway station five kilometres away. Limited roadside parking near Eisingrug, four kilometres away.

RHAEADR DU

52.9306, -3.9849 / Maentwrog, Merionethshire / Swimming, paddling and plunge pool

Sequestered in woodland on the Ceunant Llennyrch National Nature Reserve, Rhaeadr Du is a tranquil waterfall and plunge pool with a large, shingle beach which leads into and out of the water. Shaded by the surrounding trees, the deep water can be chilly but makes for a refreshing and private swim, especially as a point to cool off after exploring the rest of this magical reserve. Pub meals are available at the Bryn Arms in Gellilydan or the Grapes in Maentwrog, both four kilometres away.

Access

Access via shingle beach. Difficult to reach: follow footpaths from Magnox power station down towards river – you may need to cross rough terrain. Tan-y-Bwlch to Harlech bus stops once each morning near Magnox power station, three kilometres away. Request stop on heritage Ffestiniog & Welsh Highland Railway for Plas Halt station near Maentwrog, five kilometres away. Lay-by parking near Magnox Power Station, three kilometres from swim spot.

LLYN CWMORTHIN

52.9963, -3.9718 / Tanygrisiau, Gwynedd / Swimming

Overlooked by the derelict cottages of former slate mines, Llyn Cwmorthin is a large lake with stunning views of the surrounding mountains. Grassy banks provide points from which you can lower yourself into the water, which due to its altitude is an ideal spot to cool off on a sunny day. With the twin lakes of Llynnau Diffwys roughly three kilometres further along the track, you can spend a day making your way between these swim spots, taking in Cwmorthin Waterfall along the way. Caffi Kiki in Tanygrisiau is an ideal place to stop off for a refreshing drink and bite to eat afterwards.

LLYN DINAS. © SHUTTERSTOCK/DJTAYLOR

Access

Entry to water via grassy banks. Follow track up to lake from Cwmorthin Waterfall. Car park at Cwmorthin Waterfall, a kilometre away; bus (to Blaenau Ffestiniog) leaves from stop near car park a few times a day.

LLYNNAU DIFFWYS

53.0003, -4.0001 / Tanygrisiau, Gwynedd / Swimming

At the head of the Croesor valley, Llynnau Diffwys is a pair of lakes which both have grassy banks leading into the water. The stones on the lakebeds can be slippery, so water shoes are advisable, and due to their altitude the waters here can be particularly cool. With spectacular views down the valley, these are the perfect places to cool off after the walk up and are a soothing, tranquil swim. Take the time to admire Cwmorthin Waterfall and to stop by the ruins of the former slate mine which dot the trail up. Afterwards, head to the Lakeside Cafe in Tanygrisiau for a warming drink and hearty jacket potato.

Access

Access via grassy banks, with some slippery stones. Strenuous four-kilometre walk up generally well-surfaced tracks from Croesor or Tanygrisiau; parking near the road end at both villages. Frequent buses to Blaenau Ffestiniog (with train station) near Tanygrisiau car park.

LLYN LLAGI

53.0133, -4.0166 / Croesor, Gwynedd /
Swimming

Tucked away in a cwm, Llyn Llagi is a small, enchanting lake bursting with captivating atmosphere, which has views over the Snowdonia National Park. The grassy banks adorning the lake serve as entry points into the chilly water. With mists curling around the rocky face which looms above the lake, this is a mystical and enticing swim spot, as well as the perfect place to stop off on a hike up to Cnicht and Llyn yr Adar. You can also pay a visit to Hafod Garregog National Nature Reserve before heading to the Plas Brondanw Cafe.

Access
Entry to water via grassy banks. Long, steep walk to water on trails and rough paths. Difficult to reach via public transport. Cnicht car park in Croesor six kilometres away.

LLYN DINAS

53.0222, -4.0672 / Beddgelert, Gwynedd /
Swimming

Located south of Snowdon (Yr Wyddfa), Llyn Dinas is a large lake reaching from the National Trust's Craflwyn and Beddgelert reserve to Llyndy Isaf farm. A grassy bank leads down to a small patch of shingle, from which you can ease yourself into the cool, clear water. With views stretching up and down the lake, this is an enchanting place. A dip here can be combined with a walk up Dinas Emrys, where Merlin is said to have witnessed the battle between dragons foretelling the coming of Arthur and where the red dragon now slumbers. The swim spot is easy to reach from the road; a path leads down to a footbridge over the river to reach the other side of the llyn. Alternatively, it is a pleasant three-kilometre riverside walk to Beddgelert, where you can get a bite to eat at Caffi Colwyn or Glaslyn Artisan Ice Cream & Pizza.

Access
Access via shingle beach and grassy banks. A498 road next to lake; footpath may be followed to south side of lake. Caernarfon bus stops on A498, at least four times daily, a kilometre away; Beddgelert on heritage Ffestiniog & Welsh Highland Railway. Parking in lay-by on A498, lakeside.

CWM PENNANT

53.0233, -4.1663 / Beddgelert, Gwynedd /
Swimming

Tucked away in a cleft of the Snowdonia National Park, Cwm Pennant is a small lake surrounded by a majestic landscape. Grassy banks make for comfortable points from which you can lower yourself into the chilly water, as well as an ideal spot for a post-swim picnic. The clear-blue waters of this lake are great to combine with exploring the nearby ruins of old mines, as well as taking advantage of the beautiful walks this area has to offer. You can find a hot drink and snack at the Tyddyn Mawr Tearoom.

Access
Access via gentle grassy banks. Follow bridle-way up from Beudy'r Ddol or footpaths through Beddgelert Forest; requires navigation. Meillionen halt on Welsh Highland Heritage Railway four kilometres away; buses from Beddgelert to Caernarfon stop every two hours on A4085 main road. Roadside parking at Beudy'r Ddol farmhouses, a kilometre away.

WATKIN PATH WATERFALLS. © *SHUTTERSTOCK/GAIL JOHNSON*

WATKIN PATH WATERFALLS

53.0442, -4.0551 / Beddgelert, Gwynedd / Swimming and plunge pool

Cascading down the side of Snowdon (Yr Wyddfa), the Watkin Path Waterfalls are a series of falls and plunge pools with crystal-clear water and breathtaking views down into the valley. Rocky edges to the pools serve as good platforms for launching into the water, which can warm pleasantly in the sun. Due to its proximity to the Watkin Path, this is an excellent spot to cool off on the descent from Snowdon, or can be tied in with a dip in Llyn Dinas, a little way down the road. You can pick up a well-deserved hot drink and snack, or something more substantial, at Caffi Gwynant.

Access
Access via rocky slabs and bouldered banks. Pay-and-display car park (with public toilets) by A498, a kilometre and a half away; bus service from Beddgelert and Caernarfon stops by car park.

LLYN GWYNANT

53.0460, -4.0215 / Beddgelert, Gwynedd / Swimming

Tucked around the base of Snowdon (Yr Wyddfa), Llyn Gwynant is a large lake with a pebbled beach. From here you can swim over to Elephant Rock on the far shore, where you can find stunning views over the llyn and of the hills beyond. This fantastic swim spot is within easy reach of the Watkin Path, making it a perfect place to cool off after descending from Snowdon. Alternatively, you could spend a day wild swimming and head down the road to Llyn Dinas for two dips in one trip. A refreshing drink and snack can be found afterwards at Caffi Gwynant.

Access
Entry to water via shingle beach, close to road. Caernarfon buses (at least four daily) stop on A498, 500 metres away. Roadside parking next to water.

GLASLYN

53.0720, -4.0644 / Llanberis, Gwynedd / Swimming

Overlooked by the Pyg and Miners' tracks to Snowdon (Yr Wyddfa), Glaslyn is a large mountain lake with a curving, shingle beach which provides access into the clear water. With the impressive peak of Snowdon looming above, the blue waters here make for an awe-inspiring swim, as well as the perfect place for a refreshing break on the climb up the mountain. A dip here can be worked into either of the Pyg or Miners' tracks due to its convenient location near their confluence

LLYN DU'R ARDDU. © *JOHN COEFIELD*   GLASLYN AND SNOWDON. © *JOHN COEFIELD*

point, and you can find a drink and refuelling snack at Hafod Eryri, or at Caffi Gorphwysfa at the start of the trails.

Access

Access via grassy banks. Miners' Track (towards Snowdon summit) passes lake's shore; uneven path and steep inclines. S2 and S4 Snowdon Sherpa services stop at Pen-y-Pass, five kilometres away, where there is also a car park.

LLYN DU'R ARDDU

53.0806, -4.0891 / Llanberis, Gwynedd / Swimming

Nestled beneath the shadow of a monolithic rock wall, Llyn Du'r Arddu is a large lake familiar to walkers of Snowdon's (Yr Wyddfa's) Llanberis Path. The beach on the near side provides an easy point of access in and out of the water, the depth of which increases closer to the rock wall. With timeless views down into the valley and stretching to Llanberis beyond, this is an iconic swim spot and the perfect point to catch your breath while climbing Snowdon. You can find a drink and snack at the Hafod Eryri on Snowdon's peak, where there are also toilets to hand, or at one of the many charming cafes in Llanberis.

Access

Entry into water via beach or rocky banks. Lake is close to Llanberis Path (to Snowdon

summit), which is uneven and steep. Clogwyn railway station on Snowdon Mountain Railway stops less than a kilometre from the llyn. Pay-and-display car park in Llanberis, six kilometres away.

LLYN GLAS

53.0809, -4.0642 / Llanberis, Gwynedd / Swimming

A modest lake located on Crib Goch, Llyn Glas is home to a small island and has patches of soft, grassy banks which lead into the cold mountain waters. With glorious views down into the valley, this is a peaceful, private spot with the open air above and the magnificent, imposing faces of Crib Goch and Bwlch Coch behind. After a day of hiking and swimming, drop in at Caffi Gorphwysfa in Pen-y-Pass for a rewarding hot drink and meal.

Access

Entry to water via grassy banks. Challenging walk from Llanberis, over rough, uneven ground with steep inclines and rough scrambling areas; only suitable for experienced hillwalkers with navigational skills. S1 and S2 Snowdon Sherpa bus services stop two and half kilometres away on Llanberis Pass a few times a day. Roadside parking at Llanberis Pass.

SNOWDONIA WATER SPORTS

53.1257, -4.1337 / Unit 2, Y Glyn, Llanberis, Gwynedd, LL55 4EL / 01286 879001 / Swimming / *snowdoniawatersports.com*

Snowdonia Water Sports have extended their portfolio to offer open water swim sessions at weekends between April and October at Llyn Padarn, already a popular wild swim spot. There are taster sessions (although swimmers must already be confident in the water) and a 500-metre course for experienced open water swimmers. There are safety paddlers on hand, as well as changing facilities, showers and an on-site cafe. With Snowdon (Yr Wyddfa) as your backdrop, this is the perfect location to develop your open air swimming skills.

Access

Entry to water via shingle shores. Frequent buses to Bangor, Caernarfon and Llanberis from A4086, 500 metres away. On-site parking, on water's edge.

LLYN PADARN

53.1264, -4.1328 / Llanberis, Gwynedd / Swimming

Stretching alongside Llanberis, one of the Snowdonia National Park's best-known towns, Llyn Padarn is a long lake with a couple of small lagoons. In 2014, the llyn was designated the first freshwater lake in Wales to achieve bathing water quality. A shingle beach makes for quick access into the llyn, where you can find wonderful panoramic views of the surrounding hills and of Snowdon (Yr Wyddfa) rising in the distance. A swim here can easily be tied into a day of exploring Llanberis, with its Lake Railway and the National Slate Museum on the other side of the water. Toilets are to hand at the Snowdonia Water Sports car park and afterwards you can stop by at Pete's Eats for a drink and a snack, or pick up some fish and chips to eat by the lake.

LLYNNAU MYMBYR. © *SHUTTERSTOCK/VALERY EGOROV*

Access

Entry to water is via shingle shores. Frequent buses to Bangor, Caernarfon and Llanberis from A4086, 500 metres away. Parking near Snowdonia Water Sports, on water's edge.

LLYN IDWAL

53.1190, -4.0263 / Bethesda, Gwynedd / Swimming

Found at the base of Glyder Fawr, Llyn Idwal is a large lake which stretches towards the bowl-like rock face of the mountain ahead. A long, shingle beach makes it easy to wade into the shallows and acclimatise to the cool mountain water. With enchanting views of the surrounding landscape, this is a terrific swim spot which can be tied in with some breathtaking walking routes around the nearby mountains as well as the Cwm Idwal National Nature Reserve, where you can observe the diverse wildlife of the region. Hot drinks, snacks and toilet facilities are available at Ogwen Centre.

Access

Entry to water via shingle beaches. Follow stone-slabbed trail. 6B and S6 (Snowdon Sherpa) buses stop near YHA Idwal Cottage, a kilometre away. Parking at National Trust Carneddau and Glyderau car park, near YHA Idwal Cottage, a kilometre away.

LLYN BOCHLWYD

53.1144, -4.0097 / Capel Curig, Conwy /
Swimming

High up in the Glyderau, Llyn Bochlwyd is
a lake tucked among majestic peaks, with
views down into the valley below. The banks
which lead to the water are a mixture of grass
and rock, although you should be mindful
of the stones underfoot. Surrounded by a
breathtaking landscape, this spot is great to
combine with a swim in nearby Llyn Idwal, or
a hike up the trail overlooking Cwm Bochlwyd
to the Devil's Kitchen and Glyder Fawr. Grab
a drink and bite to eat from Ogwen Snack Bar
back at the Carneddau and Glyderau car park,
where toilet facilities are also available.

Access

Entry to water via rocky, grassy shores.
Sometimes steep, stone-slabbed trail to lake.
6B and S6 (Snowdon Sherpa) buses stop near
YHA Idwal Cottage, a kilometre away. Parking
at National Trust Carneddau and Glyderau
car park, near YHA Idwal Cottage, a kilometre
away.

LLYNNAU MYMBYR

53.0985, -3.9324 / Capel Curig, Gwynedd /
Swimming

Situated in the north of the Snowdonia
National Park, Llynau Mymbyr is a vast,
sunglasses-shaped lake managed by the
Plas y Brenin National Outdoor Centre. Paid,
supervised sessions are available here, ideal
for newcomers to open water swimming,
however the centre focuses more on water
sports training and so the lake is also open to
unsupervised swimmers. The boulder-littered
banks mean a slight scramble is required to
access the water, but once over the rocks
these stone platforms serve as solid bases
for getting in and out of the water. A swim
here can easily be tied in with a trip to Gwydir

Forest Park, and on the way you can find a
drink and snack at Ty Hyll or Moel Siabod Cafe.

Access

Access via stony banks. Plas y Brenin bus stop,
a kilometre away, served by S2 and S6 buses
to Llanberis and other local destinations a few
times a day. Limited parking available beside
the A4086, less than 100 metres from banks
of the lake.

FAIRY GLEN

53.0727, -3.7912 / Betws-y-Coed, Caernarfon-
shire / Swimming and plunge pool

Situated at the confluence of two streams,
Fairy Glen is a gorge section of the Afon
Conwy with moss-laden rock walls on either
side. Large boulders provide platforms for
getting into and out of the water, however
they require a slight scramble and may be
slippery. The water can get deep quickly here,
and it is not advised to swim after periods
of heavy rainfall. With the stunning, lush
greenery of the trees overhanging the gorge,
this is a secluded spot which is great to tie in
with a visit to the nearby Fairy Falls further
along the river, or to the National Trust's
Ysbyty Ifan. You can find hot drinks and cake
afterwards at Conwy Falls Cafe. The Fairy Glen
is on privately owned land; there is a small
charge to enter the gorge.

Access

Access via slippery boulders; requires scrambling. Follow private path through gorge. Buses
stop on A470 main road, 500 metres away,
near Pont yr Afanc for Blaenau Ffestiniog and
Llandudno, approximately five times a day.
Parking available at the Fairy Glen car park,
less than 500 metres from the gorge.

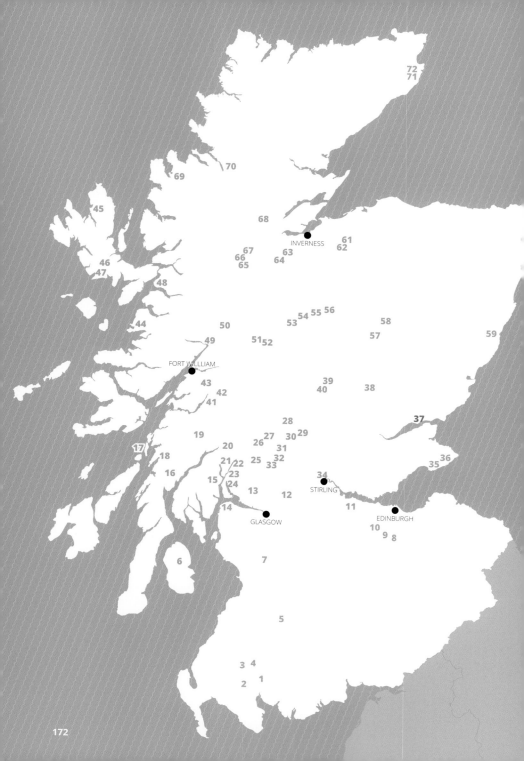

INVERNESS

72
71

70

69

68

67
66
65

61
62

63
64

50

49

51 52

53 54 55 56

58

57

59

FORT WILLLIAM

43

42
41

39
40

38

37

44

48

45

46
47

17

18

16

19

20

21 22
23
24

25

26 27
31
32
33

28

30 29

35 36

34

STIRLING

15

13

12

11

EDINBURGH

14

GLASGOW

10
9 8

7

6

5

3 4
2 1

Scotland

THE TRINKIE. © *FERGUS MATHER*

GREY MARE'S TAIL BURN. © *WALKINGENGLISHMAN.COM*

GREY MARE'S TAIL BURN

55.0253, -4.3621 / Newton Stewart, Dumfries & Galloway / Swimming and plunge pool

Adorned with fern-strewn, grassy banks, Grey Mare's Tail Burn is a stretch of river with several waterfalls and plunge pools dotted along its path. Natural stone platforms around the plunge pools provide points from which you can step or slip into the water, though there may be a large, sudden step. Surrounded by charming wild flowers and with a view stretching down the river which is shaded by overhanging trees, this idyllic location can be combined with a walk around the Black Loch or a hike up to Murray's Monument. You can find a snack and a drink at the Clatteringshaws Visitor Centre & Cafe.

Access

Access via stone platforms. Not easily accessible by public transport: nearest bus stop on outskirts of Newton Stewart, eleven kilometres away. Parking at Black Loch car park within a kilometre; path to swim spot covers some uneven ground.

PULHOWAN BURN IN THE WOOD OF CREE

55.0105, -4.5323 / Newton Stewart, Dumfries & Galloway / Swimming and plunge pool

Concealed in ancient woodland, Pulhowan Burn is a small river and home to several plunge pools which are ideal for anyone seeking a quick and exhilarating dip. The banks are a mixture of soft grass and stone boulders, providing various entry points into the water. With bracken-covered ground, the woodland here creates a mesmerising background to the stepped waterfall. On a trip to this RSPB reserve, it is worth taking your time to explore the woods and wildlife more thoroughly, with a chance to see otters and even pied flycatchers. You can find refreshments in Newton Stewart.

Access

Stony banks provide access into water. Not easily reached by public transport: closest bus stop over six kilometres away in Newton Stewart. Parking available approximately two kilometres away at Wood of Cree car park, five kilometres north-west of Newton Stewart.

WATER OF MINNOCH. © *STUART TAYLOR, HIGHLANDERIMAGES PHOTOGRAPHY*

WATER OF MINNOCH

55.0743, -4.5523 / Glentrool, Dumfries & Galloway / Swimming and plunge pool

Flowing through the Galloway Forest Park, the Water of Minnoch is a river and small waterfall which can be accessed close to the Glentrool Visitor Centre. The slower-flowing water above the waterfall can be accessed through grassy banks, although the river area directly next to the bridge is very rocky. The pools beneath the waterfall require a little more scrambling to access, over some large boulders. From here, you can swim up beneath the bridge and take in the atmosphere of this stunning location, lined with pines. You can reward yourself afterwards with refreshments in the Glentrool Visitor Centre, and a swim here can be tied in with an exploration of the area on one of the many wildlife-packed walking routes and mountain biking trails.

Access
Grassy banks or rocks access the water. 359 service operates every couple of hours from the Post Office bus stop in Glentrool, just over a kilometre away. Glentrool Visitor Centre car park provides pay-and-display parking less than 100 metres away.

LOCH TROOL

55.0847, -4.5021 / Glentrool, Dumfries & Galloway / Swimming

Deep in the Galloway Forest Park, Loch Trool is a lake imbued with history. The mixture of grass and scrub lining the sloping banks make for soft points of entry into the cool water, where you can connect with the landscape in which Robert the Bruce fought and won the Battle of Glen Trool, more than 700 years ago. A swim here can conclude a walk around this astonishingly beautiful location, incorporating Bruce's Stone, which gives picture-perfect views over the lake. You can find refreshments and more information about the area at the Glentrool Visitor Centre.

Access
Access via sloping grass and scrub banks. Buses to Newton Stewart and Girvan stop five kilometres away in Glentrool. Loch Trool Trail car park provides parking less than a kilometre away from the swim spot, which can be reached via an established trail.

GLEN ROSA WATER. © SHUTTERSTOCK/BIG JOCK

TAMAR MANOUKIAN NEW CUMNOCK POOL

55.3965, -4.1835 / 22 Castle, New Cumnock, Cumnock, East Ayrshire, KA18 4AN / 01290 333891 / Swimming / *dumfries-house.org.uk/attractions/new-cumnock-pool*

Located in a historic mining town within East Ayrshire, the Tamar Manoukian New Cumnock Pool is one of Scotland's most popular lidos, attracting thousands of visitors each year. The pool's timetable accommodates swimmers of all abilities and features a variety of public swimming, adult-only and aqua fit sessions. The lido itself is twenty-five metres long and is always kept at around 30 °C. The pool closed in 2016 for a major revamp and was reopened in June 2017 once it had been fully refurbished by the Dumfries House Trust. The process took nine months to complete and was part of a £4 million refurbishment scheme undertaken by The Prince's Foundation. After your swim, several takeaway refreshment options can be found just down the road.

Access

Entry into pool via ladders; pool area wheelchair accessible. Castlehill bus stop 150 metres away, served by regular buses to Ayr, Tarbolton and Sanquhar. New Cumnock railway station 700 metres away. On-site parking.

GLEN ROSA WATER

55.6020, -5.2044 / Brodick, Isle of Arran / Swimming and plunge pool

In the heart of the Isle of Arran, Glen Rosa Water is a waterfall and plunge pool on Glenrosa Water. Stone boulders and platforms around the water's edge provide perfect points from which to descend into the water, which is usually cold but serves as a refreshing swim after the hike to the swim spot. Surrounded by timeless mountains, Glen Rosa is a wild and captivating swim, and can be combined with a hike to Goat Fell. Nearby Brodick offers plenty of options for grabbing a snack and a drink, such as Janie's and the Little Rock cafe.

Access

Stone boulders and natural stone platforms allow access to water. Glen Rosa Waterfall can only be accessed on foot; 322 bus stops regularly three and a half kilometres away at Glen Rosa Road End stop. Parking available approximately four kilometres away in Brodick, opposite Brodick Primary School.

WHITE LOCH

55.7413, -4.4058 / Newton Mearns, East Renfrewshire / Swimming

Not far from the outskirts of Glasgow, White Loch is a modest reservoir tucked beside the B769. The water can be notoriously cold and swimmers are advised to wear a wetsuit, as well as swim shoes to make the shingle underfoot more comfortable. With a fantastic view over the loch and the hills beyond, this swim spot is exposed to the elements, so take plenty of warm layers for enjoying its raw, natural beauty. You can find cafes up the road in Barrhead, Neilston and Newton Mearns.

Access

Muddy, stony banks provide entry points. Buses to and from Glasgow stop five kilometres away in Malletsheugh. Lay-by parking on B769 beside the northern shore of the loch, less than 100 metres away.

GLENCORSE RESERVOIR

55.8597, -3.2446 / Penicuik, Midlothian / Swimming

At the foot of Castlelaw Hill, Glencorse Reservoir is a reservoir with tree-lined banks and a small island to one end. Grassy banks form soft entry points into the cool water, as well as excellent spots for picnics. A swim here can offer a refreshing opportunity to cool off from walking in the Pentland Hills Regional Park or hiking up to Castlelaw Hill, taking in the Iron Age Castlelaw Hill Fort on the way. The nearby Pentland Hills Cafe Express is the perfect place to grab a post-swim snack and drink.

Access

Access via grassy banks. Flotterstone Inn bus stop a kilometre and a half away, with services to Edinburgh, Dumfries and Biggar. Pentland Hills Regional Park Flotterstone car park rests a kilometre and a half away, and can be accessed from A702 by Flotterstone Inn.

THREIPMUIR RESERVOIR. © *SHUTTERSTOCK/VITO HORAK*

THREIPMUIR RESERVOIR

55.8642, -3.3208 / Balerno, Edinburgh / Swimming and paddling

Set in the countryside only a few miles from Edinburgh, Threipmuir Reservoir is a large lake with a long, sandy beach which provides an excellent entry point into the water for both swimming and paddling. The fields beyond the water provide a tranquil backdrop, and with the open sky above, this is a great swim spot for anyone looking to escape from the city. You can also take the time to walk around Threipmuir and Harlaw reservoirs on a gentle trail, or around Red Moss of Balerno Nature Reserve. Refreshments can be found afterwards at Carlyle's Bar and Kitchen or the Mill at St Joseph's in nearby Balerno.

Access

Access via sandy beach. Three kilometres away, Cockburn Crescent bus stop served by frequent buses to Whitecraig. Parking available at Threipmuir Reservoir car park, less than a kilometre away.

LOUP OF FINTRY. © *SHUTTERSTOCK/MOUNTAINTREKS*

GATEWAY, JUPITER ARTLAND

55.9070, -3.4237 / Bonnington House Steadings, Wilkieston, Edinburgh, EH27 8BY / 01506 889900 / Swimming and paddling / *www.jupiterartland. org/art/gateway*

The colourful, circular Gateway pool is not for the serious swimmer. At only nine metres wide, this blend of artwork and lido is more of a plunge pool, however it is rare that you get to swim and become part of an art installation. One of Jupiter Artland's permanent outdoor exhibits, the Gateway pool opened in 2019 and hosts public swimming sessions, although you will have to book a slot. The swirling lines that criss-cross the pool represent ley lines that supposedly run through the sculpture park, and the pool is surrounded by sculpted yew hedges. There are changing facilities in the geodesic dome by the pool, although if you forget your costume, Jupiter Artland sell swimming trunks decorated with the Gateway's vibrant swirls. This unique pool is the perfect accompaniment to a day out at the sculpture park and art gallery, and afterwards the Grapes pub can provide refreshments.

Access

Access to the water via steps. Wheelchair access to much of sculpture park, including the pool; accessible toilets available. Frequent buses to Edinburgh/Whitburn stop at sculpture park entrance. Kirknewton railway station three kilometres away. On-site parking.

AVON LAGOON

55.9726, -3.6334 / Linlithgow, West Lothian / Swimming

A stone's throw from Linlithgow, Avon Lagoon is a small lake beside the River Avon Heritage Trail which is shaded by copses of trees dotted around the lake's edge. With the peace of the countryside as well as the convenience of the nearby town, this is a great swim spot if you're not looking to travel far. A visit here can easily be combined with a day of outdoor activity, with the Kettlestoun Mains Woodland Walk and Muiravonside Country Park all within easy reach. A variety of refreshment options are available nearby, including cake and hot drinks at Steading Cafe and meals at the West Port Hotel.

Access

Access via grassy banks. Buses between Livingston and Bathgate stop hourly at Kettlestoun Mains bus stop, less than a kilometre away; Linlithgow railway station under three kilometres away. Parking available at West Port car park, less than two kilometres from Avon Lagoon. Established path through the woods leads to lake.

LOUP OF FINTRY

56.0495, -4.1500 / Fintry, Stirling / Swimming and plunge pool

Tumbling from a grass-topped, rocky outcrop, the Loup of Fintry is a picturesque waterfall hidden in a small grove of trees. Rocky banks provide platforms for getting into the invigorating water, where you can swim up to the base of the waterfall and enjoy lush, idyllic views of the gorge and trees stretching out before you. Combine a dip here with a walk through the woodland around Carron Valley Reservoir, or walk up to the old site of Sir John de Graham Castle and absorb some of the landscape's rich heritage. Further along the road is the Bunny Coffee Hutch, where you can get a cake and a hot drink.

GOUROCK OUTDOOR POOL © *SARAH THELWALL*.

Access

Water accessed via rocky banks. Five and a half kilometres away, Church Hall bus stop in Fintry served by infrequent buses to Balfron. Limited parking available at Loup of Fintry car park, a dedicated lay-by on B818 beside entrance to the trail, which covers grassy and sometimes uneven ground.

DUMBROCK LOCH

55.9752, -4.3256 / Milngavie, East Dunbartonshire / Swimming

Just outside Milngavie and Strathblane, Dumbrock Loch is a small lake in Mugdock Country Park. Grassy banks and sloping stone edges provide a choice of entry points into the water, and are also a great place to dry off in sunny weather. The loch, which can be reedy, is fringed by trees and has a peaceful feel. A dip here can easily be part of a day exploring the rest of Mugdock Country Park

and its ruined castle, or the nearby Scottish Wildlife Trust reserve at Loch Ardinning. You can find refreshments afterwards at Charlie's Coffee Bar in the country park.

Access

Grassy banks and stone edges lead into the water. Frequent bus services from Glasgow and Stirling call at the Milndavie Road stop in Strathblane, a kilometre and a half from the loch. Ample parking available at Mugdock Country Park car park, less than 500 metres away.

GOUROCK OUTDOOR POOL

55.9612, -4.8219 / Albert Road, Gourock, Inverclyde, PA19 1NQ / 01475 213122 / Swimming and paddling / *www. inverclydeleisure.com/facilities/ gourock-pool*

Originally opened in 1909, Gourock Outdoor Pool is the oldest heated lido in Scotland. Maintained at a

temperature of 29 °C, the pool uses saltwater taken from the Firth of Clyde. The thirty-three-by-fifteen-metre lido slopes to a depth of three and a half metres, and there is also a shallower pool for young children and toddlers. Thanks to a large renovation project, the lido offers modern changing facilities, improved disabled access and a terraced area and traditional patio with spectacular views of the Clyde Estuary. Throughout the summer, visitors can also enjoy a unique swimming experience under the stars by taking part in the pool's Starlight Swim evening sessions. A variety of options to grab a drink and bite to eat are within easy walking distance.

Access

Entry into pool via steps and ladders. Pool area wheelchair accessible; hoist available. Just outside the lido buses to Glasgow and Greenock stop approximately every thirty minutes. Gourock railway station 500 metres away. On-site parking.

LETTERMAY BURN

56.1610, -4.9304 / Lochgoilhead, Argyll & Bute / Swimming, paddling and plunge pool

Gushing from natural stone platforms and winding its way through enchanting woodland, Lettermay Burn is a stretch of river home to several small waterfalls and plunge pools. The smooth banks provide easy points of access to the river and its plunge pools, which can have low water levels after long, dry spells. A trip to this serene and secluded location can be tied in with a visit to Loch Goil, as well as an exploration of the Cormonachan Wood, which are teeming with wildlife. Afterwards, you can grab a hot drink and snack at the Boat Shed Cafe, just by Loch Goil Cruisers.

Access
Access via smooth banks. Infrequent buses services to Helensburgh and Arrochar stop at Drimsynie Caravan Park stop, a kilometre and a half away. Parking available at car park off the B839 in Lochgoilhead, three kilometres from Lettermay Burn; first section of the path follows established track, however later stages are narrower.

LOCH TUNNAIG

56.1594, -5.3599 / Ford, Argyll & Bute / Swimming

Isolated among the Scottish hills, Loch Tunnaig is a small stretch of water within a cluster of six lochs. With no nearby roads or villages, this is the perfect place to experience a truly wild swim beneath the serenity of the open sky. The water here can be cold, and with no facilities bringing a picnic and flask of a warming drink are a must. You can also take the time to explore the other lochs around Loch Tunnaig, including the much larger and aptly named Loch Awe.

Access
Soft, grassy banks provide access to water. Only accessible on foot; the walk covers uneven ground and can be steep at times. Infrequent 421 bus stops at the Hatchery stop in Ford, seven kilometres away. Parking available six kilometres away at lay-by beside a wooded area on the B840.

EASDALE ISLAND

56.2906, -5.6532 / Ellenabeich, Isle of Seil / Swimming

Dotting Easdale Island are numerous flooded slate quarries with clear, blue water and captivating views of the sea beyond. As a precaution, you should check which quarries are open for swimming during your visit as this is subject to change. This relaxing location, which can be cold, is perfect to combine with a visit to the Easdale Island Folk Museum, where you can learn more of the island's heritage and history, or a walk along the island's trail around the other quarries. You can grab a warming meal afterwards at the Puffer Bar and Restaurant.

Access
Access via shingle beach. Easdale Island is car free and can only be accessed by ferry; the bus service from Oban stops a few times a day at Turning Area in Ellenabeich, within 200 metres of ferry. On the island, follow grassy path past Easedale Island Folk Museum towards quarry. Parking available at Ellenabeich car park before making the crossing.

RIVER OUDE

56.2928, -5.4681 / Kilmelford, Argyll & Bute / Swimming

Meandering through grassy and tree-covered hills, the River Oude is a clear, lively river which opens out into a dam downstream of where it is crossed by the A816. Soft, sloping banks provide easy access points into the water, which is shaded further along by the over-

LOCH AWE. © SHUTTERSTOCK/R K HILL

hanging trees. You can swim in the river or make your way towards the lake formed by the dam, however be cautious of boulders beneath the surface. Surrounded by the contrasting hues of gorse and lush tree foliage, this swim spot is perfect for passers-by looking to take a plunge. The Catchacarrot Vegan Pop-up Cafe in Kilmelford offers the chance to grab some well-earned refreshments.

Access

Sloping banks into water; getting down to bank may involve a scramble down a gentle slope. Buses to Oban and Ardrishaig stop a few times a day four and a half kilometres away at Car Park stop in Kilmelford. Lay-by before bridge provides space to park within 200 metres of riverbank.

LOCH AWE

56.4060, -5.0300 / Lochawe, Argyll & Bute / Swimming and paddling

Suitably named, Loch Awe is a vast, forty-kilometre lake home to islands and castle ruins, encased by the timeless Trossachs. Accessing the water is easily done from a large, sandy beach, making this loch both swimmer and paddler friendly. From here, you can experience picturesque views of the loch stretching into the distance, as well as sights of the derelict and mysterious Kilchurn Castle, which can be further explored on foot. You can also enjoy a visit to St Conan's Kirk, comprising a church, gardens and tearoom, or one of the several adventurous walks around Loch Awe, which can lead you to the Duncan Ban MacIntyre Monument.

Access

Easy access from sandy beach. Cruachan Cottages bus stop served several times a day to Oban, Taynuilt and Dalmally, less than two kilometres from the swim spot. Parking at Kilchurn Castle car park, within a kilometre.

FIRKIN POINT, LOCH LOMOND. © *SHUTTERSTOCK/IAN WOOLCOCK*

FALLS OF FALLOCH

56.3501, -4.6930 / Crianlarich, Stirling /
Swimming and plunge pool

Tumbling from a rocky outcrop, the Falls of
Falloch is a majestic waterfall and plunge pool
also known as Rob Roy's Bathtub, although it is
not known if the famous Scottish outlaw ever
bathed here. The trees enveloping the stony
walls of the pool make this legendary swim
spot feel peaceful, and as you dip your feet in
the peaty water it is easy to feel in awe of the
scenery around you. The force of the waterfall
is powerful enough to hold a swimmer under
the water and caution should be taken. After
your swim you can get a well-deserved hot
meal at the Drovers Inn in Inverarnan.

Access

Slabs of stone surrounding the pool provide
access; may be slippery. Three and a half
kilometres away, Hotel stop on A82 served by
buses to Uig, Portree and Fort William. Parking
at Falls of Falloch car park just off A82, within
200 metres of swim spot.

LOCH ARKLET

56.2515, -4.5915 / Stronachlachar, Stirling /
Swimming

At the heart of the Loch Lomond and the
Trossachs National Park and by neighbouring
Loch Katrine, Loch Arklet is a smaller loch
overlooked by tree-blanketed hills and
mountains in the far distance. Grassy banks
provide entry points to the cool waters of this
stunning swim spot, which was also reputedly
the home of Rob Roy MacGregor's wife, Mary
of Comar. After taking a dip beneath the open
sky, you can journey on to nearby Stronachlachar for a post-swim pick-me-up
at the Pier Cafe.

Access

Grassy banks lead into water. Not easily
accessible by public transport: Sir Walter Scott
Steamship, which runs from the Trossachs
Pier at the southern tip of Loch Katrine to
Stronachlachar Pier, is just over a kilometre
away. Parking available at lay-by on B829,
beside the sign for Queen Elizabeth Forest
Park, a kilometre and a half away.

LOCH KATRINE

56.2609, -4.5791 / Stronachlachar, Stirling / Swimming and paddling

Snaking across the Trossachs, Loch Katrine is a vast, curving lake with a mysterious air about its tranquil waters. Grass and scrub banks provide soft entry points, although they may require a little scramble to get to, and can provide a great place for a picnic after a revitalising swim. A dip in Loch Katrine can be combined with a trip across the loch on the steamboat which runs from the jetty at Stronachlachar to the Trossachs Pier, enabling you to take in the immense splendour of the surrounding landscape. The Pier Cafe offers the perfect place to enjoy refreshments at the water's edge.

Access
Grassy banks give access to water. Difficult to access by public transport: nearest railway station and buses in Crianlarich, twenty-eight kilometres away. Parking available at the Stronachlachar Pier car park, less than a kilometre away.

FIRKIN POINT, LOCH LOMOND

56.1706, -4.6762 / Tarbet, Argyll & Bute / Swimming and paddling

Along the western shore of Loch Lomond, Firkin Point is a picturesque stretch of shingle beach with a stunning view of Ben Lomond rising above the opposite bank. The stony bank is an easy point of access to wade into the deep, cool waters of the loch, as well as a great location for paddling. With the convenience of public toilets close at hand in the car park, take the time to enjoy the serenity of this swim spot by walking along the woodland trail beside the loch's shore. Afterwards, head up to the Bonnie and Ben Cafe for a snack and a hot drink.

Access
Access via shingle beach. Hotel bus stop three and a half kilometres away in Inverbeg served several times a day by services from Glasgow, Fort William, Portree, Uig, Campbeltown, Oban and Lochgoilhead. Arrochar and Tarbet railway station five kilometres away. Parking available at Firkin Point car park off the A82, 100 metres from shore.

MILARROCHY BAY, LOCH LOMOND

56.0962, -4.5566 / Balmaha, Stirling / Swimming and paddling

A sheltered area of the vast Loch Lomond, Milarrochy Bay looks out on to the relaxing waters of the loch and to the mountains of the Trossachs. A long, shingle beach with nearby public toilets provides the perfect base point for getting in and out of the water, which can be cold due to the loch's depth. As Loch Lomond is also a popular location with canoes and boats, swimmers are advised to use tow floats for safety. This gorgeous location can easily be tied in with a walk up to Conic Hill, where you will find spectacular panoramic views overlooking the loch. Afterwards, head to St Mocha Coffee Shop and Ice Cream Parlour in Balmaha for welcome refreshments.

Access
Shingle beach. Car Park bus stop two kilometres away in Balmaha, served by buses from Alexandria approximately every ninety minutes. On-site car park situated along the West Highland Way, less than 200 metres from water's edge.

LOCH ARD. © *JAMES CARRON*

LOCH ARD

56.1880, -4.4886 / Kinlochard, Stirling / Swimming and paddling

At the heart of the Queen Elizabeth Forest Park, Loch Ard is a modest loch with a wide, enchanting view of the surrounding hills and mountains. A mixture of grassy and muddy banks leads into the chilly water, and at over four kilometres in length the loch is ideal for anyone looking for a long training swim. With plenty of trail routes for walking, running and cycling, a swim in Loch Ard can be a perfect stop to cool off or to start a day of outdoors exploration, and afterwards you can find refreshments at the Wee Blether Tearoom in Kinlochard.

Access
Grassy and muddy banks lead to water. Bus stop at Tourist Information Centre in Aberfoyle approximately seven kilometres away, for regular services between Glasgow and Stirling. Roadside parking at lay-by on B829 beside the

two benches marking the swim spot.

LOCH DOINE

56.3393, -4.4901 / Balquhidder, Stirling / Swimming and paddling

A small loch beside Loch Voil, Loch Doine has all the charm of its neighbour as well as soft, grassy banks providing quick entry points into the water. With swathes of fir trees rising up into the hills on either side, this swim spot is bracing and private, and can easily be combined with a walk into the timeless and majestic Crianlarich Hills with picturesque views back over the valley. There are no nearby cafes, so make sure you bring a hot drink and filling snack to warm yourself up after a dip.

Access
Access via grassy banks. Not easily accessible by public transport: nearest bus stop twelve kilometres away near Kingshouse for buses from Callander. Parking available at signed car park at the

far end of the track running alongside Loch Voil and Loch Doine, two kilometres west of swim spot.

LOCH VOIL

56.3465, -4.4465 / Balquhidder, Stirling / Swimming and paddling

In the shadow of Creag Mhòr, Loch Voil is a narrow loch with soothing, calm water. A stony beach serves as a great entry point, allowing you to wade into the water. With nothing but the quiet road and trees behind and the open loch and mountains before you, this is an idyllic location for a peaceful swim and picnic. After your dip, take the time to wander up to the mirrored cabin called the LookOut, or head the other way along the loch towards Balquhidder, where you can see the grave of the famed Scottish outlaw and folk hero Rob Roy MacGregor. Those looking for refreshments will have to travel to Strathyre.

LOCH TAY. © JAMES CARRON

Access

Access via stony beach. Not easy to reach by public transport: nearest bus stop just over eight kilometres away near Kingshouse, served by buses from Callander. Extremely limited parking available along the road, fifty metres away.

LOCH TAY

56.4727, -4.3028/ Killin, Stirling / Swimming and paddling

Stretching along the foot of Ben Lawers, Loch Tay is a large lake with banks swathed in woodland. A small, sandy beach provides an access point into the cool, calm waters of the loch – perfect for both paddling and swimming. With a view of the lake stretching out ahead and grassland behind, this is a picturesque location to relax while absorbing the beauty of the surrounding landscape. On a visit here you can also take the time to see the stunning Falls of Dochart or visit the Scottish Crannog Centre in Kenmore to find out more about the Iron Age dwellings that dot the loch side. Public toilets are available in Killin, as are a number of hotel restaurants, where you can end the day with a meal.

Access

Access via sandy beach. Callander stop at the Station Road Turning Circle in Killin served by buses from Callander a few times a day, a kilometre from the lake. Roadside parking along Pier Road, less than a kilometre away. Path to lake is a grassy and sometimes uneven track.

LOCH BOLTACHAN

56.4083, -4.1094 / St Fillans, Perth & Kinross / Swimming

A small loch sequestered among the hills and knolls of the Trossachs, Loch Boltachan has a mixture of stony and grassy banks from which you can ease yourself into the water. Due to its height, the water can be very cold and in winter will ice over.

Remote and private, this is a memorable swim spot with a breathtaking panorama of the surrounding hills. Due to its isolated location, be sure to take a hot drink and something to eat, as well as plenty of warm layers for once you leave the water. You can also make the hike out part of a round trip to include Little Port Hill and The Girron.

Access

Grassy banks into water; challenging hike over hilly terrain to lochside. Two kilometres away, Station Road bus stop in St Fillans served by infrequent buses to Perth. Roadside parking by Loch Earn in St Fillans, approximately three kilometres away.

LOCH EARN

56.3935, -4.1719 / St Fillans, Perth & Kinross / Swimming and paddling

Spanning from Lochearnhead to St Fillans in the Loch Lomond and the Trossachs National Park, Loch Earn is a vast lake with distant views of Ben Vorlich. A stony beach slopes into the water, which due to its depth is usually cold. Although swimmers should be mindful of the boulders in the shallows, this location is perfect for paddling as well as swimming, and serves as a great location for a family picnic. If you're looking for a day of water-packed fun, CAG Adventures in Lochearnhead offers guided paddleboard and canoe trips, or you could explore the nearby glens and drink in the beauty of this national park. Broch Cafe in nearby Strathyre offers the reward of hot drinks and cake.

Access

Stony beach leads into water. Buses to Perth, Crieff and Killin stop infrequently at Four Seasons Hotel in St Fillans, just over three kilometres away. Parking available at large lay-by in wooded area halfway along the loch, off the A85.

LOCH LUBNAIG

56.2779, -4.2841 / Callander, Stirling / Swimming and paddling

Nestled in the Loch Lomond and the Trossachs National Park, Loch Lubnaig curves around the base of its mountains, creating breath-taking panoramic views while you swim. A wide, shingle beach makes it easy to ease yourself into the loch's cool, still waters and also serves as a great place to paddle. You can kick back and relax with a picnic here or hike up to the top of Beinn Each, where you will find stunning vistas of the surrounding mountains and loch below. On the bank of the loch, the Cabin is a great place to get a post-swim snack.

Access

Access via shingle beach. Not easy to reach by public transport: closest bus stop six and a half kilometres away in Strathyre, for infrequent buses from Killin. Signposted car park for Loch Lubnaig just off A84, less than 100 metres away.

LOCH RUSKY

56.2058, -4.2345 / Callander, Stirling / Swimming

A small loch in the Queen Elizabeth Forest Park, Loch Rusky has a concrete jetty which provides the perfect platform for slipping into the water. This site is also used by boats and is a popular fishing spot, so a tow float is recommended for visibility. With a wide view and trees lining the banks, this is a charming swim spot. Watch out for glimpses of ospreys during the spring and summer months, but be sure to observe any restrictions which might be in place. Head to Callander for a well-earned pick-me-up at Pip's Coffee House or Mhor Bread tearoom.

Access

Access via concrete jetty. Bus services from Glasgow stop four and a half kilometres away at Inchmoy stop. Lay-by parking close to gate for Loch Rusky on A81, approximately 300 metres from loch, or a little further north by a forestry track.

LAKE OF MENTEITH

56.1777, -4.2780 / Aberfoyle, Stirling / Swimming and paddling

On the edge of the Queen Elizabeth Forest Park, the Lake of Menteith is a medium-sized lake with two small isles, one of which is home to Inchmahome Priory. You can paddle in the shallows by the sandy shore or wade further in for a bracing and revitalising swim. After your dip, you can soak up the calming atmosphere with a picnic or connect with the lake's history by visiting the ruins of the priory. Afterwards, head to the Station Coffee Shop in Aberfoyle for a hot drink.

LOCH LUBNAIG. © *JAMES CARRON*

Access

Sandy shore leads into water. X10A bus service between Glasgow and Stirling stops a kilometre away at Inchmoy every couple of hours. Small car park in a wooded area directly off B8034, less than fifty metres from the lake's shore.

DEVIL'S BUCKET

56.1872, -3.9046 / Dunblane, Stirling / Swimming and plunge pool

Devil's Bucket on Wharry Burn is a small waterfall and plunge pool, which can fall to a low level during prolonged dry spells. With open countryside all around and a wooded area home to more pools just along the river, this is a great location to enjoy a picnic in the sun. A swim here can be tied in with a day of exploration in nearby Stirling, where you can also visit the National Wallace Monument, Stirling Castle and Cambuskenneth Abbey. A variety of cafes are

available in Stirling, or you can opt for the Beech Tree Cafe in Dunblane.

Access

Access from grassy banks and stony (sometimes slippery) platforms. Poor public transport links: closest bus stop four kilometres away on outskirts of Stirling. Roadside parking on Sheriffmuir Road by bridge on Wharry Burn, approximately a kilometre from Devil's Bucket.

PITTENWEEM TIDAL POOL

56.2105, -2.7376 / 10 West Braes, Pittenweem, Anstruther, Fife, KY10 2PT / Swimming and paddling / *thewestbraes. blogspot.com*

Pittenweem Tidal Pool is a man-made outdoor swimming pool located in the West Braes area of Pittenweem. It is approximately fifty metres long and twenty metres wide, and is estimated to have been around since the

nineteenth century. The walls surrounding the pool offer a feeling of protection from the waters beyond, but it is recommended that people only use the pool at mid to low tide when the walls are visible. With the Firth of Forth lapping before you, this is a great spot to inject a bit of wilderness into your swim without having to travel into Scotland's countryside. A community group called the West Braes Project are currently overseeing plans to renovate the pool and the surrounding areas. Nearby Pittenweem has a variety of cafes and restaurants.

Access

Sloping beach leads into water. Pool can be reached on foot via steps leading down from the clifftop. Pool rests 300 metres away from Tollcross bus stop, where buses from Edinburgh and Leven stop approximately every hour. Parking available at the car park next to West Braes Crazy Golf on the clifftop.

CELLARDYKE TIDAL POOL. © SHUTTERSTOCK/ALANF

CELLARDYKE TIDAL POOL

56.2279, -2.6804 / Cellardyke Play Park, East End, Cellardyke, Anstruther, Fife, KY10 3AW / Swimming and paddling

Nestled next to a small play park, Cellardyke Tidal Pool (formerly known as the Cardinal's Steps) is an old bathing pool originally developed by local volunteers in the 1930s. Although it is no longer maintained, the pool is still used by the local outdoor sports and adventure centre for water-based activities. The tidal pool itself is an ideal size and depth for swimming, however it is advised that you only swim in the pool at mid to low tide when the walls are visible. Jumping and diving is also discouraged. On the side of the pool nearest to the play park is a smaller, shallower, rectangular-shaped section which might appeal to less-confident swimmers. Cellardyke has a variety of refreshment options.

Access
Entry into pool via a slightly rocky beach. Pool is 700 metres from March Crescent bus stop, served by buses to Edinburgh and St Andrews hourly. On-site parking.

WILD SHORE DUNDEE

56.4611, -2.9630 / West Victoria Dock Road, Dundee, DD1 3JP / 01382 214484 / Swimming / www.wildshoredundee.co.uk

A five-star visitor attraction, Wild Shore is Scotland's biggest aqua park and the only city-based aqua park in the UK. Based at Dundee's City Quay, Wild Shore is a fully accredited British Waterski and Wakeboard site, perfect for family days out and ideal for anyone interested in water-based activities. Supervised swim sessions are run for those over twelve years old on Wednesday evenings and Saturday mornings – swimmers must book in advance and wear a brightly coloured cap. Swimmers must be able to confidently swim twenty-five metres unaided. If you are looking to add extra excitement to your day, the aqua park also offers cable wakeboarding, stand-up paddleboarding and Ringo riding. Wild Shore's biggest attraction, however, is its floating adventure course. A variety of pubs and cafes sit a short walk away.

Access
Entry into water via jetties. Dundee Bus Station is 300 metres away, served frequently by a variety of buses to Aberdeen, St Andrews and Perth. Dundee railway station just under a kilometre away. Parking is available at the Olympia multi-storey car park, 300 metres from Wild Shore.

BLACK WATER

56.7235, -3.3962 / Dalrulzion, Perth & Kinross / Swimming

Cutting its way past the Drumfork Estate, Black Water is a river with a section of rapids which flows beneath an arched stone bridge. Further along the river there are several pools, however rocks may line the riverbed and caution should be taken in drier spells. With open fields stretching out on either side and mountains in the distance, this is a truly wild swim, and can be tied in as a diversion on the Cateran Trail. You can find refreshments at the Wee House of Glenshee several kilometres north.

Access

Access via steep banks; a little scrambling required to reach water. Road End bus stop, less than a kilometre away, served by infrequent buses to Blairgowrie. Limited parking at lay-by on A93, two and a half kilometres away; river can be accessed by walking to the bridge via the road.

SOLDIER'S LEAP

56.7422, -3.7745 / Killiecrankie, Perth & Kinross / Swimming

Beneath the railway line on the River Garry, Soldier's Leap is a wide river pool with a white pebble beach. Accessing the spot requires some scrambling, but a spectacular swim awaits, with privacy provided by the trees on all sides. Named for a soldier who reputedly once leapt the breadth of the river during the Battle of Killiecrankie, this spot is peaceful and secluded. Refreshments are available in Blair Atholl, where options range from Blair Atholl Watermill to the Loft.

Access

Access via pebbly beach; some scrambling to reach water. Just over 300 metres away, bus stop at Killiecrankie Village Hall provides a stop for services to Struan and Pitlochry. Parking at Visitor Centre car park within 500 metres of Soldier's Leap.

WADE'S BRIDGE. © SHUTTERSTOCK/JOHN PAUL SLINGER

WADE'S BRIDGE

56.6193, -3.8756 / Aberfeldy, Perth & Kinross / Swimming and paddling

Linking Aberfeldy to the countryside beyond, Wade's Bridge spans the River Tay, whose refreshing waters are perfect for swimming. A large, shingle beach beside the lush, tree-lined banks provides an excellent spot for wading into the deeper water of the river, while grassy banks further along also provide soft entry points. Once in the water, you can swim up towards this historic bridge and enjoy the peace of this tranquil spot. This location is great to combine with a visit to the Birks of Aberfeldy or a walk to St David's Well in Weem Wood. You can find a wide range of refreshment options in Aberfeldy.

Access

Access via shingle beach. Taybridge Drive bus stop rests 500 metres away, served by regular buses to Perth. Roadside parking beside the Black Watch Memorial, approximately 300 metres from the swim spot.

GLENCOE LOCHAN. © *SHUTTERSTOCK/DAVE CLAYTON*

LOWER GLEN ETIVE

56.6162, -4.9674 / Glencoe, Highland / Swimming and plunge pool

Coursing through the Trossachs, the River Etive can be split into two sections based on their location within Glen Etive. At Lower Glen Etive, a small and brief section of rapids gives way to a deep, tranquil river canyon with high stone walls. Crossing the shallower stretch of river before the rapids enables you to access a soft grassy bank, which provides an access point into the river. An idyllic location for wild camping, the luscious, dark water makes Glen Etive stand apart from other wild swims, and can easily be combined with a dip further up the river in Higher Glen Etive. The Glencoe Visitor Centre offers a chance to grab drinks and snacks, or for something more filling head to their Highland Coo Cafe.

Access

Grassy banks and rocky ledges lead to water. Not easily accessible by public transport: nearest bus stops eleven kilometres away at Chairlift Road End for infrequent services to Glasgow. Lay-by parking beside the river, less than 100 metres away.

HIGHER GLEN ETIVE

56.6253, -4.9062 / Glencoe, Highland / Swimming and plunge pool

Home to a modest waterfall and plunge pool, Higher Glen Etive is nestled within a river gorge with high, sloping hills on either side of its rocky walls. Steep, grassy banks lead down to small patches of shingle beach, and blocky sections of stone provide access points into the water; from here you can make your way back up the river towards the waterfall. This location is ideal to combine with a tour of the other picture-perfect points in the Glen Coe area, such as the Meeting of Three Waters, the Glencoe Waterfalls, the historic Signal Rock and the Three Sisters Viewpoint. You can refuel at the Glencoe Visitor Centre's cafe.

Access

Varied access to water: grassy banks, shingle beach and blocky stone. Not easily accessible by public transport: Chairlift Road End bus stop served by infrequent buses to Glasgow, seven kilometres away. Lay-by parking within 100 metres of the swim spot.

GLENCOE LOCHAN

56.6904, -5.0981 / Glencoe, Highland / Swimming and paddling

Tucked away in a patch of woodland beside Loch Leven, Glencoe Lochan is a small lake with muddy but soft banks leading into the water, which can be cold due to

LOCH MORAR. © SHUTTERSTOCK/TIM KNIGHT

RHA WATERFALL

57.5928, -6.3607 / Uig, Isle of Skye / Swimming and plunge pool

Spilling from a stepped rocky outcrop, the Rha Waterfall is in fact two waterfalls located on the River Rha. Boulders along the banks form points from which you can slip into the cool waters of the plunge pool below and experience stunning views of the wood-shaded river stretching into the distance. A magical swim here is perfect to combine with a trip to the Fairy Glen, where enchanting drumlins dot the landscape, as well as the imposing Castle Ewen. After a day of discovery, you can get a hot drink and snack at the Galley Seafood Cafe and Takeaway, or alternatively the Ferry Inn.

Access

Access to water over boulders. Park View Terrace bus stop on the A855 300 metres away for service to Portree, which runs several times a day; Intercity buses also depart for Glasgow from A87 main road. Roadside parking area at the junction of the A855 and A87, within a kilometre of Rha Waterfall.

---

the shelter provided by the trees. With its wooded shores and majestic peaks in the distance, Glencoe Lochan is the epitome of the Scottish wild swim, and is perfect to combine with a day of exploration on the Glencoe Lochan trails and the Pap of Glencoe walk, as well as the Glencoe Folk Museum. Refuel afterwards at the Glencoe Gathering.

Access

Soft, muddy banks lead to water. Services from Fort William, Portree and Uig stop several times a day at the Hotel bus stop, just under two kilometres away. Glencoe Lochan car park less than 500 metres from the lake.

LOCH MORAR

56.9695, -5.8037 / Morar, Highland / Swimming and paddling

Situated on Scotland's west coast, Loch Morar is a large lake and home to the mythical monster Morag. Due to its immense depth, the loch's waters can be very cold, and a short, concrete slipway gives way to the deeper water. With a spectacular panoramic view of the lake and Munros beyond, this spot is peaceful and refreshing, and can be combined with a trip to the gorgeous Silver Sands of Morar. You can enjoy a meal at Sunset Morar or the Silver Sands Restaurant in Morar, or venture further up the A830 to find numerous cafes in Mallaig.

Access

Access via concrete slipway. A kilometre and a half away, buses to Fort William and Mallaig stop a few times a day at Station bus stop; Morar railway station just over a kilometre away. Very limited parking at small lay-by shortly before the jetty – do not block access.

PATTACK FALLS. © *SHUTTERSTOCK/ALEX NICOL*   FAIRY POOLS. © *SHUTTERSTOCK/ELXENEIZE*

ALLT DARAICH

57.2864, -6.1625 / Sligachan, Isle of Skye / Swimming and plunge pool

In the shadow of Skye's mountains, the Allt Daraich waterfall and plunge pool are surrounded by the island's immense natural beauty. A mixture of grassy banks and stone platforms provide plenty of places from which you can ease yourself into the refreshing, clear water. The staggering backdrop of the Cuillin Hills makes this a truly remarkable swim spot, and a visit here can be incorporated into a walk taking in the other impressive waterfalls around Sligachan and the Sligachan Old Bridge, dating to 1810. You can reward yourself afterwards with a hot meal at Seumas' Bar.

Access
Access via grassy banks and stone platforms. Hotel bus stop serviced by buses to Portree and Uig – check times as some services only run on school days. Sligachan Old Bridge car park approximately a kilometre from the waterfall.

FAIRY POOLS

57.2498, -6.2552 / Carbost, Isle of Skye / Swimming and plunge pool

Cascading through the Skye wilderness, the Fairy Pools are a series of mesmerising waterfalls and plunge pools along Allt Coir' a' Mhadaidh. Entering the pools involves a bit of scrambling over rocks, so water-friendly footwear is advised for those looking to try out this spectacular location, surrounded by majestic hills and mountains. You can escape the crowds at the Fairy Pools with a longer hike through this gorgeous and raw landscape to Bruach na Frìthe, which provides breathtaking panoramic views. In summer, the area can be prone to midges. There are no cafes nearby, so be sure to take a drink and bite to eat.

Access
Scramble over rocks to access pools (footwear recommended). Hotel bus stop is nine kilometres away, serviced by buses to Portree and Uig – check times as some services only run on school days. Parking at Fairy Pools car park, just over a kilometre away; follow grit path to swim spot.

GLENELG WATERFALL

57.1924, -5.6095 / Glenelg, Highland / Swimming and plunge pool

Close to Scotland's west coast, Glenelg Waterfall is a waterfall and plunge pool tucked away among the bracken and foliage of the glen. The rocky edges to the pool provide a platform from which you can slip into the water, however they require a slight scramble to reach. With wide views, this is an idyllic spot, and you can also take the time to connect with the landscape's history by exploring the nearby ruined towers of Dun Grugaig, Gleann Beag broch and Dun Troddan. The nearest refreshments are at the Way Out West Cafe in Glenelg.

Access

Access from rocky edges; slight scramble required. Not easily accessible by public transport: nearest bus stop eighteen kilometres away in Invershiel. Parking available at lay-by opposite the Dun Troddan ruins, two kilometres away.

THE WITCH'S CAULDRON

56.9548, -5.0015 / Spean Bridge, Highland / Swimming and plunge pool

Cascading from a rocky step, the Witch's Cauldron is made up of three waterfalls with a large plunge pool at its base. The entry point into the pool is stony and often uneven underfoot, and requires a slight scramble down a short slope. Nestled in a wooded grove, this is a gorgeous swim spot with the convenience of a nearby picnic bench. The river and waterfalls can be fast-flowing following periods of heavy rain, and swimmers should check the depth of the pool before jumping from the outcrop. Located just beside the road, this is a great place for a spontaneous dip.

Access

Stony and uneven access to water; requires scrambling. Not easily accessible by public transport: nearest bus stop is approximately fifteen kilometres away in Spean Bridge. Chia-aig car park 100 metres from the waterfall.

LOCH OICH

57.0497, -4.7965 / Invergarry, Highland / Swimming and paddling

Surrounded by the raw and imposing beauty of the Highlands, Loch Oich is a long, narrow lake with tree-covered mountains rising on either side. Grassy banks serve as soft entry points for accessing the pleasant and serene waters of the loch. A swim here can be tied in with a visit to the ruins of Invergarry Castle further along the water's edge, or to Invergarry and Fort Augustus Railway Museum. After you dip, head to the Invergarry Hotel for a bite to eat.

Access

Access via grassy banks. Seven Heads Store bus stop 300 metres away, for services to Glasgow, Fort William, Inverness and Uig; buses run several times a day. Plenty of parking at Loch Oich car park, less than fifty metres away.

PATTACK FALLS

56.9816, -4.3610 / Laggan, Highland / Swimming, paddling and plunge pool

Tucked away beside the A86, Pattack Falls is a small waterfall and wide plunge pool overlooked by two grass-decked stone outcrops. A small beach area leads into the cool, tranquil plunge pool, and provides the perfect place to paddle in the shallows. This swim spot is ideal for those passing by and looking for somewhere to take a dip. You can also explore the circular path which climbs to the abandoned village of Druim an Aird and connect with the history of this awe-inspiring landscape. Roughly four kilometres up the road, the Laggan Wolftrax Centre offers a variety of refreshment options, as well as mountain biking trails.

Access

Water accessed via rocky beach. Not easily accessible by public transport: closest bus stop seven kilometres away at Drumgask Lodge. Parking available in signposted Druim an Aird car park, less than 100 metres away off the A86.

LOCH AN EILEIN. © *SHUTTERSTOCK/4KCLIPS*

LOCH CAOLDAIR

56.9786, -4.2679 / Dalwhinnie, Highland / Swimming and paddling

Encompassed by woodland and mountains, Loch Caoldair is a lake in Laggan with shingle beaches providing entrance into the water, whether for swimming or paddling. The water here can be cold, so swimmers are advised to wear a wetsuit when enjoying the loch's reviving waters. A swim here can be linked into a hike up to Creag na Doire Duibhe, which offers picturesque panoramas of the loch below and the landscape beyond. You can also explore the Dalwhinnie Distillery, as well as grab a drink and some food at the nearby Snack Shack.

Access

Water accessed by shingle beaches. Six kilometres from the loch, buses to Edinburgh and Glasgow stop a few times a day at Road End bus stop on the A9; Dalwhinnie railway station seven kilometres away. Small lay-by before Raeburn Hut on A889 provides parking within two kilometres of the loch.

FESHIEBRIDGE

57.1164, -3.8990 / Kincraig, Highland / Swimming and plunge pool

Running through a tree-shaded gorge in the Cairngorms National Park, the River Feshie is home to rapids which flow beneath the B970 and into a cool, clear and wide river pool. A shingle beach provides easy access into the water, which can sometimes have a strong current and carry log debris after periods of heavy rainfall. A swim here can be a great way to cool off after a walk around the nearby Loch Insh, or take in the picturesque views that the Invereshie & Inshriach National Nature Reserve has to offer. You can get a drink and a snack at the Old Post Office Cafe Gallery in Kincraig.

Access

Shingle beach. Buses to Carrbridge, Aviemore and Inverness stop regularly at War Memorial stop in Kincraig, three and a half kilometres away. Less than 200 metres away, Feshie-bridge car park beside the B970 provides ample parking.

LOCH AN EILEIN

57.1527, -3.8238 / Aviemore, Highland /
Swimming and paddling

Snug at the foot of the Cairngorms, Loch an Eilein is a small loch with dusty, gravel shores ensuring easy access into the water for a swim or paddling in the shallows. With woodland on all sides and bare tree roots dipping their fingers into the chilly but refreshing water, this is a truly idyllic swim and the perfect place to sit back with a picnic and immerse yourself in the landscape. A swim here can be tied in as a relaxing stop after a hike up to Torr Alvie and the Duke of Gordon Monument, with spectacular views over Strathspey below. Head to the Rothiemurchus Centre's cafe for a snack and drink, or into Aviemore for more choice.

Access
Gravel shores give access to water. Rothie-murchus car park bus stop, three and a half kilometres away, regularly served by buses from Aviemore. On-site car park less than 300 metres from the shores of the loch.

LOCH MORLICH

57.1671, -3.7022 / Glenmore, Highland /
Swimming and paddling

A popular spot for visitors to Glenmore, Loch Morlich is a large lake enveloped by the iconic pine trees of the Cairngorms National Park. The vast beach area along the eastern bank makes it easy to access the water for both swimming and paddling, and it is also the perfect location to enjoy a picnic and ice cream in the sun. A dip here can easily be combined with the wondrous woodland trails around the lake, or a visit to the nearby Cairngorm Reindeer Herd. The Boathouse Cafe and the Pine Marten Bar and Scran are both ideally located to cater for your refreshment needs.

Access
Access via large beach. Less than a kilometre from Loch Morlich, the Youth Hostel bus stop is served by the 31 bus several times a day to and from Aviemore, and Glenmore Visitor Centre car park provides ample parking.

AN LOCHAN UAINE

57.1754, -3.6548 / Glenmore, Highland /
Swimming and paddling

Sandwiched between the hills and mountains of the Cairngorms National Park, An Lochan Uaine is a small loch of clear, cool water. Shielded from the path by a border of pines, this peaceful spot has dusty gravel banks which make stepping into the water easy, whether for swimming or paddling. This spot makes a great, more secluded alternative to Loch Morlich, or can be part of a day of wild swimming as you take a dip in both. The surrounding forest offers plenty of options for adventure and discovery on its numerous woodland trails, and you can grab a post-swim drink and snack at the Glenmore Visitor Centre's cafe.

Access
Gravel banks access water. Visitor Centre bus shelter is served by the infrequent 31 service to Aviemore. Parking available three kilometres from the loch at the Glenmore Visitor Centre car park. Path to the loch is predominantly forestry track with gradual inclines.

LOCH MUICK

56.9444, -3.1556 / Ballater, Aberdeenshire / Swimming and paddling

Located on the Balmoral Estate, Loch Muick is a medium-sized loch with a long, shingle beach, dotted with driftwood. This beach makes the loch an idyllic location for a picnic and paddling, as well as easily accessible for swimming in its chilly but refreshing waters. Beneath the open sky and surrounded by timeless, majestic Munros, a dip in Loch Muick is great to combine with a walk around the loch, as well as a visit to the Spittal of Glen Muick Visitor Centre, where you can learn about the area's geology and biodiversity. There are numerous cafes and other refreshment options up the road in Ballater.

Access
Shingle beach leads to water. Not easily accessible by public transport: nearest bus stop fourteen kilometres away in Ballater, for regular services to Aberdeen. Parking available at Spittal of Glen Muick car park, just under two kilometres away.

CAMBUS O'MAY

57.0659, -2.9572 / Ballater, Aberdeenshire / Swimming and paddling

Reaching across the River Dee, the Cambus O'May footbridge is a historic

LOCH MUICK. © *JAMES CARRON*

piece of engineering and architecture, dating to 1905. Here you will find fantastic views of the surrounding countryside and hills beyond, as well as of the bridge itself, which you can swim beneath. A swim in the wide river can form part of a day of exploration when combined with a visit to the Muir of Dinnet National Nature Reserve. The nearby Courie Courie Bakery and Cafe offers the opportunity to grab a well-deserved drink and snack.

Access
Sandy and grassy banks provide access. Cambus O'May Forest Walk Centre bus stop served by 201 line between Ballater/Braemar and Aberdeen. Parking available at Cambus O'May Suspension Bridge car park, less than 100 metres from the shores.

STONEHAVEN OPEN AIR POOL

56.9698, -2.2047 / Queen Elizabeth Park, The Links, Stonehaven, Aberdeenshire, AB39 2RD / 01569 762134 / Swimming and paddling / *stonehavenopenairpool.co.uk*

Famous for being the northernmost lido in the UK, Stonehaven Open Air Pool is an Olympic-sized pool that attracts approximately 30,000 visitors each year. Open from late May to early September, the pool is filled with clean seawater heated to a pleasant 29 °C. A family friendly destination, the lido features a small shark-themed water slide and an inflatable swoopee. There is also a paddling pool for those under eight years old which features a dolphin water splash. Meanwhile, adults can enjoy relaxing on seats and loungers in sheltered sun terraces. The lido offers a variety of sessions through-out the season, including fun and inflatables sessions for kids, plus quiet

STONEHAVEN OPEN AIR POOL. © *STONEHAVEN OPEN AIR POOL*

and lane swimming sessions for adults. In peak season, the pool also runs weekly midnight swim sessions.

Access
Entry via steps, ladders and a slide. Site is wheelchair accessible; hoist available upon request. Cowie Bridge bus stop, which is served by X7 to Aberdeen approximately every twenty minutes, is 500 metres away. Stonehaven railway station a kilometre and a half away. On-site parking.

PITFOUR LAKE
57.5282, -2.0363 / Mintlaw, Aberdeenshire / Swimming

Near to the eastern coast of Scotland, Pitfour Lake is a modest lake nestled among a mixture of fields and woodland. The still, tranquil water can be cold and, due to the lack of shallows, may have a sudden step change; this is a committing swim. The perfect place to cool off and have a picnic after a walk or cycle around the trails of the Pitfour Estate, a swim here can also be tied in with a visit to Deer Abbey or to Aden Country Park. The park is also home to the Cafe at Aden, where you can grab a hot drink to warm up.

Access
Soft, grassy banks lead to water. 66 and 66A services stop approximately every ninety minutes at Aden Country Park bus stop on Station Road, less than a kilometre away. Limited parking available approximately 500 metres from the lake, just off the A950, from where even, grit paths run from road to the lake. Further car parking in Aden Country Park.

RANDOLPH'S LEAP
57.5251, -3.6713 / Forres, Moray / Swimming and paddling

Flowing through a tree-shrouded gorge, Randolph's Leap is located on the River Findhorn. The stony banks which surround it can in warm weather serve as excellent spots for sitting and enjoying the scenery and sunshine while drying off. With woodland on all sides, a swim here is great to combine with walks through the trees along the meandering river up to Logie Steading, taking in some of the fantastic wildlife Scotland has to offer. Afterwards, you can find tea and cake at the Olive Tree Cafe in Logie.

Access
Stony banks access water. Ten kilometres away, buses to Findhorn and Elgin stop a few times a day in Forres. Parking is available to side of B9007, opposite gated path down to the river, which is roughly 100 metres away through the trees.

DULSIE BRIDGE. © *SHUTTERSTOCK/IAN COOPER IMAGES*

URQUHART BAY WOODS. © *MARK HOWLEY*

DULSIE BRIDGE

57.4507, -3.7811 / Grantown-on-Spey, Highland / Swimming

Blending with the stone of the gorge, Dulsie Bridge watches over the soothing waters of the River Findhorn. You can swim in the river pools and up to a small waterfall spurting from the opposite side of the river gorge. The steep banks make it a challenging scramble in and out of the water, so exercise caution; the deep river is dangerous after heavy rain. A swim under the eye of this quietly impressive bridge can easily be tied in with a walk which runs through the woods alongside the river, providing picturesque views looking back on the bridge through the trees. You can find a pick-me-up piece of cake and drink at the Olive Tree Cafe in Logie.

Access

Access via rocky banks; some scrambling required down occasionally steep banks. Difficult to reach via public transport: nearest bus stop eleven kilometres away at Littlemill, for daily services to Nairn and Cawdor. Limited roadside parking shortly before the bridge beside a grassy area, within 100 metres of the river.

DORES BEACH, LOCH NESS

57.3827, -4.3340 / Dores, Highland / Swimming and paddling

Lining the north-eastern shore of Loch Ness beside the village of Dores, Dores Beach is a 500-metre stretch of shingle bank which provides easy access into the chilly waters of the loch. From here, you can experience stunning views down the length of Loch Ness, lined with mountains which eventually stretch into the horizon beyond. You could also factor in a visit to the nearby McBean Memorial Park or treat yourself to a hot meal at the Dores Inn.

Access

Access via shingle beach. Regular buses to Inverness stop at the Inn bus stop, 200 metres away. Free public parking available beside the church just beyond Dores, less than 500 metres from the beach.

URQUHART BAY WOODS, LOCH NESS

57.3307, -4.4530 / Drumnadrochit, Highland / Swimming and paddling

In the shadow of Urquhart Castle, Loch Ness is one of Scotland's most iconic lochs, spanning from Fort Augustus to Lochend. This awe-inspiring location, infused with myth and

PLODDA FALLS. © SHUTTERSTOCK/CLIFF HANDS

is Scotland's second highest waterfall, and has a deep plunge pool below. Blocky stone banks provide solid points of entry to the water, however they can be slippery at times. Submerged in both water and woodland, the waterfall provides a peaceful soundtrack to a swim here, which can be combined with the walking trails through the Douglas firs or a visit to the Glen Affric National Nature Reserve. You can find refreshments afterwards at the Coach House Cafe in Tomich.

Access

Blocky stone banks access the water – slippery at times. Tomich Post Office stop served by buses to Drumnadrochit a few times a day. Ample parking available at Plodda Falls car park, less than 500 metres away. Firm gravel trail leads to swim spot – some segments can be muddy and steep.

legend, is easy to access from Urquhart Bay Woods, where a dusty, shingle beach provides plenty of spots to get into the water. Due to its depth, the loch can be mercilessly cold and swimmers should wear a wetsuit. It is worth braving the chill for a dip in this stunning spot, which can easily be tied in with a trip to the Loch Ness Exhibition Centre, Urquhart Castle or a walk along the banks to take in the scenery. Refreshments and toilets can be found in nearby Kilmore, including Cafe Eighty2.

Access

Access via shingle beach. Borlum Farm bus stop 500 metres away served a few times a day by 917 and 919 bus lines to Fort William and Portree. Parking available at Cemetery car park in Kilmore, a kilometre from swim spot. During summer, parking can be extremely busy.

PLODDA FALLS

57.2724, -4.8601 / Cannich, Highland / Swimming and plunge pool

Plunging from a high, rocky outcrop in the midst of sheltered woodland, Plodda Falls

LOCH BEINN A' MHEADHOIN

57.2954, -4.9096 / Cannich, Highland / Swimming and paddling

Nestled in the Highlands and surrounded by Caledonian pinewoods, Loch Beinn a' Mheadhoin is a loch whose northernmost tip stretches to Glen Affric. The grassy banks offer soft entry points into the water, which can be cold due to the loch's depth. With beautifully clear water offering mirror images of the sky and trees, this location is truly idyllic. Further exploration of the glen can lead you to Plodda Falls and Dog Falls, both also excellent swim spots. Alternatively, you could lie back with a picnic and soak in the rare wildlife of this isolated, stunning setting.

Access

Grassy banks access the water. Not easily accessible by public transport: nearest bus stop twelve kilometres away in Tomich. Parking available at Coille Ruigh na Cuileige car park, less than a kilometre from swim spot.

DOG FALLS

57.3122, -4.8519 / Cannich, Highland / Swimming and plunge pool

On the River Affric, Dog Falls is a small waterfall which spills into a wide plunge pool. The river can be accessed from the bridge, where sloping stone banks provide points over which you can scramble into the water. From here you can swim in the cool, peaceful waters of the river pools, or you can swim upstream towards the waterfall itself. A dip at this secluded location lends itself to an exploration of the Glen Affric National Nature Reserve, as well as a trip to nearby Plodda Falls, if you're looking for two dips in one trip. You can grab a snack and a hot drink in Tomich at the Coach House Cafe.

Access
Scramble into water over stone banks. Not easily reached by public transport: nearest stop ten kilometres away at Tomich Post Office. Dog Falls has a designated car park less than 100 metres from the swim spot.

LITTLE GARVE BRIDGE

57.6272, -4.6870 / Garve, Highland / Swimming

A timeless piece of the High-lands' landscape, Little Garve Bridge spans the Black Water, which is home to several river

pools perfect for swimming. The rocky banks of the gorge make firm points from which you can slip into the water, though they may require some scrambling and can be slippery if wet. Surrounded by dense woodland, a trip here can be incorporated into a visit to the nearby Black Water Falls, where there are public toilets, the Ben Wyvis National Nature Reserve or down to Rogie Falls. You can grab a snack and a drink down the road at Tarvies.

Access
Access via rocky banks – some scrambling may be required. Hotel bus stop two and a half kilometres away for services to Inverness and Ullapool a few times a day; Garve rail-way station two kilometres from the swim spot. Parking available at the public car park less than 500 metres from the bridge.

LOCH MAREE

57.7418, -5.5822 / Poolewe, Highland / Swimming

According to local folklore, the long, stretching waters of Loch Maree are home to the monster Muc-sheilch, and surrounded by Munros, trees and crags, it isn't hard to see how this loch can capture the imagination. A small, stony beach enables easy access into the water, as well as the perfect place to paddle and enjoy views of the loch

stretching away before you. After a swim here, why not head to Inverewe Gardens in Poolewe to discover local wildlife and grab a drink and snack from Osgood's Cafe, or venture to the impressive Victoria Falls.

Access
Stony beach accesses the water. Farm Road End bus stop caters for services between Poolewe, Gairloch and Dingwall. Small car park beside the loch at the end of a small track off the A832, less than fifty metres away.

RIVER DOUCHARY

57.8720, -4.9563 / Ullapool, Highland / Swimming, paddling and plunge pool

Isolated in the Scottish heathland, the River Douchary is a lengthy river home to beautiful, cascading waterfalls as well as deep, refreshing plunge pools. The rocky banks of the plunge pools form platforms from which you can slip into the water and enjoy the soundtrack of the babbling waterfalls. Due to its remote location, a trip to River Douchary is a day out in itself, enabling swimmers to immerse themselves in this spectacular landscape with a picnic. After a day of adventure, you can find a variety of refreshment options in Ullapool.

DOG FALLS. © *SHUTTERSTOCK/ONDREJ_NOVOTNY_92*   THE NORTH BATHS. © *FERGUS MATHER*

Access

Access via rocky banks; River Douchary can only be accessed on foot and will require covering uneven ground. Closest bus stop nine kilometres from the swim spot in Leckmelm, for infrequent buses to Ullapool and Inverness. Parking available at Lael Forest Garden car park off the A835, eleven kilometres away.

THE TRINKIE

58.4288, -3.0702 / Wick, Caithness, KW1 5TN / Swimming and paddling

🚇 🅿️

The Trinkie is a man-made tidal pool located on Wick's South Head in Caithness. It is easy to find from the road above, as its name is painted in large white letters on an area of flat rock below. The walk to the Trinkie can be treacherous when wet, so it is recommended that you visit it on a dry day. The pool was created in the mid-twentieth century from part of a quarry, and before Wick's first indoor

pool was opened in 1994 the Trinkie was a huge attraction in the summer months, with many townspeople learning to swim here. The pool has gradually fallen into a state of disrepair and neglect over the years, however the Trinkie Heritage Preservation Group is currently working towards repairing and refurbishing the pool with the aim of returning it to its former glory.

Access

No steps/ladders provided as the ground naturally slopes into the water. Just under a kilometre away, buses to Thurso stop several times a day at Caberfeidh Court bus stop. On-site parking available in adjacent lay-by.

THE NORTH BATHS

58.4422, -3.0774 / Wick, Caithness, KW1 4JJ / Swimming and paddling

🚇 🅿️ ❌ 🚻

Officially opened in 1904, the North Baths is a man-made

tidal pool located just outside Wick Harbour on the north side. While it can reach a depth of just over two metres in the deep section, the gently sloping shallow end of the pool near the steps is separated from the deep end by a railing and is ideal for paddling. Generations of local residents have taken a dip in these waters, and it is a great spot to cool off while gazing out into Wick Bay. After your swim, you can grab a bite to eat in one of Wick's many cafes or pubs.

Access

Entry into pool via steps in shallow section. Can be reached on foot via a path which commences at the Seaview bed and breakfast. Hillhead Road bus stop is 400 metres away, and is served by buses to Thurso a few times a day. Wick railway station just over a kilometre away. Some roadside parking in Wick, or Riverside car park just under a kilometre away.

Swims at a glance

WILD SWIMMING SPOTS

OPEN AIR SWIMMING

PEN-FFORD-GOCH POND, WALES. © *JOHN COEFIELD*

Also available